5/96

City-Building in America

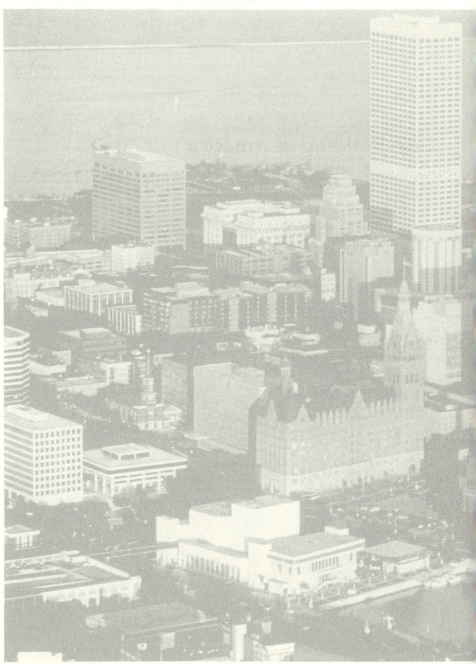

Milwaukee Journal Photo

City-Building in America

ANTHONY M. ORUM

WESTVIEW PRESS

Boulder • San Francisco • Oxford

Published in 1995 in the United States of America by Westview Press, Inc., 5500 Central Avenue, Boulder, Colorado 80301-2877, and in the United Kingdom by Westview Press, 12 Hid's Copse Road, Cumnor Hill, Oxford OX2 9JJ

Library of Congress Cataloging-in-Publication Data
Orum, Anthony M.
  City-building in America / Anthony M. Orum.
    p. cm.
  Includes bibliographical references and index.
  ISBN 0-8133-0842-9. — ISBN 0-8133-0843-7 (pbk.)
  1. Cities and towns—United States—Growth.   2. Urban policy—
United States.   3. Milwaukee (Wis.)—Economic conditions.
4. Milwaukee (Wis.)—Social conditions.   I. Title.
HT384.U5078   1995
307.76'0973—dc20   94-38969
                                                                         CIP

Printed and bound in the United States of America

The paper used in this publication meets the requirements
of the American National Standard for Permanence of Paper
for Printed Library Materials Z39.48-1984.

10   9   8   7   6   5   4   3   2   1

To my mother, Alma Orum,
my grandmother, Edith Ostermann,
and my wife, Susan Jorjorian

Contents

Part Four   Conclusion   193

Illustrations

Acknowledgments

I want to begin by thanking all those librarians and archivists who helped to guide me to materials that made these histories possible. I am particularly grateful to Stanley Mallach, the former archivist of the Fromkin Collection at the University of Wisconsin–Milwaukee (UWM) Library. Stanley provided me with my first introduction to the historical resources on the city of Milwaukee and provided indispensable information on people and works to which I should turn. I also am very grateful to Allan Kovan, an archivist at the Milwaukee Area Research Center and a former colleague of Stanley's, for his initial help.

I want to thank Judith Simonsen, the curator of research collections at the Milwaukee County Historical Society. Judy introduced me to the array of wonderful materials at the Historical Society and helped to guide me to particular family collections that proved essential to my research. I am especially thankful that she guided me to the Falk family materials, for these provided the foundations for my analysis of the links among the German families of Milwaukee.

I also am very indebted to David Hall, a former staff archivist at the Legislative Reference Bureau of the City of Milwaukee. Dave helped direct me to particular collections as well as to the materials contained in various City of Milwaukee documents. He was most generous with his time, as were the other staff members of this bureau. I should add that if every city in America had a library the equal of the Legislative Reference Bureau, our histories of American cities would all be the richer and more substantial for it.

I probably would never have started this book had it not been for the generous support of the Newberry Library here in the city of Chicago. They provided me with a fellowship in 1991–1992 that gave me some free time to think and work on the book. More importantly, other scholars there helped to shape and direct my thinking. During my particular year there, the people who were especially helpful to me were Tim Mahoney, an associate professor at the University of Nebraska at Lincoln, and Jim Grossman, the director of the Scholl Center on Family Studies. I also want to thank the other Fellows who shared their comments with me in reactions to an early version of this work. In particular, I am very grateful to the following: Susan Rosa, Bruce Calder, Michael Grossberg, Paul Cohen, Jan Rieff, Laura Edwards, and Fred Hoxie. It was to say the least quite a challenge to be a social scientist living and working amid such a collection of classical scholars and American historians as these. I am also very grateful to Kathleen Conzen for having provided encouragement for this work very early on, in the course of a conversation I had with her about Milwaukee history in February 1987.

Along the way, many other people also have helped me enormously. In Milwaukee, Professor Margo Anderson of the History Department at UWM very generously gave me copies of materials that she had collected on economic and social issues in contemporary Milwaukee. I also want to thank her for having provided me with copies of several unpublished papers that were helpful to my research. In addition, Jack Norman, a journalist for *The Milwaukee Journal,* very kindly allowed me to interview him and provided me with fuller insight about the organizations and families that are important to the directions of modern Milwaukee. John Zipp, a friend and member of the Sociology Department at UWM, also has been enormously and continuously helpful, from pointing me to important research materials to reading the first draft of the final manuscript.

In the Twin Cities, I am especially indebted to John Adams, professor of geography at the University of Minnesota, for allowing me to read a pre-publication examination of a manuscript he and Barbara VanDrasek have written on the history of Minneapolis–St. Paul. I also want to thank him and his wife for a delightful dinner at their home; it helped to make my lonely research task a good deal more enjoyable. While in the Twin Cities, I also had important conversations with John Kostouros, a journalist in the area. Myron Orfield, a state legislator who is full of wonderful ideas and enormous energy, also was very kind and generous with his time, especially in giving me a quick tour of Minneapolis by car.

In Cleveland, the research librarians at the Western Reserve Historical Society were very helpful during my brief stay in the city. Professor Michael Grossberg of the History Department at Case Western Reserve also was very kind and gracious to me there, allowing me to test my ideas, as a sociologist, against the views of his fellow historians. He is not to be held responsible for their rather quizzical response to some of my claims.

In Austin, Texas, I have been aided over time by countless people. For my first work on the city, I am particularly grateful for the kind help of Audray Bateman. In my more recent work at the Austin Historical Society, I am especially indebted to Biruta Kearl, Audray's successor as the curator at the Austin History Center. I also am very thankful to the staff members who permitted me to do such outrageous things as copy materials without immediately paying for them. These sorts of simple acts of kindness and generosity, incidentally, were numerous throughout the course of this research venture and represent just one of the many small ways that the staffs at libraries and research centers throughout this country aid scholars.

Over the course of this work, several people were particularly helpful in aiding me in gathering materials, reading newspapers, and gaining personal interviews. They include Lynn Kleinman, who became a good friend and was very helpful in tracking down a good deal of information in the *Milwaukee Sentinel*. Jean Peterman, a graduate of the Department of Sociology at the University of Illinois at Chicago (UIC), also proved a very able research assistant and had the opportunity and privilege of interviewing such major Milwaukee figures as former Mayor Frank P. Zeidler and the legendary city historian Frederick Olson. And Neal McCrillis, a doctoral student at the time in the History Department at UIC, was especially helpful in providing readings and summaries of historical materials on the several cities involved in the analysis for this book.

I also am grateful for the opportunity to have presented some of the materials in this book at various places where I received both encouragement and useful criticisms and insights. I am grateful to Janis and John Notz for having helped to arrange and to host a presentation at the Newberry Library in May 1992 on the German families of Milwaukee. Several members of those families actually were in attendance at my presentation. I also am grateful to Michael Ebner, professor of history at Lake Forest College, for having arranged my presentation on the history of Milwaukee at the Chicago Urban History Seminar in December 1993. I found the questions there from the audience extremely helpful. Michael has been most supportive of this effort throughout its history.

At the University of Illinois at Chicago, I have been granted a group of colleagues who are both patient and too kind to refuse to listen to me test out my arguments on them. They include James Norr, Xiangming Chen, John Johnstone, and Melvin Holli. I also am very grateful to my close friend, Harvey Choldin, installed at the University of Illinois campus some miles south of Chicago. Harvey has provided indispensable words of encouragement along the way. I also am indebted to the dean of my college, Jay Levine, for his continuing support and interest in this project.

In the last stages of the manuscript, there were several people who provided me with very penetrating and careful reviews. They include Professor Arnold Fleischmann of the University of Georgia. Arnie has provided encouragement for this project over a long period of time. As someone who, like myself, was raised in the Milwaukee area, he has had a special interest in the history of the city and has always provided me with considerable insights. I thank him both for his general insights and for his particular comments on the first draft of the manuscript. I also am particularly grateful to Faith Paul, a fellow member of the Public Policy Research Consortium here at UIC, for taking the time to read and comment extensively on the first draft of my manuscript.

One critic of the major drafts of the manuscript, Gregory D. Squires, proved enormously helpful. He has played an important part in helping to shape the final document.

I must reserve a special place in these acknowledgments for my longtime friend, Joe Feagin. Joe was with me at the very start of this research in 1982. We have had so many conversations, including some strong disagreements, that at times I almost felt as though he were a co-author of the entire project. He also has supported me through my disappointments over this work and shared my occasional sense of satisfaction. In the last stages of this book, he provided me with a set of comments that proved indispensable to the revisions. I can never thank Joe enough for his kindness as a friend as well as for his candor as a critic. These qualities, together with his remarkable record of productivity, are the standard by which both friends and scholars should always be measured.

I also want to record my debt of gratitude to Jennifer Knerr. For some reason of which I am unaware, Jennifer was sufficiently impressed by my first book on Austin to be willing to tender me a contract for this book. That sign of commitment helped to carry me over the rough times of this work, when it seemed that it might never get done. She has throughout been very supportive and even has been willing to endure a few of my outbursts over a review no author should ever have had to receive. Because of her patience and gentle encouragement, this book has become a much better book than it might otherwise have been.

Lastly I want to thank Susan for providing those constant moments of encouragement. There were times when the sheer intellectual effort required by this book seemed to overwhelm me. Susan was there to comfort me and to reassure me that the book would get done. Yet there were other occasions when a critic had offered advice on my ideas, advice that seemed impossible to follow. Again Susan was there to encourage me to be more open about the suggestions of fellow scholars. Her gentle and repeated assurances that this would become a good work have enabled it to make its way into this world. The strongest praise I can give her is to group her along with my mother and grandmother as the three women who have stood behind me throughout my life and tried to show me how to become both a better person and a better scholar. I thank them for their tacit confidence in my capacity to grow.

Anthony M. Orum

PART ONE

Introduction

1

Building, Unbuilding, and Rebuilding American Cities

American cities face a moment of truth. Many cities today show evidence of considerable decline. The loss of industrial jobs has eaten away at their cores. Many residents have been left jobless, which contributes to family instability, crime, and a host of other problems. At the same time, the suburbs and peripheral areas of the city seem to be booming. New developments go up almost constantly; schools are flush in substantial resources. But such affluence is likely to be temporary, partly because of the declines now happening at the middle level of corporate management and partly because the problems of the central city are gradually overwhelming the metropolitan area as a whole.

Some cities seem to suffer less than others. They are essentially the newer, postindustrial cities in America. Characteristically, their growth has been most rapid in the period since World War II. Fed in large part by the disproportionate share of monies coming from the federal government for air bases, naval installations, and new public works projects, such cities have grown rapidly, changing from small towns into major metropolises almost overnight. Though such cities do not suffer the fate of many older industrial cities—now divided into a dying core and a somewhat flourishing outer ring—they nonetheless suffer their own set of problems. Growth has been so explosive that their infrastructures often cannot accommodate the rapidly expanding numbers of people. Highways prove inadequate; utilities are overburdened, or, if not, they become part of a modern passion play in which the overlords are landed developers.

At both ends of the spectrum, then, among older industrial cities and among newer post-industrial cities, problems are in abundance. Since the New Deal, many of these problems have been solved by the federal government. It has been the only institution with sufficient public revenues to help cities in decline, particularly the impoverished residents of the inner city, who have suffered the most from the loss of industrial jobs. But the federal government is overburdened. It is clear that the effort for revival of the declining older industrial cities must begin by making changes from within and, by the same token, that the need to control the problems of explosive growth in the newer, post-industrial cities must take place either at the city or state level.

This book deals with both kinds of cities. It speaks to the problems that are happening today within America's cities. Though it will concentrate on the structural and institutional features of cities, it is more concerned with helping the human inhabitants—the impoverished, unemployed people of color who tend to reside in the inner city as well as the middle- and upper-class residents who tend to ring the central city and whose lives now hang in the balance with companies that are making major decisions to streamline (i.e., to reduce their number of employees). There are many important books on the lives of city inhabitants, which are crafted in terms of how people have come to increasingly suffer. This is a book about the nature of the city itself—how it has come to be the way it is and how it has become transformed over time. It is also a book that assumes if cities are built, they can also be unbuilt, and rebuilt to better meet the needs of local residents.

The main focus of this book is on the older industrial cities that are undergoing substantial change and uneven development. By uneven development I mean, along with other writers, the simple fact that the inner cities lose population, wealth, and jobs while the outer ring of suburbs flourishes. The book is about cities like Detroit, Michigan; Pittsburgh, Pennsylvania; and St. Louis, Missouri; cities that once were the spectacle of industrial grandeur but now seem a shadow of their former selves. These are cities that since 1950 have lost large numbers of people from their central cores—along with jobs—a loss that has left behind poverty and despair, little employment, and schools in a sad state of disarray.

The book proceeds by focusing at length on one such declining industrial center: Milwaukee, Wisconsin. Milwaukee is typical of many such cities, as a glance at Table 1.1 reveals. It, like other such centers, has lost thousands of people from its inner core, has grown in the suburbs, but has been left with an extreme degree of uneven metropolitan development. I show how Milwaukee became a city and how it became transformed over time through a matter of critical events and specific stages.

I also consider whether the happenings to industrial Milwaukee are unique or whether they also parallel events in other industrial cities. Here I do so by making a comparison between Cleveland, Ohio, and Milwaukee. For all intents and purposes, I show that the two cities went through the same process of construction and destruction, leaving them with massive social and economic problems in their inner cores, but also with problems that are now spreading outward, into the suburban areas.

Next, I turn to look at one of those flourishing post-industrial cities of the South and the West. I consider Austin, Texas, partly because it is so prototypical of the boom cities of the post–World War II era. It possesses a highly educated

TABLE 1.1   Population Figures of Selected Cities with Declining Fortunes, 1950, 1980, and 1990

	1950	*1980*	*1990*
Cleveland, OH PMSA[a]	1,383,599	1,898,825	1,831,122
Cleveland	914,808	573,822	505,616
Outside central city	468,791	1,325,003	1,325,506
Detroit, MI PMSA	2,659,398	4,488,024	4,382,299
Inside central cities	1,849,568	1,404,725	1,222,120
Outside central cities	809,830	3,083,299	3,160,179
Milwaukee, WI PMSA	829,495	1,397,020	1,432,149
Milwaukee	637,292	636,298	628,088
Waukesha	—	50,365	56,958
Outside central cities	192,103	710,357	747,103
Pittsburgh, PA PMSA	1,532,953	2,218,870	2,056,905
Pittsburgh	678,806	423,960	369,879
McKeesport	—	31,012	26,016
Outside central cities	856,147	1,763,898	1,660,810

[a]Primary Metropolitan Statistical Area, 1990.
SOURCE: Bureau of the Census. 1950 data from Table 6, "Population of All Incorporated Places of 1,000 or More," and Table 9, "Population of Urbanized Areas, 1950," *1950 Census of the Population*. Volume 1: *Number of Inhabitants* (Washington, D.C., 1952).

population, never developed a strong industrial base like Cleveland and Milwaukee, is home to a major state university, and in the past decade has witnessed the growth and development of many high technological companies, including Dell Computers, among others. As Table 1.2 demonstrates, Austin's expansion follows the same post–World War II pattern as a number of other cities in the South and West. A relatively small college town prior to the war, it has grown by leaps and bounds in subsequent decades.

The differences between Milwaukee and Austin are striking. But what is perhaps most notable are the similarities. Based on a systematic comparison of Austin, Cleveland, and Milwaukee, it is possible to conclude that the stages through which Austin has grown, as a city, recapitulate parallel stages in the development of both Cleveland and Milwaukee. I suggest, then, that if one accepts the parallels and the evolution of cities by stages, residents of places like Austin— the high-growth cities—would be well advised to prepare in advance for their own decline at some point in the future. This means several specific things, but, among others, it means that municipal government needs to plan ahead for that day when members of the local population are likely to be a drain on public revenues simply because of the anticipated job losses that inevitably will occur.

Finally, I consider one other kind of city here. It is a hybrid city, one that developed in the heartland of industries, the Midwest, but also has been very successful in recent decades, particularly in terms of generating new post-industrial gains without suffering the same degree of inner-city decline as places like Detroit,

TABLE 1.2   Population Figures of Selected Cities with Rising Fortunes, 1950, 1980, and 1990

	1950	1980	1990
Austin, TX MSA[a]	135,971	536,688	781,572
Austin	132,459	372,536	465,622
Outside central city	3,512	164,152	315,950
Columbus, OH MSA	437,707	1,243,827	1,377,419
Columbus	375,901	565,021	632,910
Lancaster	—	34,953	34,507
Newark	—	41,200	44,389
Outside central cities	61,806	602,653	665,613
Indianapolis, IN MSA	502,375	1,166,575	1,249,822
Indianapolis	427,173	700,974	731,327
Outside central city	75,202	465,601	518,495
Memphis, TN MSA	406,034	913,472	981,747
Memphis	396,000	646,170	610,337
West Memphis, AR	—	28,138	28,259
Outside central cities	10,034	239,164	343,151
Minneapolis–St. Paul, MN MSA	985,101	2,137,133	2,464,124
Bloomington	—	81,831	86,335
Minneapolis	521,718	370,951	368,383
St. Paul	311,349	270,230	272,235
Outside central cities	152,034	1,414,121	1,737,171
Phoenix, AZ MSA	242,724	1,509,175	2,122,101
Mesa	16,970	163,594	288,091
Phoenix	106,818	790,183	983,403
Scottsdale	2,032	89,577	130,069
Tempe	7,684	106,861	141,865
Outside central cities	109,220	358,960	578,673
Raleigh-Durham, NC MSA	151,288	560,775	735,480
Chapel Hill	9,177	32,928	38,719
Durham	71,311	113,233	136,611
Raleigh	65,679	157,517	207,951
Outside central cities	5,121	257,095	352,199

[a]Metropolitan Statistical Area.

SOURCE: Bureau of the Census. 1950 data from Table 6, "Population of All Incorporated Places of 1,000 or More," and Table 9, "Population of Urbanized Areas, 1950," *1950 Census of the Population.* Volume 1: *Number of Inhabitants* (Washington, D.C., 1952).

Cleveland, and Milwaukee. There are several such centers in the Midwest; for example, Indianapolis, Indiana, and Columbus, Ohio (see Table 1.2). However, I examine the development of the Twin Cities of Minnesota—Minneapolis and St. Paul—to learn why they have proven so successful in terms of retaining a highly educated population, generating new industries, and creating a metropolitan government structure that can enable cities and suburbs to share limited resources. The lessons of the Twin Cities are very important; one among them being that a commitment from the leading business and political leaders was essential to the development of the cities into post-industrial success stories. Milwaukee, by contrast, possesses a leadership that has been conservative and timid, unwilling especially to deal with the critical social and economic inequalities that beset its residents.

I tell the stories of these several cities because even though I believe they are in some sense unique and special stories, much of what takes place in Milwaukee, Cleveland, Austin, and Minneapolis–St. Paul also occurs in many other cities today. I hope that the stories prove enlightening, especially about the ways in which American cities have been built. I am particularly eager, however, that they prove sufficiently illuminating so that novel and imaginative steps can be taken to improve the lives of all their residents, from the very poorest who inhabit the inner cities, to the very richest who dwell in the suburbs. Fundamentally, I believe, the city is a community—one in which the lives of all people are intertwined. If we accept that premise, then it is obligatory that every effort be made to overcome the inequities that exist in all manner and form, from those of housing to those especially of schooling. As Rodney King said so plaintively into the television cameras two years ago on the conclusion of the trial of the Los Angeles police officers who beat him—"Can't we all get along together." I believe we can and must. I hope I have provided lessons in this work that may be used for achieving more harmonious community within the American city.

2

Themes and Perspectives on the American City

In order to undertake this study of the growth and development of cities in America, it would be useful to begin with a common definition of the city.[1] Unfortunately, it is difficult to find agreement among scholars about the character of cities. Some scholars, for example, treat the city much as would a student of architecture and fasten on the physical structures. Others treat the city as a conglomerate of population, subject to the ebb and flow of demographic pressures and forces. And yet others think of the city as the site essentially of major economic transactions and forces and thus see within it the processes of the production and distribution of goods and services.

Here, in this study of the city-building process in America, I want to focus on the range of political and economic forces that can influence the lives of urban residents and that can shape the destiny of any single urban center. For the purposes of this book, then, the city will be construed as *a site in which political power is mobilized and economic processes occur.* But I do not intend to simply objectify the city, though objective forces will play a large part in defining it. The city *assumes important meaning as well,* particularly for its residents, those who live in its neighborhoods and who work in its business firms. Mark Gottdiener, a leading authority on cities, speaks of this element, writing that "settlement places are always *meaningful* places."[2] John Logan and Harvey Molotch, two equally eminent scholars of the city, also draw attention to this feature, referring to the attachment to "place" that exists for many of us. "Places have a certain *preciousness* for their users," they write, "that are not part of the conventional concept of a commodity."[3] Indeed, it is because the city represents the confluence both of objective forces and of the meaning that we attach to it that it often becomes the site of considerable conflict and tension. For it is within the city that the currents of history run their course, alongside our efforts, as local residents, to channel them.

Theoretical Background

For many years, the analysis of cities among social scientists was dominated by the ideas of the Chicago school of sociology.[4] This group included a number of key intellectual figures—among them, Robert Park, Ernest Burgess, and Louis Wirth. They identified their common area of concern as that of human ecology, insisting that human beings' broad environment, where they lived and worked, exercised a decisive influence over their lives.[5] Drawing on the imagery of ecological study more generally, scholars of the Chicago school insisted on defining the basic processes of the city in terms such as *population competition* and *succession*.[6] They insisted that such processes were fundamentally normal among the residents of any given area—as normal as such processes are among any other living species. Though they also believed that the elements of culture and of government, for example, were equally decisive to the lives of human beings, they clearly drew their imagery of urban life from the realm of biology and ecology.[7]

The empirical research of students operating under the aegis of the Chicago school tended to focus on the aspects of social disorganization and disarray in the city. Writing at a time when tens of thousands of European immigrants were pouring into American cities, the students wrote wonderfully sympathetic examinations of the lives of the downtrodden, the outcast, and the misfit, including works on gangs, hoboes, and prostitutes.[8] The students' intentions, in effect, were to make visible the noxious aspects of life in the city. Often, they hoped, these works could be used in the effort to reform and to improve local governments.[9]

Among the most lasting contributions of the Chicago school are both a physical depiction of the city and a theoretical synthesis on the way of life in the city. Burgess, in particular, has developed a portrait of the city of Chicago that depicts it in terms of a series of concentric circles.[10] Circles closer to the center of the city are those wherein the competition for land is the most intense and thus are places where the land values tend to be the highest.[11] Accordingly, business institutions are most likely to be found there as they can most easily afford the rental prices. Circles farther out from the center are areas both of somewhat lower land value because demand is less and sites in which the homes of urban commuters are most apt to be found. But there is all manner of variation contained within each of the concentric circles, or zones as Burgess calls them. For example, he has identified one zone close to downtown Chicago as the zone of transition, in which light manufacturing would be found.[12] Rather quickly, then, this portrait of the city of Chicago became transformed into a theoretical portrait of how urban centers, created out of the processes of competition and succession among human populations, would emerge.

The theoretical synthesis about life in the city comes from the pen of Wirth.[13] It remains to this very day one of the classic pieces of analysis about life in the American city—though it is also highly overdrawn and very controversial.[14] Influenced by the writings of Georg Simmel, a German sociologist with whom Park had studied in Germany, Wirth insists that life in the city produces a unique set of experiences for its residents. Individuals who live in the city tend to meet one another in specialized circumstances; to deal with one another in anonymous, often superficial fashion; and to treat one another in the most impersonal manner. The city, he argues, breaks down the close personal bonds of the rural areas, substituting for them universal and impersonal connections. Accordingly, the city tends to contribute to higher rates of suicide as well as mental instability. To offset the loss of close personal bonds, involving especially extended family members, Wirth maintains that the individual now is free to engage in such new groups as voluntary associations, thus "joining with others of similar interest into organized groups to obtain his (sic) ends."[15]

Both the physical representation and the broad way of life came to highlight the work of these sociologists. Over time, further embellishments would be added, including further refinements of the basic scheme underlying the conception that the environment shaped the life of human beings. Some scholars would demonstrate that, in fact, the pattern of concentric circles, so descriptive of the population and residences of Chicago inhabitants, failed to capture the patterns in other cities.[16] Other scholars would add considerable elegance and substance to the ecological point of view. Singular among them was Amos Hawley, who provided a broad and comprehensive theory of human communities based on a refined and more powerful conception of basic ecological elements.[17]

These general themes, which depicted the human community as an ecological site, dominated much of the urban literature, particularly in the United States, until the 1970s. The ecological paradigm was able to withstand even the most vigorous intellectual assaults, including the criticisms of such personages as Walter Firey, who insisted that symbolic elements figured far more prominently in shaping life in cities than the ecologists had assumed.[18] Then, in the wake of major upheavals in cities, including, among other things, the default on loan payments by New York City, various strikes by tenant groups, and a host of similar critical events, new views came to be developed about cities and how they operate. Much of this new work, not surprisingly, was inspired by the writings of Karl Marx and represented an effort to extend many of his most fundamental insights and concepts to life in the city.

One major intellectual contributor to the effort to rethink the city was Manuel Castells. Castells had been a student of Louis Althusser, the famous French structuralist, and had adopted a number of Althusser's essential principles in the effort to reconstrue the city in Marxian terms. Althusser, himself, had sought to draw out the scientific principles and method in Marx, and, in so doing, claimed to have uncovered the basic structures and processes that operated under conditions of modern capitalism.[19] Castells, among other things, offered a ringing critique of the work of the Chicago school, arguing that scholars like Burgess had improperly conceived of the nature of the city.[20] Instead of depicting the city in physical terms, Castells maintained, sociologists should seek to understand the basic forces and processes that shaped and reshaped the urban center. In particular, he insisted, if one concedes that urban life under modern capitalism is subject to the same relentless forces as any other element, then, in fact, the city comes to occupy a special niche. That niche, under advanced capitalism, is focused around patterns of consumption by people, such as housing, and it is in these terms that the analysis of urban life must be understood.[21] Moreover, Castells maintained, cities are penetrated by the other structures of capitalism, such as the state and ideological apparatus, and life within cities is determined accordingly.

The other major figure to exercise a decisive influence on the thinking of social scientists at this time was David Harvey. A young English geographer employed at Johns Hopkins University, Harvey himself underwent a profound change in intellectual orientation toward urban space, one that left him convinced that the philosophy of Marx offered the only way to understand the origins of inequities within cities, at the same time as it provided the only possible solutions for removing those inequities.[22] Harvey introduced and elaborated upon certain key Marxian concepts as a means of reorienting thought about urban areas. One key insight, which subsequently became influential among a number of other students of cities, was Harvey's idea to adapt from Marx the notion of a difference between the *exchange value* and the *use value* of a commodity.[23] Exchange value, in essence, referred to the value of land, for example, as a commodity on the market, whereas use value connoted the manner in which land might be used by urban residents, among which Harvey included such forms as shelter and neighborhood.[24] The opposition between the two forms of value, in fact, plays a central role in Marx's conceptual underpinnings of the exploitative nature of modern capitalism, for it is the difference between the two that captures the central tension between the way in which capitalism marks things and the way that ordinary people would otherwise construe (or use) them. Harvey went on to explore systematically other ways in which the insights and concepts of Marx could be helpful in understanding the modern metropolis and provided original work that would prove to be influential among a range of other urban scholars.[25]

But other scholars also made significant contributions to the intellectual reorientation that took place in the early 1970s toward the city. Harvey Molotch, for example, a graduate of the University of Chicago in the late 1960s, proposed a fundamentally new way of thinking about the nature of cities in America. In a seminal article, he insisted that the primary goal of any city is that of *growth,* or *expansion,* and that those who dominate the life of the city represent a "growth machine." He argued that certain local interests in cities mobilized themselves around the issue of growth, making it the central and overriding goal of the city.[26]

Such interests included local businessmen, particularly property owners and investors who stood to accumulate considerable financial gain from the competition over the sale and disposition of local lands.[27] Moreover, as Molotch has insisted, growth was so effective a banner that it could capture and secure a wide range of local support, including that of local government officials, who, themselves, stood to benefit from expansionist policies.[28]

This original piece of Molotch's was followed some ten years later by an award-winning work written with John Logan.[29] In it, the two urbanists expanded on the ideas set forth in the "growth machine" article, but they also elaborated on other key principles, including the contrast between urban land as exchange value and as use value, a contrast they acknowledged as having adopted from Harvey. They developed this antinomy into one of the central pivots of their work, arguing, for instance, that the tension evident between many urban residents and the business (especially real estate) interests of a city is rooted in the fact that residents would prefer to use land in any of several different ways rather than be compelled to treat it merely as a commodity.[30]

Today many of us who seek to make sense of the nature of the city-building process are greatly indebted to these thinkers, including even some of the human ecologists. They have helped to furnish us with the intellectual tools to begin to understand life in the city, in general, and to appreciate especially the processes that so often seem to dominate urban life, such as outrage and uprising. Let us now turn from this general background to consider a number of more specific themes that shall serve to inform the historical studies here of several American cities.

Guiding Themes and Ideas

In this work, we want to learn how cities are built and how they can change over time. We want to think of this as an effort to examine the city-building process as it has occurred in American cities, with an eye to making discoveries that might be helpful in understanding how cities in other nations can be built, as well as how cities might be transformed.

There are several key themes and ideas that will help guide this effort, a number of them arising out of the most recent research and reflections about the city, including those of, among others, Castells and Harvey. Some of this work has come to be identified as the "new urban sociology," a phrase that includes the recent textbook by Gottdiener, as well as writings by Gottdiener and fellow sociologist, Joe Feagin.[31] One of the most distinctive traits of this recent thinking is that it moves the agenda for urban research from an effort simply to document the ebb and flow of objective dimensions, such as the size of the metropolis, to one of seeking to understand how urban residents themselves can transform their immediate surroundings. Susan Fainstein, for one, is particularly emphatic in her concern that "(b)ecause places still matter profoundly to the people who occupy them, they cannot be disregarded by any progressive movement," though she cautions that such concerns must today necessarily be incorporated as part of a broad national strategy to effect change.[32]

City growth, or city-building, can be construed in terms of several elements. When we think of the process of city-building, we can conceive of it in different forms. For instance, Logan and Molotch speak of the process as one of "growth" in a basic sense, and they mean by this concept any action that produces an expansion of some key element of the urban structure, be it land or space.[33] There is some appeal in simply construing our intellectual task in such terms, in part, because as Logan and Molotch have so well documented, many different interests in the city seem to congregate easily and freely under the banner of "growth." But the elements of the city that do grow also differ from one another in distinctive ways. Land development and expansion, for example, are clearly very different from expansion simply in terms of new jobs. Moreover, actors are likely to have different stakes in the outcomes over different growth elements. Municipal governments, for instance, are apt to smile on efforts designed to extend their landed boundaries, but they are likely to resist simple expansion of the density of their respective populations.

There is no single right way then to construe the various elements of the city-building process. Equally good scholars differ among themselves as to which, of the several features, might be considered most significant. For instance, Gottdiener, drawing on the seminal work of the French neo-Marxist Henri Lefebvre, who also served as inspiration for the writings of Harvey, insists that we think of the city in socio-spatial terms.[34] It is the social use of urban space, Gottdiener insists, that will reveal to us how forces in the modern world dominate key decisions in the urban environment. Harvey, in contrast, considers that both urban space and the built environment, those structures created in cities, play a central role in defining the character of the city, and so both deserve to be studied in understanding city-building.[35] And Feagin, in his richly textured work on Houston, is eager to insist that land-use patterns are absolutely central to understanding the development of modern cities, particularly the way in which real estate interests dominate the city-building process.[36]

Synthesizing these writings, then, let us think of city-building in several complementary respects. First, let us think of it as an *expansion in the size of the population.* This clearly is an element that underlies many of the basic conceptions that have been offered about cities. Next, let us consider it in terms of an *expansion in the amount of capital invested in a city.* As both Castells and Harvey suggest, for example—and as I shall shortly elaborate—capital and capitalism have played a decisive role in shaping the urban environment in America. Any expansion whatsoever in the capital wealth of a city represents an important feature of the city-building process. Finally, let us also think of city-building in terms of an *expansion in the use of or amount of land or both.* Land, as well as its valorization, as writers as different as Harvey and Burgess remind us, is perhaps the most central element of the making of the city.[37]

In our historical studies, therefore, we shall focus attention on changes in the extent and/or use of land, capital, and population as part of the process whereby a city is built. Molotch, for example, recommends precisely such a comprehensive strategy, observing that "(intensive) land development, higher population density, and increased levels of financial activity" represent "(the) entire syndrome of associated events that is meant by the general term 'growth.'"[38]

In the process of city-building, larger social forces play a critical role. Cities, from one angle, can be seen merely as the condensations of the play of larger forces of a nation. They represent the social constructions created by these forces. Thus, inasmuch as capitalism plays so decisive a part in shaping the destiny of people in the United States, it necessarily must play an equally prominent role in shaping the creation of cities. And, by the same token, since governments play so central a role in our lives, they, too, must play a key part in urban life.

Of course, such claims are rather obvious. But different schools of thought, even among the new urban sociologists, are likely to emphasize one or the other of these forces. Thus, those who adopt a neo-Marxist point of view are likely to insist that the mode of production and the relations among social classes are fundamental to the construction of cities. It is in the nature of such production that the energies that will form the city lie—in particular, the effort by enterprises to accumulate capital. Moreover, different fractions of capitalism will become involved in different degrees in the accumulation process. Some, such as the second circuit of capital—the interests identified with real estate and development—have a particularly strong motivation to act in ways that will decisively shape the urban landscape.[39]

Nevertheless, because of the failures of classical, or orthodox, Marxism—specifically the failure of capitalism to be toppled by the forces of the working classes—there have been a number of attempts to emphasize the part played both by local and by federal government.[40] Sometimes the role assigned to government is basically a subsidiary one that merely seems to complement the efforts of capitalist enterprises. When Logan and Molotch, for example, speak of the "growth machine," that coalition often is dominated by real estate interests, with local government officials serving the role of collaborators, or facilitators, of growth. But other scholars recognize, even if they adopt many of the assumptions of the new urbanists, that governments can exercise more than a subsidiary role. For instance, Raymond Pahl, a British urbanist, has been a leading exponent of the view that state managers are crucial to the creation of cities under modern capitalism.[41] And Desmond King, another British scholar, takes a similar tack, insisting that the state may take the lead in promoting urban development.[42] Extensive research by Feagin in his study of Houston, for example, suggests that government officials may exercise their influence in myriad ways.[43]

One of the major benefits of studying history—and particularly of tracing out the city-building process over a long period of time—is that it permits one to discover how and when institutions come to exercise their influence. What urbanists sometimes fail to acknowledge is that some of the variation in the influence of these two epic partners—capitalism and government—can arise primarily because of the timing, both developmental and historical, of city-building. Such timing, we would suggest, may help to unravel the mystery of who exercises power, when, and how much.[44]

Both local and extra-local forces play a central part in shaping the city-building process. In the modern era, extra-local forces, in the form of global economic institutions, seem to play a major role in setting limits on what cities can and cannot do.[45] Further, inasmuch as we are interested in tracing out the city-building process both over time and over the life span of cities, we must be sensitive to the changes that may occur in the role of local and extra-local forces. In the nineteenth century, for instance, well before the birth of the modern administrative state, local forces were held to be prominent in the creation of towns, villages, and even small cities. Countless stories existed of heroic entrepreneurs who were decisive in the early construction of places.[46]

But such individual actors were not entirely determinative in shaping the destiny of a place. There are some scholars who claim, for example, that the efforts of entrepreneurs pale by comparison to the impact of broader environmental circumstances. In a recent award-winning work, historian William Cronon shows that Chicago's larger environment proved essential to its emergence as a great metropolitan center.[47] In a masterful fashion, he demonstrates that the unlimited raw materials, such as wheat and livestock, coupled with an effective network of railroads enabled Chicago to become a premiere Midwestern site, far more accomplished than such lesser rivals as St. Louis or Milwaukee.

Thus, in undertaking our examination of the city-building process over time, we shall be particularly attentive to the impact of extra-local conditions, such as railroads and broader economic circumstances, as well as to how their significance might come to vary, becoming especially powerful in recent decades.

Human agency and historical contingency have a hand in shaping the outcomes of city-building in any particular site. If the growth of cities simply were determined by the play of larger forces, there would be no reason at all to examine the process. Analyses of capitalism, for instance, would prove so powerful in their scope and predictive capacity as to render specific circumstance and particular actors superfluous. But such, of course, is not the case. Rather, it is not only how these larger forces make themselves felt but the manner in which they generate responses in the actions of specific human beings, that commend us to examine the historical construction of specific sites in detail.

Neo-Marxist writers, in general, and those who have written about the city, in particular, have wrestled with these issues in the most illuminating and provocative fashion. In large part they have been prompted to do so because Marx, himself, appeared divided on matters pertaining to the exercise of human will and the significance of historically contingent conditions. In his early work, for example, Castells took the view that the laws of modern capitalism were strictly determinative of specific urban outcomes.[48] Among other things, he argued that the structures of modern capitalism produced a special function for cities, one of serving as "collective consumption units," rather than as sites of production, as orthodox Marxism maintained. But in his later writings, particularly about urban social movements, Castells totally abandoned his earlier position, suggesting that both human agency and historical contingency exercise decisive influence.[49]

In the historical studies that follow, I shall assume that both human agency and historical contingency are operative factors. Moreover, I shall further assume that particular kinds of social actors exercise an influence over the outcomes of the city-building process. Among them, we shall include *place entrepreneurs.* Such figures, environmental conditions notwithstanding, do seem important to the way in which cities develop. These figures seem particularly critical, in fact, to the early stages of urban expansion, helping to mobilize various resources and energies in communities.[50]

But, in keeping with the spirit of the new urban sociology, I would insist that collective actors, in general, exercise an even more decisive role than individual actors in urban expansion. Indeed, there appear to be a host of such actors. They include, among others, segments of particular *social classes,* including members both of the upper class and of the working class. They also include groups that may be more specific to the city, especially ones such as *neighborhood organizations.* Writers such as Susan Fainstein and Norman Fainstein have proven especially instructive on the activities of neighborhood groups, noting that they can be successful in various locales and under very specific sets of conditions.[51] And, of course, there are also *coalitions* of key actors who have proven so critical to the success of city-building efforts in many modern cities. Logan and Molotch are especially insightful on the role of such coalitions, as well as the ways in which these groups gain the upper hand in battles over urban growth.[52] Similarly, Clarence Stone, a political scientist, has revealed much about the operations of coalitions in his pioneering work on politics and development in Atlanta.[53]

Finally, I want to propose that *corporate bodies* also figure as important actors in the city-building process. This is not the same as claiming that groups of government officials serve as members of the growth coalition. This latter claim, which derives from the writings of Logan and Molotch, would appear to suggest that all the key actors of the coalition share the same goals—in essence, growth. Instead, I wish to argue not only that public corporate bodies hold goals that are different from those of private actors in the city but also that such goals, in fact, are best understood as the effort by government to exercise its sovereign powers.[54]

Sovereignty is something, of course, that, like the effort to secure profit, is socially constructed over a long period. Furthermore, sovereignty plays a central role in the capacity of public corporate bodies to command and to manipulate the actions of citizens, capitalist and otherwise. The urban scholar to best appreciate and understand this facet of municipal government is historian Eric Monkkonen. In his extremely insightful work, *America Becomes Urban,* Monkkonen has written that in "the transition to the modern urban nation ... city government has changed its role radically. ... The city government that emerged from the late

nineteenth and early twentieth century emphasizes active service, not passive reg-
ulation."[55]

Accordingly, we can anticipate that the actions of local corporate bodies—in
particular, municipal governments—may or may not coincide with the interests
of local capitalists to accumulate capital.[56] Furthermore, I propose, if there is no
such convergence of interest, major divisions can result even among the leading
sectors of a city—differences of opinion that can effectively render the actions of a
growth coalition null and void.

Cities are the sites of fundamental conflict and tension. The city is, as John
Mollenkopf so aptly put it, a place that is "contested."[57] Contests dominate its life
and that of its residents. Some depict contests, as Harvey suggested, in the struggle between exchange value and use value. Thus, many of the modern contests assume the form of a struggle between those who wish only to treat land as a commodity and those who wish to use land or see within it something other than its
market value. In an earlier work on Austin, Texas, I put it in this way:

> Today there exist, in fact, two very different meanings that people in Austin attach to
> the land. ... On the one hand, there are those people who today define the land
> purely and simply in terms of modern-day capitalism, that is, as a commodity. ... On
> the other hand, there exists ... an entirely different conception of land. ... To (those
> who hold this conception), the land is to be preserved as much as possible in its natu-
> ral, primitive state, and equally as much to be used for the enjoyment of the broad
> public rather than simply the large-scale developer.[58]

Quite clearly, the process whereby land is turned into a commodity underlies a
good deal of the tension and conflict in the city. But there is more than simply
capitalism at work. There are countless political actors, collective and otherwise,
who become involved in the contest for control of the city. In the modern city,
there are various neighborhood groups, even neighborhood coalitions, that are at
work in the effort to enhance the lives of local urban residents. In his recent work,
Castells has been especially attentive to the role of the "grassroots," discovering
that urban movements in different places and at different times seek to transform
urban space. Further, he argues, these movements seek transformations in any of
several key respects—as patterns of meaning, power, and consumption.[59]

Thus, in the course of my historical studies, I want both to be aware of the dimensions and strands of the conflict that can permeate the life of the city and to
be especially sensitive to the manner in which conflict can figure into the city-
building process.

*A considerable part of the conflict in cities springs from the struggle to balance two
competing goals—growth, on the one hand, and equality, on the other.* In the process of building cities, certain interests are more likely to be satisfied than others.
In particular, those who hold capital are more likely to find that their investments, in industries or in land, provide them a greater return than the return provided to the general public. Of course, these capitalists would insist, such is only

natural for they have put up the capital. But the disparities often prove to be substantial, and even more tragically, they happen after the public has been assured that everyone is likely to benefit from the new industry, the new development, or the new jobs.

As Logan and Molotch so clearly recognize, the public often is appeased by the growth coalition with claims that growth is something like progress—it is natural, and it will benefit everyone. But growth is neither natural nor does it benefit everyone.[60] Various studies, for instance, reveal that the costs of growth are borne more directly by the public—and more often by the poor—than by the wielders of capital themselves. In his important work on Houston, for example, Feagin discovers that urban growth actually promotes a wide variety of "external" costs, ranging from toxic wastes to air pollution in the city.[61] Various other case studies, primarily on older cities, tend to reveal much the same pattern of unequal costs and unequal development.[62]

In one of the more illuminating recent studies of this issue, Todd Swanstrom paid particularly close attention to how the division over growth and equality was adjudicated in the politics of Cleveland. He observes that there are fundamental dilemmas involved in the politics of growth, especially when resources are scarce. Decisions come down to making a choice between serving the interests of business, on the one hand, and providing for the well-being of the public, especially the low-income citizens, on the other. Swanstrom notes, for example, that "urban renewal forced the external costs of economic growth—for example, the removal of slums to build new office towers—on those who could least afford them: inner-city slum dwellers and small businesses. ... (whereas) the benefit of the expanding service sector went mostly to downtown corporations and suburbanites."[63]

What proves particularly instructive about the social history of city-building in this regard is that it permits us to gain some insight into how the dilemma, or struggle, between the forces on behalf of equality and those on behalf of growth is resolved. Sometimes sharp insight is provided by particularly persuasive histories of these matters. One of the best is by Ira Katznelson.[64] He undertook a study of the development of working-class politics in New York City in the nineteenth and twentieth centuries. After an illuminating historical analysis, he concludes that the failure of working-class politics in New York—and, more generally, in America—happened because of the sharp separation brought about between work and home, labor and residence, for the working class. This separation, he argues, accounts for a kind of political schizophrenia in the working class, something that critically distinguishes America from its European counterparts.

In the histories I examine in this book, I shall be especially attentive to how the trade-off between growth and equality is played out. Two historical moments will prove instructive: the one that came at the turn of the century, when the working class of many industrial cities had become especially powerful; and the one that arrived at mid-twentieth century, when efforts began to redress some of the inequities within the metropolis, especially the inequity that had developed between the wealthy suburbs and the impoverished inner cities. This book's most extensive case study, that of Milwaukee, will help shed considerable light on these matters since that city is one of the few cities in America where the Social Democrats actually came to hold power in municipal government.

The nature of the city changes over time; there is evidence not only that cities change in response to historical features of the particular circumstances in which they emerge but also that they go through specific stages of development. In this as well as the final theme informing the historical studies in this work, I want to move somewhat beyond the frame of reference so effectively promoted by the new urban sociology. In particular, I want to propose some specific ideas regarding the nature of change in cities.

Assuming, as we have, that cities are influenced by the play of larger social forces, both internal and external, cities must come to reflect in some manner the central features of their epoch. Thus, for example, there are a number of cities in America that developed in the midst of the great transformations that took place as industrial capitalism entered—and reshaped—the American city. Many of these cities, such as Detroit and Pittsburgh, Cleveland and Milwaukee (the latter two of which we shall study here), were marked in a definite fashion by the emergence of industrial capitalism. Worklife and residence, daily politics and government—all were changed profoundly. Moreover, many of these same cities today are finding it difficult to disengage themselves from the dominance of industrialization—which, of course, accounts in part for the decline of each.

In one sense, then, the changes that have taken place in these cities quite clearly reflect the play of larger social and economic circumstances. If industry refashioned worklife within them, for example, industry also left them vulnerable as the character of the larger economy under modern capitalism shifted from an emphasis on manufacturing to a stress on service occupations.[65]

However, there is another kind of change that appears likely to occur in cities, one that shapes the internal life of the city itself. It appears, in fact, that cities move through a series of stages and that in each stage they take on a special character. Some analysts have referred to this development of the city in rather plain terms, as a change from urbanization to suburbanization, or as a change from rapid growth to decline.[66]

I wish to propose here that the internal configuration of a city can change as well—in particular, the configuration of local institutions and the effectiveness of their operations in promoting growth or ensuring equality or both. In a sense, this hypothesis runs against the grain of some of the ideas of the new urban sociologists. Logan and Molotch, for example, appear to suggest that the "growth machine" may change character very slightly over time but that it pretty much remains intact over the life course of a city.[67]

Important research supports the hypothesis of an internal and sequential development of cities in America. Two political economists, R. D. Norton and Ann Markusen, the latter one of the most brilliant students today of American cities and regions, provide an argument that underscores the developmental aspects of city-building. Norton, for example, argues that the older and newer cities of to-day, cities, on the one hand, like Cleveland, and, on the other hand, like Phoenix, each seem similar to one another when they were at similar points in their development—that is, when they experienced rapid initial growth, and then leveled off to more stable growth.[68] Both the growth of local industry and the activities of local government seemed to run parallel courses at similar stages in their development—courses that were aggressive in the rapid expansion of jobs and in the annexation of land, respectively. In a somewhat parallel fashion, though attending more closely to the life cycle of industries, Markusen has suggested that cities and regions are themselves likely to reflect the profit cycle of local businesses. There is an invariant sequence of stages, she suggests, in the profitability of any industrial sector, one that moves from zero profit through a stage of superprofit and then concludes in a stage of negative profit.[69] Furthermore, she maintains, the fates of cities and regions are so closely tied to the stage of profit cycle of industries that it would prove futile for residents to seek to revive the moribund industries. Concluding on a hopeful note, she observes that "the preservation of our communities and the fates of our regions lie in the development of new mechanisms for industrial planning that will acknowledge the costs of community change as an integral part of the choice to set up and to close down production facilities."[70]

Building on the insights of both scholars, I wish to suggest that the very character of the institutions of a city is apt to change from one stage to another, with an alternation between political and economic institutions in the part they play in the city-building process. Thus, for example, in the stages of early growth, both for the local industries and for the city as a whole, it is likely that economic institutions will play a large role in shaping the destiny of the city, particularly insofar as they promote the rapid influx of migrants eager to take on new jobs. However, in later stages, as the economy tends to stabilize or even to decline, I suggest, a greater burden begins to fall on political institutions, particularly local political institutions that now face the burden of diminishing capital input as well as higher unemployment rates, poverty, and other such consequences.

Such changes are by no means insignificant. Indeed, they suggest, as Markusen argues, that if cities can anticipate their own decline, owing to the circumstances influencing local industries, cities could plan accordingly and seek such options as the aggressive pursuit of new industries or the active provision by local government of an effort to redistribute revenues such that predictably high levels of unemployment will not prove so devastating to the local community.

In the studies in this book, then, I shall carefully examine the stages through which cities are apt to pass and shall seek to discover whether there is an invariant sequence—and, if so, its particular character—in a manner suggested both by Markusen and Norton. If the hypothesis about stages and about the internal configuration of local institutions proves correct, I would argue, it suggests an additional set of constraints and forces within which urban residents must seek to lead

their lives—and it commends local officials to do everything possible to anticipate and to offset the predictable local decline.

Finally, cities are continuous, and they have a history. They are places where the
past, inscribed in local institutions, weighs very heavily on the present. Ultimately, I would argue, the reason for studying the history of places is to discover
what this past is and how it weighs upon the present generations, so that present
generations can learn enough about the structures that influence their lives to
change them.

Perhaps this last claim of mine is obvious. However, often we as scholars think
and act as though there were only tomorrow and no yesterday. We make much
out of apparent changes in the present, but we fail to take account of the full and
complex nature of the past. We who study the history of cities are under a special
obligation to show how—and why—the city changes over time, the nature of
those changes, and what features of the city remain the same. For within those elements impervious to change we are apt to find the underlying forces that deeply
animate the life of the city, affecting both its growth and the opportunities for the
attainment of equity by its residents.

The weight of urban institutions in America, it seems to me, is most clearly inscribed in two dimensions: the nature of local institutions, such as municipal
government, and the nature of the boundaries that divide the city from its suburbs. Historians of the city have done much to reveal the elements both of these
institutions and of the boundaries that define cities. Kenneth Jackson, an eminent
urban historian, has described at length how Americans came to fall in love with
suburbs.[71] Jon Teaford, an equally eminent historian of urban institutions, also
has examined in depth the manner in which urban institutions were developed in
American cities, particularly at the close of the nineteenth century.[72]

These historians, and many others, commend us to attend, therefore, to the
lasting character of these aspects of the urban landscape. For it is within them that
we are likely to uncover many of the unique and powerful features of the city under modern capitalism and as influenced by the modern state. In particular, it is
the historic character of the city-suburban division that truly reflects the deep
overlap between social and spatial inequalities in the American city. These inequalities, we shall discover, are not simply the products of the past three or four
decades. They are, in fact, products that reveal the very ways in which cities in
America have been built. And they thereby portray both the limits and the possibilities for rebuilding these cities.

PART TWO

The Rise and Fall of Milwaukee

3

Pre-Industrial Milwaukee: 1818–1870

High above Lake Michigan, nestled among bluffs of oaks and elms, a small town began to take shape in approximately the year 1818. The town eventually would grow to become one of the major urban centers of the American Midwest. It began, as so many others had, in the possession of certain natural advantages over rival villages. It lay at a confluence of three rivers near Lake Michigan and thus provided ready accessibility to travelers who came by land or by water. Moreover, the town was in a beautiful and wild setting, remembered years later by one settler who described it thusly: "To say that it was simply beautiful, does not express it; it was more than beautiful—with bluffs so round and bold, covered with just sufficient timber to shade them well, and from whose tops could be seen the lake, extending beyond the reach of human vision, while between them ran the river, like a silver thread ... in which the Indian could detect and spear fish at the depth of twelve and even eighteen feet, and upon whose surface sparkled the rays of the morning sun as upon a mirror."[1]

This will be the story of Milwaukee, Wisconsin. It will be the story of the forces that created this place and particularly of the role that social agents and institutions played in its development. I begin my story by assuming that the creation of Milwaukee was primarily a social act. Yet it was a social act whose players would change over time and whose drama would be played out in different stages as it evolved. The threads of this story concern the creation of the place, Milwaukee; but the fabric that has been woven over the course of the past century and a half is a fabric that, though all of a piece, looks much like a patchwork quilt. Indeed, it is a patchwork quilt that could be said to be much like that of many other cities in America.

The Drive to Settle and to Expand Milwaukee

A City of Entrepreneurs

However much nature may have blessed Milwaukee, with its waters and its lands easy to traverse, the real story of its beginnings is to be uncovered in the work of a band of entrepreneurs. They were the men who founded and who settled the area first and who claimed the area as their own. Further, in exercising their roles as entrepreneurs, they would be like the bands of men who helped initiate the city-building process in so many other small towns and villages across America.

Three figures dominate the early years of the settlement. The first was Solomon Juneau, or "Solomo," as he was called by the Indians in the area. Juneau came to Milwaukee first in 1818. A man of French-Canadian ancestry, his business was, at the beginning, that of trade, and trade in furs and pelts especially. Before the arrival of the settlers of English ancestry, Juneau dealt with the Indians. He married Josette, a woman from among the Indians, and within just a few short years, he and his family had the makings of a substantial settlement along the banks of the Milwaukee River.[2]

In October 1833, Morgan Martin, a lawyer and financier from Green Bay, which at that time was a far more prosperous and thriving settlement than Milwaukee, met Juneau in Milwaukee. Martin, it appears, had come to the area with one explicit purpose in mind—to buy and to develop the new parcels of land that were becoming available to settlers on the frontier. He wanted to make a profit from speculation in land, and he convinced Juneau to become his able partner in this particular endeavor. The two men set about buying up as much property in the area as possible, through agreements both with the Indians and the Michigan territorial legislature.[3]

The first years were occupied in enclosing the available lands once held by the Indians. Juneau wrote to Martin in 1833 that he was developing the settlement quickly and that he had sought to lay claim to the land as best he could:

> You must be aware that being much busy about the interests of the American Fur Company, I am not able to do as much as I would wish for my present concern. Notwithstanding these daily occupations, I have not neglected to do what was necessary in order to substantiate my rights on the said premises. ... This winter I shall have logs drawn up on the spot, and early next spring I will build a handsome little building as a dwelling house. This improvement will establish more for the right claims. ... I have already enclosed the best parts of land on my side, and intend to make more inclosures.[4]

By late 1834, word of the new settlement and of the available lands had reached a number of people in other places, particularly Chicago, and the land business began to boom. Writing on behalf of Juneau in 1834, Albert Fowler, Juneau's new fellow settler and interpreter, told Martin:

We have had a number of gentlemen here to look at the country and all are well pleased. And there are three of them here now from Chicago and have all built themselves houses and say that they will come here with their families in the Spring to live. … The prospects of our country are beginning on us. There has lately been as many as four locations made on Root River below Skunk Grove. Mr. Juneau has had 36 lots laid out on survey by Judge King and there is great enquiring when they are to be sold here and at Chicago.[5]

Martin and Juneau were not the only entrepreneurs who sought to make a new settlement through engaging in intense land speculation. In 1834, they were joined at the new community by Byron Kilbourn. Kilbourn had first seen the possibilities in the development of Milwaukee in his work as a surveyor and civil engineer in Ohio. The work involved surveying and making assessments of the new frontier, and Milwaukee, it seemed to him, offered great possibilities for personal gains.[6] He arrived at the city intent on making his own special settlement—to rival that of Juneau and Martin—and took up residence on the western banks of the Milwaukee River.

The topography of early Milwaukee lent itself to the development of divisions between settlers. The Milwaukee River, which emptied its waters directly into Lake Michigan, divided the eastern section of land rather neatly from the western section. On the east side, the settlement abutted the Great Lake. The land jutted out, almost like a peninsula, and it had easy access to any traffic that traveled to the area by way of the lake. The west, however, was directly connected to the interior of the land, and settlers who traveled by wagon from Chicago or Madison would first come upon the western settlement. Kilbourn and many others sensed that the western side of town would most likely be the most prosperous, directly owing to its ease of access.

Land speculation lay at the very heart of the development of this urban enterprise by the shores of Lake Michigan, as it did for so many new settlements on the American frontier; and Kilbourn was well aware of the gains to be had if he and his companions were able to offer a more attractive setting than that provided by Juneau and Martin. Thus, he sought in every way to develop a settlement that was far superior to that of his self-created rivals.

Writing to Micajah Williams in 1837, Kilbourn observed that "(on the other side of the Milwaukee River) Martin has built two very respectable houses, and several other original owners of minor interest have contributed considerably in actual improvements. This action on their part, together with a year the start of us, has given them an apparent advantage thus far, and it is necessary that we should take a similar course to turn the tide in our favor." Seeking to gain whatever advantages he could, Kilbourn further wrote that he intended to scuttle whatever efforts might be made by those on the other side of the river to employ a bridge that would enable traffic to cross the river without ferries: "As to a bridge over the river I consider it out of the question; but if they should succeed, contrary to all expectations, in erecting it, I will take good care that they shall have no use of it—for we can construct a couple of small steamboats for harbor use, and pass them through the bridge so frequently that it can never be closed."[7] This rivalry would soon come to dominate much of the life of the early settlements on opposite sides of the river.

The period of the mid-1830s was a time of heady speculation, land grabbing, and wildfire profits. Money was easily available, and financiers in the East, who sought to make profits from the opening up of the frontier, made every effort to invest their monies in places like Milwaukee. A. F. Pratt later recalled the period in this manner:

> Everybody had money enough, and some more. Many of the most careful businessmen in the East came here, so anxious to invest their money that they often bought thousands of dollars' worth of land unseen before sleeping, with a full assurance that it would double in value before morning. One man paid his all—$15,000—as a quarter payment down, and gave his notes, secured by a mortgage, for the balance, for a tract of land, and was compelled to borrow money to return home.[8]

"Sellers were as reckless as buyers, for everybody was a seller, and everybody was a buyer," remarked Silas Chapman some years later. "There was no limit to the prices and expectation of prices. ... (As a sign of these times) it was gravely announced one morning in a New York paper that two paupers had escaped from a county asylum, and before they could be recaptured, each had made $40,000 by speculating in lots."[9]

Gains were to be had, often amounting to tens of thousands of dollars, quite a considerable amount of money at the time.[10] It has been estimated, for example, that Juneau at this time must have made something on the order of a couple of hundred thousand dollars.[11] Martin himself purchased land from Juneau, in late 1835, at a cost of something just over $200 per acre, and only months later Juneau had written to Martin that land was now selling at a cost of anywhere between $2,000 and $4,000 per acre.[12] Moreover, Daniel Wells, Jr., another early entrepreneur of whom we shall hear considerably more soon, wrote a friend in August 1835, almost thunderstruck at the great profits to be made in Milwaukee: "One particular case," he wrote, "I know where the settler got 160 acres for 1.25 cts. per acre [and] has since been offered $50 per acre amounting to $8,000 for his lot—I bought some adjoining it for which I paid $250 & could now take a small advance on it. I think it will double in a year."[13]

But the bubble burst quickly, as such land schemes are wont to do. The new village of Milwaukee, without its own marketplace and capacity to survive the exigencies of the time, was completely dependent for its survival on the broader financial marketplaces of the country. Thus, when the great financial panics of 1837 swept across America, they swept Milwaukee along with them. Men, who by virtue of their land speculation had made substantial profits in the mid-1830s, now saw their wealth disappear overnight.

Juneau and Martin both fell victim to the panic. Martin managed to survive because he maintained business interests in Green Bay and elsewhere. But Juneau seems to have had no such protection and lost much of what he had gained. By 1842, he was compelled to declare himself bankrupt to the tune of $20,000 in debt. His losses quickly became visible to the Milwaukee public, leaving others to talk of his great misfortune. Indeed, by 1852 he chose to depart the village and to move elsewhere in the state, to Theresa. He died in 1856 among the Indians he much admired and loved.

The great financial panics could have wiped out the fortunes of Milwaukee altogether, as they did those of other settlements at the time. But this particular community was fortunate in that it did not have to rely exclusively on the energies and fortunes of Martin and Juneau. Kilbourn managed to hang on to his properties—indeed, to expand his wealth. There were other entrepreneurs, too—men who engaged in land speculation as well as other business enterprises—who managed to keep the fledgling city afloat in spite of its very severe financial losses.

Among this second band were two men, Daniel Wells, Jr., and Alexander Mitchell. Like Juneau and Martin, as well as Kilbourn, the two did much of their business in financial speculation on land. Both appeared to have shown greater business acumen than Martin and especially more than their fellow Milwaukeean, Solomon Juneau. Wells came from a family in the East, in Maine, as so many other migrants had. He arrived in Milwaukee in mid-1835, and like many of his fellow settlers, he began the business of buying up and selling lands, writing to a close friend, Jacob Kimball, that "I have purchased considerable real estate at Milwaukee—principally in village property."[14] By the 1840s, Wells had managed to secure a great amount of property in the city, in part owing to his wisdom and thrift in the handling of finances. He was an industrious and ambitious capitalist and, within the space of a decade, managed to hold as debtors many residents of Milwaukee as well as of southeastern Wisconsin.[15]

Equally important to the expansion of this new settlement were the energies and imagination of Mitchell. Mitchell, as time soon would prove, was a man of substantial energy and thrift, the stereotype of the nineteenth-century Scotsman—in fact, perhaps, the original source of the stereotype. Born in Aberdeen, Scotland, in 1817, Mitchell came first to Milwaukee in 1839 to act as the local banking agent of George Smith.[16] Smith, a resident of Chicago, had six years earlier begun a career as a banker in Chicago. In 1839, he managed to secure the permission of the Michigan territorial legislature for the incorporation of a new banking enterprise, the Wisconsin Marine and Fire Insurance Company. Although ostensibly intended to deal in the matter of fire insurance, in fact the bank did business in a wide variety of areas, including the issuance of certificates of deposit and the lending of money through the bank's creation of currency notes. It also engaged in the purchase of large tracts of real estate and, by the early 1840s, the bank held the notes to almost $100,000 worth of real estate in and around Milwaukee. Eventually, Smith sold his interests to Mitchell, and Mitchell came to be one of the wealthiest of Milwaukee citizens. He was regarded by his contemporaries as someone blessed with great wisdom and foresight and, in later years, frequently would be called upon by his fellow settlers for his advice.[17]

Possibly the most notable thing about Wells and Mitchell is that, like the founding entrepreneurs of other American settlements, they were regarded by their contemporaries as men possessed of a *vision* of and for the future—a vision they employed to help and to promote the development of their village. Vision, of course, is an elusive phenomenon—something often identified more clearly in hindsight, after the fruits of a person's labors have been realized, than recognized during the visionary's own lifetime. But there is clearly something to this quality in the effort of the early entrepreneurs of the city, something about the energy and the imagination for the future of the city that was common, among others, both to Wells and to Mitchell. Of Wells, for example, it once was written by a biographer that "(he) had vision (and) … imagination. … He determined that the great wagon roads, the canals, and the railroads should lead to Lake Michigan; more particularly Milwaukee. It had the position. It must become the metropolis of the great North West."[18] Daniel Madden, the author of an excellent political history of nineteenth-century Milwaukee, perhaps puts it best when he writes:

> The single most important drive in the settlement of Milwaukee was not land, but speculative vision. The men who controlled the destiny of the city purchased land because they had imagination. They believed that their vision of the future Milwaukee was prophetic. They invested their own capital in this dream and expected to attract more capital from the East.[19]

Moreover, Wells himself had written to Kimball in 1835 that the "land about the Milwaukee River and south of there is the best in the Territory and as Milwaukee is the only harbour for some distance either way on the lake it must necessarily become a place of considerable importance."[20]

Visions such as these were crucial in helping to drive the city forward and in creating for it a sense of purpose—a sense and spirit that captured the imagination of many settlers to this part of the new western frontier. Visions such as these also gave notice that wealthy capitalists, who engaged in the purchase and sale of land, were central to the creation of the frontier community.

Commercial Enterprises and Business Alliances

The entrepreneurial spirit, concentrated in abundance in men like Juneau and Kilbourn, certainly was the first and most critical impulse that led to the creation of Milwaukee. Entrepreneurs cannot by themselves, however, promote the successful expansion of a new settlement, as the histories of many abortive attempts at American settlements show.[22] The growth of a city also demands the development of a viable and prosperous market. In this regard, the prospects of Milwaukee were aided in no little measure by the slow and gradual development of a strong group of commercial enterprises.

By 1840, the settlement of Milwaukee numbered just over 1,700 residents. They were now divided among three sections of town—the eastern part, known as Juneautown; the western part, known as Kilbournville; and the southern section, known as "Walker's Point" in honor of its founding figure, George Walker. Among the settlers, there was the usual array of business practitioners, including small merchants who ran dry-goods stores, a handful of physicians, blacksmiths, and other small businessmen.[22] Over the next decade, the town assumed all the qualities of a lively village, reaching a population of more than 20,000 by 1850.

During the 1840s, commerce and trade in the town had taken an important turn, measurably assisted by the natural advantages of Milwaukee's setting. Because the city lay at the eastern edges of the frontier of the American West, and had ready access to a hinterland that soon became rich with forests of grains, Milwaukee businessmen were able to develop a strong market presence, anchored in the trade of wheat, barley, and oats. Financing for a number of these early ventures in grain trade came, not surprisingly, from the generous coffers of Alexander Mitchell. In 1844, for instance, he lent a young settler, Daniel Newhall, $300 to set about the development of a business in the trade of grain. Very quickly, Newhall came to be regarded as something of a market genius, a risk-taker with savvy, and became the largest grain dealer in the Midwest at that time. He put ships under charter to himself and made phenomenal profits—on the order of $250,000—in a very short time.[23] About the same time, Mitchell also provided a loan to Peter McGeogh, a man who turned his own attention to trading on the Milwaukee and Chicago grain markets, and he, too, became a man of overnight prosperity in Milwaukee.[24]

Owing to the rapid success of people like Newhall and McGeogh, the economic well-being of the community, once threatened with extinction by the failure of the financial markets, began to flourish. Over the course of the 1840s and 1850s, not only had the amount of trade both within and by the community expanded, but the net wealth of its residents, in turn, had risen rapidly. More and more it became known as the prominent center of grain trade in America, and its position, set alongside the shores of Lake Michigan, provided yet another advantage over rival communities, especially those of the interior. Table 3.1 shows us the amount of exports of flour and grain for Milwaukee between 1845 and 1870. Note, in particular, that the number of bushels of wheat shipped from Milwaukee grew from 95,510 in 1845 to more than two and one-half million bushels only ten years later. Aided by the continuing supply of grains from its hinterlands, Milwaukee's marketplace soon became populated with a handful of millers who turned the wheat into flour. In the space of a few years, Milwaukee's lake traffic grew as well, and soon the city began to compete successfully with rival port cities, notably cities like Chicago and Cleveland.[25]

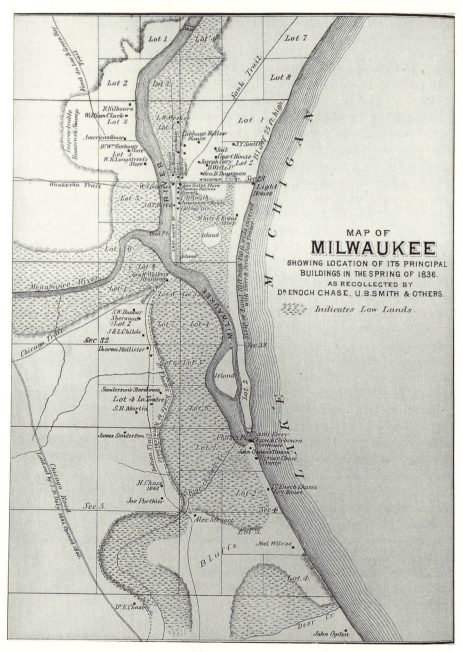

MAP OF
MILWAUKEE
SHOWING LOCATION OF ITS PRINCIPAL
BUILDINGS IN THE SPRING OF 1836.
AS RECOLLECTED BY
D*r* ENOCH CHASE, U.B.SMITH & OTHERS.

Indicates Low Lands.

Map of Milwaukee (1836)

TABLE 3.1   Milwaukee Flour and Grain Exports, 1845–1870 (five-year intervals)

Year	Flour (Barrels)	Grain		
		Wheat (Bushels)	Oats (Bushels)	Barley (Bushels)
1845	7,550	95,510	—	—
1850	100,017	297,518	2,100	15,270
1855	181,568	2,641,746	13,833	63,379
1860	457,343	7,568,608	64,682	28,056
1865	567,576	10,479,777	326,472	29,597
1870	1,225,941	16,127,838	210,187	469,325

SOURCE: *Thirteenth Annual Statement of the Trade and Commerce of Milwaukee, for the Year Ending December 31, 1870* (Milwaukee: Evening Wisconsin Printing House, 1871), p. 17.

Although Milwaukee soon came to live off its reputation as the leading grain center of America, the city's market surely was not dominated by grain alone. Clothiers and tanneries developed in the city as well, partly a result of the growing influx of immigrants from Europe, and Germany in particular.[26] Such businesses added to the growing prosperity of the city. Between 1850 and 1860, for example, the value of the products manufactured in Milwaukee increased markedly, from $1,871,661 to $6,659,070; likewise, the capital investment in businesses in the city increased over the same period, from $587,175 to almost $3,000,000.[27] Additionally, with these increases in the wealth of the community came an increase in employment opportunities as well, with the number of employees in various Milwaukee firms more than doubling in the decade of the 1850s—to 3,406 in 1860.[28]

Yet, in this pre-industrial period of its history, the 1860s represented perhaps the one decade of the greatest change and prosperity for Milwaukee. It was in this decade that the building blocks were laid for the great industrial boom that took place in the 1870s. During the 1860s, for one thing, the grain trade grew enormously. By 1870, Milwaukee businesses were importing almost 20,000,000 bushels of wheat annually and exporting more than 15,000,000 bushels.[29] The city's millers had become the most productive in the country, producing upwards of 1.2 million barrels of flour annually.[30] The trade in barley and rye continued to rise, the former aiding the fledgling development of breweries in the city. Numbers of new banks opened. Furthermore, as perhaps the surest sign that financial success finally had been secured by the city, a new life insurance company, the Northwestern Mutual Life Insurance Company, opened its doors in 1859 and by 1870 represented one of the dominant life insurance companies in America, with assets of almost $9,000,000.[31]

As the commercial enterprises of the city grew, they helped drive Milwaukee to expand. Over the same decades that Milwaukee grew into a major grain center in America and its commercial base expanded, the city population expanded accordingly. By 1870, the city numbered just over 70,000 residents, making it one of the larger urban settlements of the period in America. At the same time, it had outstripped many of its rival cities in Wisconsin, such as Green Bay, and had become, even at this early date, the major site of business activity in the state.[32]

But if commercial enterprise, and its growth in Milwaukee, helped the city to expand by providing new jobs and a vital economic core, these circumstances alone could not promote the rise of a dynamic and self-sufficient marketplace. Businesses that competed with one another were one component in the mix, but businessmen themselves soon came to realize that alliances among themselves were just as essential as competition, to expand the marketplace—alliances that would prove effective in promoting the interests of the Milwaukee marketplace against the competitive marketplaces of other settlements like Chicago. Thus, in the early 1850s several different attempts were made to create alliances of businessmen; but it was not until 1858 that the first effective alliance resulted—the Milwaukee Chamber of Commerce.

The Chamber sought to keep a continuing record of the business done in Milwaukee and sought to serve as a gathering place at which ideas would be shared and exchanged about how best to promote the interests of the city. Like other urban settlements, all of which seem to generate their own particular brand of alliances, Milwaukee's alliance of businessmen was designed to work to the interests of the community and to promote those interests outside Milwaukee. Later in the century, the reports of the Chamber heralded the great advantages of the city; and the meetings of the Chamber provided a forum in which people would propose new devices to upbuild the prosperity of the community.

The Chamber, though surely the most visible and dominant of the organizations among capitalists in the city, was by no means the only one. In the early 1860s, to cap off the prosperity that was gradually developing in the city, another association, the Milwaukee Merchants Association, also was formed. It, too, was designed to provide some greater common direction to the interests of the business community and to work to secure a greater presence of capitalism in Milwaukee.

These sorts of alliances—of the businessmen, in general, and of merchants—were a critical piece of the effort to promote the expansion of the city. While key figures, like Mitchell, handed out money easily and sought to promote the interests of ideas that they thought held eventual benefits, it was the common alliances, among the several groups, that eventually worked to promote the overall economic well-being of the city and, with that, produced its expansion as well. Composed of people like Alexander Mitchell and Daniel Wells, Jr., these alliances helped to solidify the gains and achievements made by the entrepreneurs and by those who engaged in commercial enterprises in the city.

Thus, by the late 1860s all the essential elements for a vital marketplace had emerged in Milwaukee, contributing to a strong economic presence that drove the fortunes of the city and creating new wealth and providing opportunities for hundreds, if not thousands, of migrants that now sought refuge in the city. The success of entrepreneurs such as Kilbourn and Mitchell represented the first mo-

Milwaukee Harbor and city (1856)

ment of an emerging market presence on the frontier; the second and third moments came with the development of a stable and viable economic presence and with the creation of a set of alliances, spearheaded by the Chamber of Commerce, among Milwaukee capitalists. These forces together drove the expansion of the city. In addition, as the story of the city unfolded, they also became the forces that began to write the tale of public authority in the city.

The Stirrings of Public Authority

Creating a stable public authority in the city of Milwaukee proved a considerably more difficult enterprise than that of fostering the growth of private enterprise. For a long while, well into the 1870s, one could properly say that private enterprise, alone, exercised public authority; or, to put it more precisely, public authority virtually served the exclusive needs and interests of private enterprise. When people sought to exercise authority in Milwaukee, they argued that their decisions were important to promoting the business and growth of the city. Charles Beard's stunning and controversial thesis, that America was fashioned not to be a democracy but to be a citadel of property-holders, was transparently and obviously true in Milwaukee.[33] Moreover, in this early period we gain certain insight into how local authority came into being—an insight that goes beyond the somewhat formal and mechanistic claims that capitalism and government tend to work hand in hand. Indeed, in this early period the entire city was, in effect, simply imbued with the spirit of capitalism.

Entrepreneurs Fashion Public Projects

One of the most striking facts about the beginnings of Milwaukee is that, as in other frontier outposts in America, the exercise of public authority in the city was left largely in the hands of private entrepreneurs and other prominent members of the business community. Indeed, it was they who began to fashion the public setting of the city and who sought to lay the very foundations for the community. Writing of this early period in Milwaukee, one authority, Laurence Larson, puts it this way: "What was accomplished (in the way of public projects) was largely the result of private enterprise. The earliest bridges, schools, streets, and roads were built by public-spirited citizens with private funds."[34] Whatever their motives— and one could speculate almost endlessly on such a matter—the early entrepreneurs made the first substantial donations of land, bridges, and other property to benefit the new settlement. Morgan Martin, looking back on these early years, remembered that he and Juneau had made a number of important gifts to the new settlers. "[Juneau and I]," Martin recalled in 1876, "acted in concert in laying out and building up the town, erected the Court-house, Milwaukee House; [we] opened and graded streets, in fact, [we] expended together nearly $100,000 in improving the property, and contributing to the public convenience."[35] Other settlers remembered much the same story about the contributions of the first entrepreneurs. Most even remembered that Juneau had been a man who was generous to a fault—"a noble and honest man," it was often said—in providing funds for civic projects and for needy settlers in the early settlement.[36] Another early settler, Alexander Pratt, recollected that "money seemed to be of no earthly use to [Juneau]. If a man called upon him to subscribe for a public improvement or a charitable object, whatever was required he subscribed, without asking why or wherefore."[37]

One could, of course, ascribe Juneau's contributions to simply the act of a generous man, an honest figure, as many contemporaries did. But other entrepreneurs, less inclined both to trust and to be trusted by their contemporaries, made equally munificent contributions to laying the foundations of public authority in Milwaukee—men not otherwise remembered as honest or noble; they did so because they felt the need to fill a vacuum of public authority that had not yet emerged in the fledgling city. Daniel Wells, Jr., and several others, for example, helped to secure the funding that created a bridge crossing the Milwaukee River at Oneida Street in 1844. Further, Alexander Mitchell provided the monies that helped with the construction of new wooden-plank roads that provided transportation access into and out of the town.[38]

Further, when the city, as a struggling corporate entity, ran into financial troubles, Mitchell often was available to help rescue it from possible failure. In 1861, to offer but one example, the city was about to run out of funds to finance some of its services. This had happened because the city had overextended itself to issue bonds that would assist the construction of new railroads. A number of the railroads reneged on their commitments to the city, and as a result, the city languished in debt. Mitchell stepped forth to straighten out the city's finances, prompting other Milwaukeeans to recall later that "[the new] measures were, in a large degree, due to Mr. Mitchell, and were fully effectual in restoring the credit of the city, and in keeping its financial affairs henceforward upon a sound basis."[39]

In short, private entrepreneurs, the leading ones at least, created many of the most essential public instruments for the young city, and they served thereby to advance the common welfare. Although obviously motivated by their commercial ambitions, a number seemed equally moved to undertake acts that would benefit the entire community, believing that their own peculiar and pecuniary self-interests were virtually one and the same with those of Milwaukee—as indeed they were.

Creating a Sovereign City

A great part of the challenge of effecting a new community on the western frontier of America lay in the political wheelings-and-dealings required to make an autonomous settlement. Milwaukee, like other urban outposts, was, from its outset, an authority created by the territorial and subsequently, the state, legislatures. Thus, as a corporate entity, it constantly had to fight to determine the range and extent of its own authority and to fashion a strong political identity relative to that of the state. Milwaukee was created, in effect, as a *sovereign corporate entity,* but it was an entity that was required to be constantly vigilant about the limits on its own powers.[40]

The early political struggles of Milwaukeeans to achieve independence were surely as significant as those the settlers fought against Wisconsin winters that often were harsh and interminable. Representatives of the city in the 1840s and 1850s spent a good deal of their time in the capital of Madison, seventy-five miles to the west, seeking to persuade state legislators of the wisdom of supporting projects that would aid the fortunes of the new community. Among others, such projects included canals and railways—novel methods of transportation that, it was hoped, would extend the market of the community and further reinforce the growing prospects of its success.

In the absence of any but the most rudimentary public authority—the new city had but a bare handful of practicing officials well into the 1860s—it was not surprising that the very same men who served to build up the internal community of Milwaukee were the ones who primarily represented the city in dealings at Madison. Byron Kilbourn, for example, doubtlessly motivated by his own commercial ambitions, nonetheless frequently lobbied state legislators for projects, such as the Rock River Canal, intended to link the Rock River to Lake Michigan, or for works like bridges, intended to serve the interests of the entire community.[41] Daniel Wells, Jr., having secured abundant wealth in city properties over the space of just a few years, was another frequent participant in the state legislature, acting again to advance the interests of the city. He assisted Kilbourn, for example, in lobbying on behalf of the canal, believing that "such a canal would be a boon to the business of the growing city of Milwaukee."[42] Further, Alexander Mitchell was a frequent visitor to Madison, too, seeking to gain special benefits for Milwaukee banks and his railroads, among other interests.[43]

Gains from all these efforts to establish a sovereign political authority in Milwaukee came about gradually. In 1837, the territorial legislature had created a county in Milwaukee, and shortly thereafter, in 1839, the territorial legislature authorized the first village of Milwaukee. Seven years later, in 1846, the legislature established the first actual city, thereby merging the three wards of the settlement into a single corporate entity that had its own specific charter.

The Body Politic Primeval

Just as it had been the Milwaukee entrepreneurs who argued and who fought to help the city achieve a distinctive political identity, so, too, it was they who became the figures that would serve as the symbolic heads of the new settlement. Once again, it was their entrepreneurial energy that became both the leitmotiv and the underlying principle dictating the life of the early city.

When Milwaukee County first came into being, on March 13, 1837, the leading financial speculators, among them, Kilbourn, Juneau, and Wells, were those who constituted the committee that fashioned the various rules and regulations governing property rights in the region. Kilbourn was the dominant figure in the group's deliberations, serving as their chairman.[44] Later, in 1846, when the village of Milwaukee was itself authorized by an act of the Wisconsin State Legislature, the man elected to serve as the first "president of the village," an office later transformed into that of "mayoralty," was Solomon Juneau. His contemporary settlers especially revered Juneau and found him to be the symbolic presence of the new settlement; Buck once described him as "in truth one of the noblest works of God, an honest man."[45] Within the first decade of the life of Milwaukee, two other prominent entrepreneurs also came to serve as mayor of the community—Byron Kilbourn, who was elected twice to the office (in 1848 and 1854); and George Walker, founder of Walker's Point, who served as mayor from 1851 through 1854. In addition, when these men were not serving as the public authority in the community, of course, other merchants—some entrepreneurs of lesser accomplishment—were the men who acted to exercise the public authority.

However, to say that the entrepreneurs both promoted and represented public authority in pre-industrial Milwaukee is by no means the whole story. Ever so slowly, the agencies that would enforce the laws and protect the lives of citizens themselves arose. A rudimentary police force was set up in the 1850s, but it was not until the mid-1860s that anything resembling a police establishment took hold in Milwaukee. Likewise, an early fire department was created, but, like the police department, it was manned almost exclusively by a volunteer staff of Milwaukee citizens.

Indeed, it was the widespread existence of such *volunteer* activity—a phenomenon, it must be noted, that Alexis de Tocqueville would claim to be the essence of American democracy when he visited the United States in 1839 and 1840—that perhaps best captures the heart and soul of the primitive and elemental character of the *body politic* in Milwaukee, a body politic lacking in institutions of political authority.[46] While the leading businessmen fashioned and developed the laws for the new settlement, the rest of the settlers pitched in to assist in their own particular ways. They voted for elective offices, such as the newly minted Common Council, in the 1840s—putting into office people like Wells and Kilbourn to serve as their representatives. But, even more, they became involved in helping to meet the needs of their fellow settlers when no agencies or institutions of any significant size yet existed. Years later, one pioneer recalled:

> Forty years ago (the early 1840s) ... the Old Volunteers were firemen, policemen, and, if worst came to worst, they fell in with the militia, and preserved public peace. They were the boys of law and order; all the bright and plucky young men who have since built up the financial prosperity of the city and protected it from the disorders of fire and panic, belonged to that organization. They turned out and manned the brakes with a vim, and worked for the salvation of others' property with a generosity which has no parallel in "paid departments." ... the Fire Department was then composed of the very cream of the growing village, and remained so for twenty years and over. When the present paid department was organized, the scores of business and professional men who had faithfully served the city's interests in its younger and more helpless days, withdrew to engage in other pursuits.[47]

Thus, the early public community, that in which politics occurred, was one thoroughly and absolutely dominated by the major capitalists of the period. In the words of Sam Bass Warner, Jr., early Milwaukee had taken on the character of a private city, in which the ideology of privatism, or, more plainly, capitalism, clothed both private and public affairs.[48]

Territorial Disputes and the Bridge War

Our insight into the rudimentary nature of early Milwaukee is enhanced further by briefly examining the details of the Bridge War, a battle that occupied the energies of east- and westside Milwaukeeans in 1845. The story of this event, so often and so vividly remembered in later years by Milwaukee pioneers, provides a good illustration of what forces animated the life of the early settlement and of how authority came to operate in the city.

From its earliest beginnings, when Juneau and Kilbourn established their own separate settlements on the east and west sides of the Milwaukee River, respectively, there had been a strong sense of rivalry between the two sections of the town. The rivalry began with rival practical ambitions. Kilbourn wanted to gain greater profits and to create a more pleasing settlement, and Juneau and those on the east bank sought much of the same. For a time, well into the 1840s, the disputes were covered over by a series of agreements, some hammered out in contract, others understood merely by word of mouth. Once the village came into being, in 1839, two separate wards were established, an East and a West Ward—also referred to commonly as Milwaukee and Kilbournville, respectively—and the two conducted their municipal business independently of one another, though they met in the same setting, the courthouse that Juneau had built on the east side of the river.[49]

The two wards divided their responsibilities as well, with the Eastsiders, for example, responsible for the upkeep of the early bridges and ferries that transported people from the interior across to the east side.[50] On the surface, the two sides tended to work together as a community of settlers. But the rivalry over lands and over access to the water, as well as the decided advantage that the west side possessed to the goods transported from the farms in the heartland, kept the sectional disputes smoldering.

By 1845, several bridges had been constructed that crossed the river—one at Oneida Street that had been built with funds secured by Daniel Wells, Jr., among others; another at Spring Street; and yet a third at Chestnut Street. (It may prove of some interest to those familiar with Milwaukee to know that the links that today bridge the east and west sides of Milwaukee, across the Milwaukee River (at Wisconsin Avenue, for example), are set at angles precisely because Juneau, on the east, and Kilbourn, on the west, even refused to create streets in common.) In May 1845, a series of happenings, most recollected in some confusion, brought about pitched battles between the two sides of town.

Two events appeared to have set off the lingering hostilities. Sometime early in May, a schooner, on the orders of the Eastsiders, had been sent downriver and rammed the bridge at Spring Street, thereby destroying it. Not to be outdone, the Westsiders, eager to get their pound of flesh, set about to dismantle the western ends of bridges that spanned the river. Westsiders reasoned that such bridges, which benefited the Eastsiders more than themselves, were built on land exclusively their own; therefore, they decided to rid themselves of these apparent inconveniences and did so. Of course, the Eastsiders quickly retaliated.

On May 9, 1845, an actual battle—perhaps it would be more appropriate to call it a skirmish—took place between the two sides of town. Eastsiders gathered their forces on the banks of the river and began pummeling the west side with all manner of objects. Cannons were aimed at the home of Byron Kilbourn on the west side. The crowd eventually was quieted by the pleas of Jonathan Arnold, who urged them to return to their homes. No deaths were reported, but the battle had brought out all the old rivalries and ambitions between the two sections of town. The memories of one passerby, a visitor from Detroit, both reproduce the commotion and reveal the lingering tensions between the two sides of Milwaukee:

E. J. Roberts, a prominent citizen of Detroit, came to Milwaukee in 1836 or '37. He landed from a boat and walked up East Water Street just as ... Arnold was addressing a crowd in relation to some bridge controversy. He returned to Detroit and did not visit Milwaukee until 1845, again happening to come up East Water Street just as Mr. Arnold was in the midst of his speech. Mr. Roberts rubbed his eyes, and, turning with amazement to a friend, exclaimed: "Great heavens! Haven't they adjourned that meeting yet?"[51]

Shortly thereafter, various meetings were held among the representatives of the two wards to mend fences—in fact, to build bridges. Further, newspaper accounts and editorials in the local *Sentinel,* representing the east side of town, and the *Courier,* representing the Westsiders, sought to make amends and to patch up the differences. By fall, representatives of each side of the settlement were determined that the rivalries must be laid to rest, once and for all. It was not a matter of good feelings or even of good fellowship, so much as of the promotion of good business and prosperity for the community. Thus, the leading figures, Kilbourn and Walker in particular, went to Madison, determined to convince the legislators of the importance of creating a new and common city in Milwaukee: By January 1846, a new city had come into being, with a charter; and the separate sides, which previously had been rivals, were somehow bound together into a common entity.[52]

The episode of the Bridge War discloses several important features of the early settlement at Milwaukee. One is, as I suggested in Chapter 1, that conflict lay at the very roots of the body politic. Milwaukeeans did not simply agree to live together. In fact, they often engaged in tempestuous struggles with one another. To keep such struggles under wraps and to approximate a consensus, they were compelled to hammer out the terms of an agreement. Such an agreement proved binding on their behavior; still, the struggles that triggered the compact would never entirely disappear. In this sense, of course, Milwaukee was little different than other frontier villages.[53]

A second fact is that the very nature of this conflict seems to have been animated by the same drives and ambitions that animated the drive for profit among the settlement's early entrepreneurs. The leading figures of the community, those driven visionaries, frankly sought to make as much profit as they could from their speculation on land—and, in the cases of Juneau and Kilbourn, to offer the most attractive and livable prospects to their fellow pioneers. Though it might stretch the point too far, it seems the case that the driving spirit to settle and to possess these new lands at Milwaukee came simply to be reconstituted in sectional and territorial terms. Third, there is little doubt that the agents that animated the life of early Milwaukee, as well as the forces that drove it to expand, were *not* explicitly political. Just as no political institutions yet existed to settle internal rivalries, so, too, there were no political institutions to enlarge the possibilities of the city. Every aspect of the early town assumed the character of economics—from the drive to grow to the deals made on land speculation. Yet again, such claims, though transparently true in early Milwaukee, would be true exclusively in this period. By the time of the early industrial city, and certainly by the time of its mature industrial stage, political institutions had emerged, *had acquired a life of their own,* and had become a strong force, *at the local level,* to drive forward the possibilities of a bigger and better Milwaukee.

Reaching Outward

As Milwaukee became transformed from a village to a city and thence grew ever larger, efforts naturally developed to expand the place outward. Most such efforts were motivated by private gain—by the attempt of businessmen to extend the reach of their marketplace into other regions and other settlements. As part and parcel of these plans, there were attempts to create a new harbor for Milwaukee, to develop canals, and, most significantly, to build railroads. Now, certain historians have suggested that railroads and other mechanical means of transportation exercised a vast influence over the topography of America, creating villages and towns where none previously lay.[54] There is some truth to such a claim. But what we must always ask is: Who—or what—lies behind such efforts? Moreover, once we explore this question, we frequently will find the very nimble fingers on the "invisible hands" of our entrepreneurs.

Railroads and the Upbuilding of Milwaukee

Two men, in particular, had central roles in the development of mechanisms of transportation for early Milwaukee—Byron Kilbourn and Alexander Mitchell. Kilbourn did so, it would appear, out of a tremendous ambition and an unquenchable thirst for new profits for what he believed to be his own urban empire; Mitchell did so, in large part, because it was he to whom everyone turned when projects were on the verge of failure, particularly when their finances had somehow run amok.

From almost the day he set foot in Milwaukee, Byron Kilbourn pursued new means and devices for transportation with a passion that could only be understood perhaps in light of his earlier profession as a civil engineer in Ohio.[55] It was Kilbourn who pushed both his fellow settlers, and many of Wisconsin's state legislators, to establish a canal that would run from Milwaukee to the Rock River and from there to the Mississippi. Other settlers, too, believed that the great economic hopes of the community were to be pinned on the successful transportation of goods across land to the Mississippi. But Kilbourn was the one with the gumption and the driving ambition to try to build such a canal and to try to construct it in such a way as to benefit his own special settlement on the western banks of the Milwaukee River, Kilbournville.

Kilbourn managed to secure a land grant from the federal government in 1838—a grant of 500,000 acres over which he and others would pursue the construction of a canal. He hoped that the canal would be built directly on his side of the Milwaukee River, that it would run to the Rock River, and that it then would pass through a country rich with lead mines—a source of possible profit through trade—emptying itself ultimately into the waters of the Mississippi. Unfortunately, others were not nearly so persuaded of the desirability of canals. This fact, coupled with the very limited capital available in the wake of the 1837 panic, spelled an early end to Kilbourn's effort to get this form of transportation constructed. Besides, the governor, James Doty, on whom Kilbourn and his allies would have had to rely in order to get all the plans completed, in 1841 came out against a canal, believing it to be a sad waste of effort. Instead, he and others believed that different modes of transportation, such as plank roads, might well prove far more desirable and successful than canals.[56] Nonetheless, Kilbourn's venture was not entirely without reward. He and the Rock River Canal Company managed to construct a small dam in the waters of the Milwaukee River that would later provide Milwaukee with its first electric power and furnish the millers with the necessary energy to turn wheat into flour.[57]

Kilbourn, however, was not to be defeated in his effort to get trade routes for the city. Within the space of a few years, he turned his attention to a different mode of transport—railroads. A contemporary of Kilbourn's remembers the vigor with which the entrepreneur pursued the dream not only of a railroad but of defeating Milwaukee's nearby urban rival, Chicago:

> [H]e said that, "look at my map of railroads. I have laid out Milwaukee and, if we build the first one, and get to the river first, Chicago will not dare to approach our territory. And if we build this first road to Dubuque, I will guarantee building up our Milwaukee system and then we can defy the world to come between us and this great northwest."[58]

Railroads, now available with the innovation of the steam engine, quickly became the preference among the wise and prudent figures of the era. Besides, their worth was already becoming known, and investments happened accordingly, in places like Chicago. Thus, Kilbourn decided to put his money on the railroads. As it would turn out later, he decided to put a little bit too much of his money not only on railroads but in the wrong hands.

His first, and major, misadventure occurred in the case of a line that became known as the Milwaukee and Mississippi Railroad.[59] Like his earlier effort with the Rock River Canal, Kilbourn and his allies hoped to eventually build a vast network of routes that would stretch from Milwaukee to the Mississippi.[60] The problem that they ran into, however, was a problem that plagued many such efforts, especially in outlying regions such as Milwaukee. There was too little money available—too little capital on which those living on the western frontier could depend. To counter the problem of too little capital, someone came up with a very

novel idea for funding. It depended on the goodwill, some might even say the na-
ïveté, of farmers whose lands lay along the proposed route from Milwaukee to the
Mississippi. The idea was that farmers would take out a mortgage on their farms
in return for stock in the railroads.[61] Eventually the railroad stock would pay sufficient dividends to cover the interest on the mortgages themselves. The net result
would be that farmers would be the collective owners of the railroad. In turn, the
Milwaukee and Mississippi Railroad Line would secure funding for construction
by selling the mortgages on eastern U.S. money markets.

It seemed an absolutely brilliant idea—indeed, perhaps a bit too brilliant.
These sorts of ideas really depended both on the hard cash to back them up and
on the goodwill and fair practices of the bankers themselves. Unfortunately, the
era of 1850s and eastern financiers were not particularly well-known either for
goodwill or for their high moral purpose.

Kilbourn worked hard to secure as much in the way of finances as he could.
The line scored some early successes, completing a short portion of the railroad
between Milwaukee and Waukesha; but this still left hundreds of miles to be completed before the line would reach the Mississippi. Eventually, Kilbourn's fellow
directors tired of his schemes and of his apparent unwillingness to assure them
that there were adequate finances for the railroad. The directors also grew to believe that Kilbourn was something of a scoundrel and a swindler. Thus, in the fall
of 1852, shortly after he returned from a visit to secure finances in the East,
Kilbourn was dismissed as president of the railroad line. Funds were in short supply, and the other directors of the line sought to make it work. Their efforts, with
Kilbourn now out of the way, turned out to be decidedly more effective.[62] Additional lines were built, linking Milwaukee to Eagle, Wisconsin. But late in the
1850s, money once more became a problem. The panic of 1857 wiped out the fortunes of many, and the financiers in the East now began to call in the mortgages
they held on the Wisconsin farms.

Eventually, the Milwaukee and Mississippi Railroad collapsed, and any effort to
create the desired link to the Mississippi looked as though it would forever be
doomed. In the meantime, Kilbourn had become president of yet another railroad, the Milwaukee and LaCrosse. A railroad that stretched from Lake Michigan
to LaCrosse, which sat just on the Wisconsin side of the Mississippi, could now
crown his dreams to link Milwaukee to the western markets. Yet, as his associates
at the Milwaukee and Mississippi Railroad had learned, Kilbourn seemed so determined to build his railroad that nothing would deter him, not even the need to
grease the palms of a few political officials. Thus, in rather short order he, and his
associate, Moses Strong, were found to have bribed a number of parties to get
their compliance in erecting the line to LaCrosse—parties that included both the
governor and a number of legislators. The deed never produced a conviction for
Kilbourn; but it did reaffirm the conviction of many Milwaukeeans, as well as of
other residents of Wisconsin, that Byron Kilbourn was nothing but a petty
schemer out to gain his own advantages. His reputation, which had been built on

his skills as a promoter and land speculator, would never again be the same, and he retired to Florida in disgrace some years later.

Between the skulduggery of Kilbourn and the rocky financial empires of eastern U.S. bankers, it appeared that Milwaukee might continue to languish at the fringes of the frontier. Although it grew to become quite a sizable settlement over the course of the 1850s, Milwaukee lagged seriously behind the fortunes of its rivals elsewhere, especially Chicago. More and more, it became clear that the natural advantages Milwaukee possessed along the shores of Lake Michigan could only take the city's prospects so far. Furthermore, it also became clear that as the frontier moved westward, the rich fields of wheat, and the markets that grew thereupon, would move west as well, into the newer frontier cities such as Minneapolis and St. Paul.

At this point, in about 1860, the fortunes of Milwaukee could have turned completely sour. The economic market and some of the thriving commercial entrepreneurs had reached a point of some success. And yet, the municipal government of the city stood at the edge of financial ruin. In large part, its decline was a direct result of the failure of the railroads. Once the farm-mortgage scheme had been found defective, the railroad developers turned to other sources of funds. The next wrinkle was to secure funding by drawing on the monies and debt of municipalities. The city of Milwaukee became the banking agent for the railroads. Soon, however, the city's limited funds dried up, and it was left with a large amount of debt that it could not cover. By 1857, the Milwaukee and Mississippi Railroad, which had once seemed to its promoters to be the great salvation both for Wisconsin farmers and for their Milwaukee brethren, lay moribund—more than $6 million in debt—and the lives and resources of hundreds of farmers had been brought to ruin.[63]

Into this obvious vacuum stepped Alexander Mitchell. Mitchell already had secured not only a sufficiently sound reputation as a banker but also more than enough wealth for himself personally; he could have left the whole matter of railroads alone. He was not only the darling of Milwaukee and Wisconsin, but also the friend and confidant of many an eastern U.S. banker.[64] Yet he became persuaded that his own best interests would be served by helping to solve the railroad crisis. For one thing, Mitchell had already figured out a way to help the city of Milwaukee recover from its problem of indebtedness, and the city lay forever almost literally in his debt. In the 1860s, he began to put together the pieces of a vast network of railroads. He first assumed the presidency of the Chicago and Milwaukee Railroad, one of the many lines whose fortunes lay on the edge of bankruptcy. Mitchell next helped to resolve the financial difficulties of the Milwaukee and La-Crosse Railroad, which, sometime after the shenanigans of Kilbourn, had been reorganized under a new name—the Milwaukee and St. Paul Railway. Finally, Mitchell came into the leadership of the old Milwaukee and Mississippi Railroad, which, itself, had undergone transformation into the Milwaukee & Prairie du Chien line.[65]

By 1870, through his considerable financial acumen and by virtue of the trust that others held in him, Mitchell had become a czar of the railroads—an empire builder of unprecedented proportions. He and his colleagues now controlled several thousand miles of railroad, including more than 2,000 miles in the state of Wisconsin alone.[66] Mitchell's energies and will now commanded much of the trade and business done by the growing firms of the city of Milwaukee. At the time, a comment in the old *Chicago Post* reflected on Mitchell's success in this manner:

> History repeats itself. The tears of Alexander the Great, because he had no more worlds to conquer, are familiar to every schoolboy, and here we have another Alexander, surnamed Mitchell, who started out with the Milwaukee and St. Paul railroad, first gobbled the old Milwaukee and La Crosse, then the Prairie du Chien. ... As there are still other lines to gobble, however, we suppose the weeping will not commence until such little side-tracks as the Union Pacific, New York Central, etc., are added to the inventory.[67]

Alexander the Great had finally figured out, among other things, how to effectively link Milwaukee to the Mississippi by rail.

Kilbourn had proven himself the schemer, and Mitchell something of the savior, for the lives of their fellow Milwaukee residents. Both had helped to launch Milwaukee into the larger regional marketplace, providing outlets for its growing numbers of new products and, simultaneously, making the city far more accessible to the thousands of new immigrants who were making their way westward at the time. Kilbourn and Mitchell's ambitions, as well as their risks, drove the city to stretch itself. Very soon, Milwaukee would arrive at the moment when it would turn from a city into something approaching a large-scale metropolis.

Summary

Milwaukee, in its earliest years, was thoroughly and absolutely captivated by the interests of its private entrepreneurs—figures such as Byron Kilbourn and Solomon Juneau who, in their efforts to accumulate ever greater profits for themselves, managed to sell—indeed, to create—the nascent village. It also was these very same figures who worked to develop a sovereign presence for the city, seeking, among other things, to gain advantages in the state capitol in Madison. In these primitive beginnings, one could not properly speak of a stable and continuous political authority. Such authority was, as some Marxist writers would put it, simply *an instrument* in the hands of early businessmen. Capitalists developed the apparatus and tools of local government; they manipulated local government; and they used local government largely for their own ends.

However, it was not as though these entrepreneurs imposed their desires on an intractable public. Citizens who were not particularly wealthy and who did not represent strong entrepreneurial concerns, willingly and voluntarily participated in public enterprises. People such as these made up the public enterprises, and they did so out of an interest in the common welfare of the community. In a sense, the entire early community was imbued with a spirit of accumulation for profit, or privatism.

Conflict, furthermore, was evident even in these earliest moments in the city's life. The Bridge War, for example, arose because of the primitive passions of some business figures to exercise control over the entire property of the community itself. In this sense, too, life in the early city was dominated by privatism—one in its most rudimentary state. The struggle to accumulate wealth and to dominate life among the early settlers led to divisions that initially pitted the east side of the city against the west side. So deep and intensely felt were these differences, moreover, that they left a permanent mark on the landscape, inscribed today in the way the two sides of Wisconsin Avenue run at sharp angles to one another as they cross the Milwaukee River in downtown Milwaukee.

As we have seen, and as one might expect, even in this early period, as entrepreneurs worked to accumulate capital that would drive the city to expand, the primitive community was vulnerable to extra-local conditions and circumstances. Both in 1837 and once again in the 1850s, the health of the national economy exercised a profound impact on the fortunes of the nascent city. Moreover, its hinterlands exercised a decisive influence on its fortunes as well, particularly as the shift occurred in the availability of grains, moving the markets farther north and westward to Minneapolis and St. Paul.

All of this suggests that the actual creation of the community, though a social act that sprang from the pecuniary interests and motives of local land speculators and entrepreneurs, also was a contingent one: The city's success depended on the right mix of external circumstances. Many another site, wishing to become the next great metropolis, failed precisely because it was not the beneficiary of such good fortune as Milwaukee's.

4

Early Industrial Milwaukee: 1870–1900

"The vision of the pioneers of industry who settled here has proved correct. The initiative of a later generation has made it a great center. … Milwaukee is a great factory town and commercial interests are secondary."[1]

"As Chicago is sure to be the great distributing center of this country, so, from necessity, Milwaukee will be its manufacturing center."[2]

Cities, like most social formations, change over time. They do not, however, become entirely altered. Instead, new events and happenings are overlaid upon and across old social constructions. The old ones remain, of course, but in a much diminished and less visible form.[3]

So it was with the city of Milwaukee. The great commercial and trade developments of the 1850s and 1860s eventually gave way to new economic developments in the 1870s. Commerce did not die overnight, but it was rendered a far less important force for the growth and expansion of the city. The early entrepreneurs, such as Alexander Mitchell and Daniel Wells, Jr., did not entirely fade from sight but proved no longer critical to the vitality of the city.

In their place rose new figures. A new brand of entrepreneurs took over the fate of the city and thereby helped to establish a different generative force for shaping and expanding Milwaukee. They were the industrial entrepreneurs—the men who would construct and benefit from the great technical advances that occurred within the confines of industry, both in Milwaukee and elsewhere.

Great industry swept across the city like wildfire and modified its landscape accordingly. Alongside the new entrepreneurs materialized a vast and tireless body of laborers—men and women who came to constitute the great body of Milwaukee citizens and who, through varying alliances, came to press their demands for a fair share of the profits that accumulated in the coffers of the great industrial entrepreneurs. Sixteen years into the era of the Industrial Revolution in the city, the first of the great labor strikes would take place, serving notice that a political alliance of workers now would press to have labor's voice heard in the city's councils.

But there was something else that would occur in the last quarter of the nineteenth century—something evidently less visible but nonetheless equally compelling for the fate of Milwaukee residents. Slowly, from within the heart of the city, a new and powerful force emerged. This was the municipal government—an institution that most residents were unaware of but that, by the turn of the twentieth century, would in fact wield considerable authority and resources. Ever so gradually, virtually silently, the elements of municipal government came into existence—a city hall, to replace the original courthouse, the gift of Solomon Juneau; a public waterworks; a strong and professional police force; a fire department composed of a large body of personnel and an array of equipment; and much else besides. To people alive at the close of the nineteenth century, these things would seem perfectly harmless—the inevitable and necessary by-products of the growth of their city. Yet very soon municipal government in Milwaukee would exercise its authority over a vast array of resources; it would wield its dominion over many acres of public land; it would modulate the sound and tone of politics; and it would exercise its will over the lives of several hundred thousand people.

The Great Industrial Transformation

The New Marketplace

Until the early 1870s, the city of Milwaukee had been acknowledged as a center for trade and traffic in grains. Lying at the northwestern edge of the United States, the city profited from the adjacent fields of wheat, barley, and oats that were the product of rural America. For a brief time, in fact, it was the leading urban entrepôt in the trade of wheat and oats; by 1873, Milwaukee imported more than 28 million bushels of wheat, exported almost 25 million bushels, and was declared by boosters to be the "wheat capital of America."[4] Business at the Milwaukee Grain Exchange was booming, and trade in futures brought thousands of dollars into play among the traders. But 1873 would be the peak year for grain trade and exchange in the city. By 1880, the exports had dropped to just under 10 million bushels of wheat annually.[5] Most of the traffic in grains had by now become concentrated farther north and west, in Minneapolis and St. Paul. Thus, while Milwaukee reported a value of just over $4 million in the products of flour- and gristmills, Minneapolis simultaneously reported a value of more than $20 million.[6] Nevertheless, Milwaukee's location, at the eastern edge of vast hinterlands, coupled with its connections by rail and by water, enabled it to continue to lead the nation in traffic in barley well into the 1890s.

Though its position as the leading center of grain traffic faded, other developments transpired to promote new business forces in the marketplace and to exercise a decisive impact on the fortunes of the city. They happened on several different fronts in industry.

One such front was that of brewing. Milwaukee gradually had come to possess two obvious advantages for such products. The first was its access to various grains, particularly barley. Barley represented the key ingredient for the production of beer. Although the grain traffic, in general, declined after 1873, that in barley, in particular, picked up considerably. By 1892, city boosters could proclaim that "Milwaukee was the leading barley center in America."[7]

The other obvious advantage was one that would come to play a part in the many dramas to unfold in the city. A large and seemingly endless flow of immigrants from Germany had begun to take up residence in the city soon after its birth. Prompted by the political upheavals of 1848, many Germans had fled their homeland, seeking shelter elsewhere, particularly in America. Word spread quickly of this "German Athens," and by 1870 fully 32 percent of Milwaukee's foreign-born population had come to the city from Germany.[8]

The Germans brought with them a variety of skills and interests, including the capacity and knowledge to make a good German lager. Brewing establishments had begun to spring up across the city in the 1840s. One such establishment occupied the energies of two young men, Franz Falk and Frederick Goes. Falk had grown up in Bavaria where he acquired the skills of a *braumeister*. In his teens, he decided to come to America and eventually he settled in Milwaukee. He and Goes started their establishment in the 1850s. By the late 1860s, their original brewery, now named for Falk, had become one of the largest operations in the city.[9]

Identical tales happened among other families. August Uihlein, raised in Wertheim-am-Main, was brought to America by his grandfather in 1850. The two of them settled in Milwaukee where Uihlein's uncle, August Krug, ran a brewery. Eventually Uihlein's six brothers—Alfred, Charles, Edward, Gustave, Henry, and William—joined him and were raised and educated in the city. In the early 1870s, the several brothers became involved in the operation of their uncle's original firm. By now it had come into the hands of Joseph Schlitz, who assumed control of the firm on the death of August Krug in 1866. In 1875, Schlitz lost his life at sea while on a voyage to Europe. According to the terms of his will, his wife, along with August, Henry, and Alfred Uihlein, assumed control of the brewery. August took over as chairman of the board and soon had the firm, renamed to honor Schlitz, turning out large profits.[10]

The German influence was felt in yet other brewing quarters. The Best Brewery had been started by Jacob Best on his arrival in Milwaukee in 1842. By the early 1860s, his son, Phillip, became owner of the establishment and renamed it for himself. Phillip Best soon was joined by his two sons-in-law, both German immigrants themselves, Captain Frederick Pabst and Emil Schandheim. Eventually, Pabst assumed complete control of the enterprise. By the 1890s, the Pabst firm was the largest brewer in the city, followed closely by Schlitz and the brewery of yet another German immigrant, Valentine Blatz.[11]

German immigrants, full of enormous energy and ambition, came to dominate other lines of business, too. Frederick Vogel was born in Kircheim in 1823 and emigrated to America in 1846. Settling first in Buffalo, New York, Vogel worked in a small tannery owned by a cousin. His work took him to many places, including Chicago and Milwaukee. In 1847, he moved to Milwaukee and soon became involved with Guido Pfister, another German immigrant. The two of them built a small tannery on the Menomonee River. Pfister already was the proprietor of a small leather shop, and by the late 1850s the two men had merged their interests. Twenty years later, the Pfister and Vogel Leather Company was the greatest tannery and producer of leather goods in Milwaukee, with branch operations in a host of other American cities. Guido Pfister and Frederick Vogel in the meantime also had joined the ranks of the leading business figures in the city.[12]

The great migration of Germans inevitably included a large contingent of Jews. They, too, sought refuge from the horrors taking place in Europe in the mid-nineteenth century. Many eventually made their homes in Milwaukee. Several among them were familiar with the clothing trade. Henry and Elias Friend were two brothers who knew the business well. They began to produce men's garments in 1847 and were joined by a third brother, Meyer, within a year. Thirty years later, the Friends were the leading clothing manufacturers in the city, their operations totaling $500,000.[13] Two other German Jews, Solomon and David Adler, also took up the manufacture of clothing in the city. By the 1880s, they had become a family firm known as Adler, Mendel and Company. Although their firm was somewhat smaller than that of the Friends, together the two businesses captured the lion's share of the clothing market in Milwaukee.[14]

Germans, in brief, had come to exercise an enormous influence over the industrial energies of Milwaukee. But other newcomers exhibited as much drive and purpose and had an equally strong hand in forging the new industrial marketplace. By the 1870s, Milwaukee housed a number of firms specializing in the manufacture and production of various forms of heavy machinery. Their growth had been due in no small measure to an ironworks built at the edge of the city in 1868. The firm was developed by Eber Brock Ward, a wealthy capitalist from Detroit. By 1870, his plant had a workforce of 600 people with an annual payroll of more than $400,000. The firm became one of the major producers of steel in the Midwest and, in 1889, part of the Illinois Steel Corporation.[15]

The leading manufacturer of heavy machinery in Milwaukee in the 1870s was the Reliance Iron Works, owned by Edward P. Allis. At its beginnings, the Works had been developed by two men, James Seville of Milwaukee and Charles Decker of Ohio, the latter of whom provided the initial funding.[16] Allis came into ownership of the firm in 1861. As with the previous owners, his firm specialized in small jobs, including the repair of machines. Yet, as the traffic in grains in Milwaukee grew, Allis turned the firm's work to the production of flour-milling equipment, taking advantage of the allied industries, both in iron and in flour milling. By the end of the 1870s, Allis's business was the leading manufacturer of flour-milling equipment in the United States. It produced machinery for the local flour- and gristmill firms and for those elsewhere, including several in Minnesota.[17]

Enterprises in brewing, tanning, clothing, and the industrial manufacture of heavy equipment, in sum, constituted the leading lines of manufacture in Milwaukee well before the dawn of the Industrial Revolution in the city. That revolution, itself, was materially assisted by several critical technical inventions. Among the most notable were those in the realm of heavy machinery. Although Edward Allis possessed a talent for business, it was his talent for identifying brilliant engineers that proved to be his forte. In the 1870s, he hired three men who would play crucial roles in the technological revolution.

Edwin Reynolds may have been the most brilliant of the three. Reynolds had been employed as a mechanical engineer with the Corliss Works in Rhode Island when Allis convinced him to come to Milwaukee to become general superintendent of Reliance Iron Works.[18] Under Reynolds's direction, the company soon developed several key innovations: a steam engine with a new, more efficient form of governor to regulate the emission and use of steam; a large pumping engine to provide the mechanical means for pumping water; a new screw pump that would help to transform the pumping of water into rivers; and new, enlarged blowing machines that would be employed in the blast furnaces and Bessemer converters at various steel plants in America.[19]

William Dixon Gray and George Madison Hinckley were the other two engineers taken on by Reliance. Gray came aboard in 1876 as the head of the design and construction department. Under his supervision, new and far more effective roller machines were manufactured for the flourmill industry. The rollers were invented to replace buhrstones, the large and unwieldy instruments that for years had been used to grind wheat into flour. Gray's breakthrough led to a machine that worked far more quickly and efficiently.[20] Altogether, Gray, himself, came to hold more than fifty patents for a variety of inventions.[21] Hinckley's speciality was sawmill equipment. Like Reynolds and Gray, Hinckley proved an ingenious engineer. He helped to oversee the manufacture of larger and more complex sawmill equipment, including the first band saw operation. So effective were his inventions that they soon provided products not only for a host of American firms but also for a number of firms abroad, including some in Japan.[22]

Critical innovations happened in other branches of manufacturing, too. In the clothing industry, large new sewing machines coupled with steam-engine devices were put into use in the Friends' firm. They enabled the business to employ large numbers of workers in the very earliest phases of mass production of clothing.[23] Likewise, in the leather and tanning industry, Pfister and Vogel's company, along with the firm of their chief rival, Albert Trostel, managed to introduce a number of labor-saving inventions that permitted them to produce goods more efficiently.

Most of these technical advances came in the 1870s and thus made that particular decade the true period of technological breakthroughs in Milwaukee. They opened the doors to the employment of increasingly large numbers of workers. Indeed, it would be during the next decade that the growth of the workforce and of profits would reach its peak in this epoch. Altogether, the era of early industrialism was one of marked expansion in the size of the labor force as well as in the magnitude of the profits gained in all four major lines of industry in Milwaukee—brewing, tanning, clothing, and the industrial manufacture of heavy equipment. Between 1870 and 1900, the net value of goods produced by manufacturing firms in the city grew from roughly $7 million to almost $60 million. Within each of the leading sectors of industrial enterprise, the story was identical: The net value of products increased. All told, manufacturing had begun in substantial ways to remake the social and physical landscape of Milwaukee. These alterations would eventually prove so complete as to render that landscape never again the same.

Remaking the Face of the Workforce: Capital Versus Labor

The conflicts that earlier prevailed in Milwaukee between the Eastsiders and the Westsiders, between the forces of Solomon Juneau and those of Byron Kilbourn, came soon to pale by comparison with the new industrial divisions that arose in the city. The new industrial marketplace had the effect of transforming the face of the city and of creating the basis for a new and enlarged Milwaukee. But the Industrial Revolution in Milwaukee also did something else, something it seemed to do everywhere in America—it laid the foundations for a profound division in the workforce. This division resulted in capitalists, on the one side, and workers, on the other.[24]

In the years after 1870, as the new industrial form of manufacturing took over the city, it helped to reinvent the very character of work. More and more, the workforce of Milwaukee became the labor force of manufacturing. In the city's earliest years, when primarily a center of commerce and traffic in grain, the majority of workers were employed in commercial occupations, as tradesmen, blacksmiths, grocers, and coopers, among others. Yet as the new firms came in and managed to employ ever larger numbers of people on specific tasks at machines, tending to the mechanical intricacies of the production processes, the labor force changed accordingly.

Consider the information in Table 4.1. As one can tell, the number of employees in the manufacturing sector grew enormously over the three-decade period, from 8,433 in 1870 to more than 56,000 by 1900. The greatest absolute increase took place over the course of the 1880s. But, of even greater note, there occurred a

TABLE 4.1   Employees in Manufacturing, 1870–1900

Year	Number of Employees in Manufacturing	Increase over Previous Decade	As Percent of Total Population	As Percent of All Occupations[a]
1870	8,433[b]	—	9	40
1880	20,886[c]	+12,453	18	51
1890	43,423[d]	+22,537	21	58
1900	56,266[e]	+12,843	20	50

[a]These figures pertain to the occupational distributions rather than the industrial distributions for the area.

[b]Figures for Milwaukee County. U.S. Bureau of the Census, *Ninth Census of the United States* (Washington, D.C., 1870), "Manufactures," Table IX, "The States of Wisconsin by Counties."

[c]Figures for the city of Milwaukee. U.S. Bureau of the Census, *Tenth Census of the United States* (Washington, D.C., 1880), "Manufactures," Table VI, "Manufactures of 100 Principal Cities, by Specified Industries."

[d]Figures for the city of Milwaukee. U.S. Bureau of the Census, *Eleventh Census of the United States* (Washington, D.C., 1890), "Manufactures," Table 3, "Manufactures in 165 Principal Cities, by Specified Industries."

[e]Figures for the city of Milwaukee. U.S. Bureau of the Census, *Twelfth Census of the United States* (Washington, D.C, 1900), "Manufactures," Table 8, "Manufactures in Cities, by Specified Industries."

SOURCE: 1870 data are from the U.S. Bureau of the Census, *Ninth Census of the United States* (Washington, D.C., 1870), "City Data, Occupational Data," Table XXXII. Figure derived by taking total for manufacturing and mining as percentage of total occupations. 1880 data are from the U.S. Bureau of the Census, *Tenth Census of the United States* (Washington D.C., 1880), "Manufactures," Table VI; and "Occupations," Table XXXVI. 1890 data are from the U.S. Bureau of the Census, *Eleventh Census of the United States* (Washington, D.C., 1890), "Manufactures," Table 3; and *Compendium of the Eleventh Census* (Washington, D.C., 1890), Table 95. 1900 data are from the U.S. Bureau of the Census, "Manufactures," Table 8; and *Compendium of the Twelfth Census* (Washington, D.C., 1900), Table 94, "Occupations by Cities."

gradual change in the proportion of workers laboring in the manufacturing sector: By 1900, roughly one of every two employees was employed in manufacturing.[25]

Within manufacturing, the fruits of the production process were by no means shared equally. Inequalities stole in almost overnight. There were, on the one hand, those few men who owned and ran the firms—the entrepreneurs such as the Friends, the Pabsts, and the Uihleins—all of whom controlled the monies and received the vast bulk of profits in Milwaukee. Some, such as the Uihleins and Guido Pfister, moved their considerable monies into other lines of investment, thereby securing, even advancing, their wealth. The Uihleins, for example, assumed control of the Second Ward Savings Bank, an investment that decades later would pay most handsome dividends.[26] They also came into control of large sections of Milwaukee real estate, including full blocks of the downtown area of the city, as well as major theaters.[27] Moreover, as the manufacturing process spread and entered into the city's inner recesses, the inequalities increased rather than diminished. Consider, for example, that over the course of the 1890s, the differen-

Factories lining Milwaukee River—rear view ca. 1890

Milwaukee River looking north from Wisconsin Avenue ca. 1890

Dredging boat on Milwaukee River ca. 1890

tial in earnings between wage workers and salaried officials actually rose. In 1890, the average salary of a male firm official amounted to $929; by 1900 it had grown to $1,030. In contrast, male operatives actually made less on the average in 1900 than in 1890—$485 as compared to $505.[28] In effect, the division that the new manufacturing enterprises laid down in the city, with the capitalist entrepreneurs and firm officials on the one side and the workers on the other, became more marked over time and thereby in its own way affected the overall fortunes of the city.

Fruits of the production process are one thing, of course; however, the social organization of labor is quite another. Here it became evident that some Milwaukee firms took steps to lighten the burdens that the new labor processes demanded of their employees. For example, International Harvester, which had developed a large plant to produce agricultural equipment in the city, took pride in the clean lunchrooms and restrooms it had built for its employees, along with other provisions for their welfare, including a well-trained medical staff.[29]

Nonetheless, one simply could not alter the fact that the production process had become an often demeaning and demoralizing way of work.[30] The Menomonee Valley of Milwaukee became transformed from a pleasant plain of roughcut weeds and lovely trees, where children played and danced among the grasses, to an array of industrial plants, manufacturing everything from leather to machinery. Smoke clung to the roofs of factories, creating something of a mountain of grey and black ash. Black, tarry refuse belched into the waters of the Menomonee River, leaving a thick film to blot out life below; when not black tar, it was the thick slime of offal that would redden the river well beyond the reach of the packinghouses.[31] In addition, deep within each factory there lay the huge machines and row upon row of men, women, and children, all of them tending to the needs of these iron monsters, churning out both products and handsome profits for their employers.

Milwaukee, indeed, over the course of just a few years, had been changed from a small city of commerce to a large one of manufacturing, a "factory city." Nineteenth-century entrepreneurs believed the change to be a good thing—to represent a "good" that all people could share. Soon it would become unmistakenly clear that all people would not share this good equally, and that some would benefit vastly more than others. Everyone gained, of course, from the development of manufacturing and the growth of the city, but some gained considerably more than others. Furthermore, it would be this imbalance, between growth and equality, that would drive an even deeper wedge between capital and labor, and fuel the growth of the resistance efforts, particularly by the Social Democrats.

The Marketplace and the City

The revolutionary transformations that swept over the marketplace of Milwaukee, producing the industrial institutions of the city as well as the split between capitalists and laborers, would hold very important and decisive consequences for the character of life in the city and for its future prosperity.

In the most immediate sense, the creation of the new industries had the effect of creating new jobs; and with the new jobs came the inevitable growth of the city in the form of vast new numbers of migrants. As the new and more prosperous firms, such as Reliance Iron Works, became more successful, profiting from the technological innovations they introduced for processes such as the milling of flour, they were able not only to garner new business opportunities for themselves but to extend their plants and to employ many new workers. Within the space of several years, Reliance Iron Works had changed form into a new corporation, Edward P. Allis & Company. It had moved its offices on several occasions and increased its staff of employees from 75 people in 1866 to more than 700 by 1880.[32]

However, something else had happened that would generate more jobs even within particular industrial branches and thereby promote the expansion of new numbers of people in the city. Inventions in one particular firm, once successfully translated into an efficient form of production, led to the proliferation of new firms exclusively devoted to their manufacture. There were several notable such stories.

In 1887, the Allis firm had an order to rebuild a traveling crane. Until this time, the crane had been operated with a system of ropes. The ropes were used to hoist items attached to the crane, then to pull them across a stretch of space, and finally to lower them. An engineer for Allis, A. J. Shaw, came up with an idea for a new crane that would operate with three separate electric motors, each one devoted to the three steps of the crane's movements—hoisting, bridge travel, and trolley travel. The device proved enormously popular and in time became easy to produce. A separate company was thereafter established, with Shaw as owner and with Henry Harnischfeger, of Pawling & Harnischfeger (a firm that made small machines), as president. Eventually Shaw retired, Pawling & Harnischfeger absorbed the company, and their own firm grew chiefly on the basis of the new cranes that it produced.[33]

Work at Pawling & Harnischfeger itself also generated new firms. New chain-belt machines were developed by one of the company's employees. The machines became such a profitable outgrowth of the firm that another business was itself developed, the Chain Belt Company of Milwaukee.[34] Similarly, the Nordberg Manufacturing Company originated to produce novel valve governors invented by Bruno Nordberg, an employee of Pawling & Harnischfeger.[35] Stories like these, of one company giving birth to another, happened throughout Milwaukee's industrial marketplace. These companies were augmented by others that seemed to grow almost naturally and inevitably—foundries, for example, that were developed by heavy-machinery producers who wished to create the raw materials for their own processes, thus saving themselves a good deal of money at the same time.[36] The lesson of all these stories was effectively the same: industrial success in Milwaukee bred even greater success and with it brought expansion of the city's fortunes.

The industrial transformation of Milwaukee held yet other decisive consequences. The division between the capitalists and the workers helped to alter the very topography of the city itself, much as this class division would do in many other industrializing cities. There arose clear working-class sections of the city, many of which, of course, grew up in sites within easy walking distance of the factories. They became the places of small, compact one-story cottages, arranged row upon row, within which the mechanics and other unskilled workers lived.[37]

Amid these topographical changes, another change occurred that ultimately would hold even greater significance for the destiny of the city and its residents. Certain companies, unhappy with their locations, decided to relocate their plants to special areas outside the city limits. Patrick Cudahy, for example, had developed a very profitable meatpacking company by the 1880s. In 1893, Cudahy founded a new town outside of Milwaukee, named after himself. It consisted of 70 acres of farmland. Although Cudahy lived elsewhere—in the most posh section of town—his employees lived in homes adjacent to the plant. So, too, there lay a similar tale in the development of West Allis, another site on the edge of the city limits. After Edward Allis's death, Charles Allis, his son, and Edwin Reynolds chose to relocate their company, now cramped for space, in a land development just outside Milwaukee. Within a few years' time, the development had become a separate city, West Allis, with an expanding workforce numbering in the thousands.[38]

Eventually, there would be several such company towns that grew out of the manufacturing process in Milwaukee. They represented a vast redefinition of the city's land and space; more than that, as we shall learn, they eventually would play a decisive role in reshaping Milwaukee's financial fortunes as well.

Alongside these changes was the growth of suburban areas, such as Shorewood to the north, Wauwatosa to the west, even ex-urban fringe locales, marking the city's eastern edges, the bluffs that overlooked Lake Michigan, where the wealthy and affluent residents came to live. These fringe locations represented areas notable for their unblemished views of the Great Lake together with the hills and trees that gave life in the city the feel of life in the country.[39] They became the areas of prime real estate for residents—the areas of greenery, far from the black soot of the plants. They grew into neighborhoods that furnished a refuge to entrepreneurs, an escape from the dense, bleak decay that lay across downtown. Moreover, precisely because they offered such a retreat, they underwent a transmutation, from a refuge into a fortress intended to keep out the laboring classes. This story, of course, was one retold across many American cities that underwent industrial transformation.[40]

The reshaping of the Milwaukee market exerted its influence in other respects as well. As the laboring classes swelled in numbers, as more and more people became employed in the large industrial enterprises, the seeds were planted for the development of a strong political effort designed to promote the interests of the workers. Once more, the European origins of many Milwaukeeans had a hand in this part of city life. Just as the Germans had brought with them special skills (e.g., making lager and helping to develop heavy industry), so, too, they brought the experience necessary to articulate the grievances of workers and to help organize and carry out small revolts.

Social Democracy, a movement that had begun to take root in Germany, found strong proponents in Milwaukee. Certain men and women emerged in the late nineteenth century, such as Paul Grottkau and Victor and Meta Berger, who took the fight on behalf of the working classes to the streets. Certainly there was no more fertile ground for their concerns than this industrial city, for it was in Milwaukee that the very doctrines of Marx and Lassalle, as well as the other socialists, found a reality so transparent as to seem absolutely ready-made for their ideas— the growth of manufacturing enterprises accompanied by the obvious and visible divorce of men and women from the fruits of their own labor. When Marx wrote of his vision of the alienating consequences of industrial capitalism, he could, in fact, simply have been depicting the topography of Milwaukee or portraying the demeaning character of work in the Menomonee Valley—work that compelled men and women to tend more closely to the needs of sewing machines than to their own.

The 1880s had proven to be the decade of the greatest expansion in Milwaukee of new jobs and of new capital. It was in this decade that more and more workers shifted from the commercial and small-craft enterprises, where products previously had been made on a piecemeal basis, to the manufacturing sector, where employment opportunities now flourished (refer again to Table 4.1). No wonder, then, that the 1880s also was the decade in which the seeds of various reform alliances, from populism to socialism, would sprout and blossom. Prior to the 1880s, there had been various efforts to unite the working-class citizens of Milwaukee behind groups that would fight on their behalf. Small-craft unions had flourished for a time in the 1860s. The Knights of Labor began to enter the city at the same time as labor itself swelled in numbers, and by the mid-1880s it was reported that approximately 16,000 workers were members.[41]

Against this backdrop, the strikes of the spring of 1886 should have come as no surprise. The strikes became part of a firestorm of revolt on behalf of the eight-hour workday that raged across America. In Milwaukee, they first mobilized about 7,000 workers. By May 2, more than 15,000 workers had abandoned their jobs.[42] Particularly virulent demonstrations took place at the Allis Company and the Bay View Rolling Mills. People displayed all manner of discontent and displeasure: Banners read that "Cooperation Must Take the Place of Wage Slavery."[43] At its conclusion—the end of the first week of May—the protest in Milwaukee had led to strikes by more than 100,000 workers, the police and state militia had arrested hundreds of people, and nine individuals lay wounded or dead in local hospitals and morgues.[44] Riots and terror had broken out south of the city, in Haymarket Square, and throughout Chicago. Though the outbreaks would never prove so violent in Milwaukee, they revealed an increasing and impassioned discontent among workers.

The developing division between capitalists and laborers in the city came to have many implications for the fates of Milwaukeeans. Demands would be made to provide more for the working class, to enable laborers to share in the fruits of their own toil, and to help the broad and ever increasing body of citizens through the creation of a city government clearly more responsive to their needs.

City Government Unleashed

The growth of the capitalist enterprises and the development of the new industrial marketplace set into motion a powerful chain of events. Not the least consequential were those that unleashed the energies of city government.

Citizen Needs and Government Response

The great industrial transformation of Milwaukee made visible and evident the many needs of the city's inhabitants. This is not to claim that the capitalist enterprises failed to care for the well-being of their employees. Rather, they failed to care for them well enough, and there were few other agencies around, except for the voluntary welfare groups, sponsored by the German community and other immigrant groups, that could minister to the needs of such a large and endlessly expanding number of migrants to the city. In fact, between 1870 and 1900, the population of the city had increased fourfold—to 285,315—making it the four-teenth-largest city in America.[45]

The growth of the needs and demands of citizens happened slowly. They arose, in part, in response to the changing material conditions of the city, itself. As industries rapidly developed, taking over vacant lands, many of them spilled their waste and garbage into the streets of Milwaukee. In 1865, the *Milwaukee Sentinel* noted the "little stream trickling down ... the sides of the city's streets ... the stench from which precludes effectually any idea ... that it is pure spring water."[46] By 1874, the health commissioner declared the Milwaukee River to be a "huge cesspool."[47] Many new residents had their own wells. Yet, as the numbers of new people expanded, the wells themselves grew insufficient to meet the growing population's many requirements.[48]

In the previous epoch of Milwaukee history, when commercial entrepreneurs had dominated the life of the city, one of the key elements to the development of projects on behalf of citizens was that the wealthy were capable of funding many of them out of their own pockets. People like Byron Kilbourn and Alexander Mitchell could afford to give over a piece of land or a building, or even to construct new roads for public use. But now, as the city grew, such developmental expenses became impossible for any small group of citizens, much less a single individual, to bear. The net effect was to create a vacuum—a growing population whose needs expanded daily but for whom there was no private agency to meet those needs.

A turning point in the public life of the city, and the life of city government, in particular, happened in 1871. For years, the municipal government of Milwaukee had tried to develop a waterworks to provide citizens with clean drinking water and to enable the sewage of the city to be directed away from homes, leaving citizens free of the dangers of waterborne diseases such as dysentery.[49] James Johnson, the new health officer appointed in 1871, had insisted that "water works and a good system of sewrage [sic] are a great necessity for our city ... [for] ... well water will become so impregnated and tainted with foreign ... material as to be dangerous to life, and the generator of disease."[50] Private firms had sought to build such works, believing handsome profits could be made from them; however, all such efforts collapsed. Consequently, if the requirements of people were to be met—if the workers were to continue to work and residents were to be able to comport themselves comfortably in the city—there seemed little alternative but to construct, through public action and funds, a city waterworks.[51]

In 1871, the Wisconsin State Legislature authorized the city to issue bonds for the financing of a new public waterworks. The city government had anticipated this action. In 1868, it had advertised in the *New York Times*, seeking designs for a new public waterworks. As a result, the city hired an engineer in 1868, Ellis Sylvester Chesborough, who previously had designed the aqueducts and reservoirs for the city of Boston. Chesborough submitted several different plans, and in the ensuing months city officials and members of the Common Council debated the merits of plans that ranged from waterworks west of the city, in Waukesha, to those that drew upon the waters of nearby Lake Michigan.[52]

The winning design was the one that drew water from Lake Michigan. The notion was that water would be pumped to a large reservoir lying above the city and from there distributed by a vast array of pipes to the thousands of city residents. Eventually, a reservoir was completed that held 21.5 million gallons of water; it held enough to satisfy the drinking needs for a city of 500,000 residents, or about five times the size of the population of that time. The project turned out to the advantage both of the citizens and of the Reliance Iron Works, because it furnished Edward Allis's company with its first real opportunity to construct a large and new type of water-pumping engine.[53] It subsequently brought the company new fame and visibility in Milwaukee as well as a handful of orders from other clients.

The new city waterworks represented an important new moment in the public life of the city. It constituted the first major construction done for the city that was to be financed by the citizens, themselves. Thus, the citizens now possessed a major financial stake in municipal government. It also represented a way in which the city government could provide a continuing and plentiful source of monies for its own programs. Fees were established to provide monies from citizens on a regular basis in order to pay off the costs of the project. By its completion, the Milwaukee Water Works cost something on the order of $2 million.[54] By 1890, however, it still was generating annual revenues of more than $300,000 that could be used by city officials for whatever they deemed significant.[55]

With revenues of this magnitude, the city government now was put in a position to change from an almost exclusively voluntary, unpaid activity, which had been run by key business figures, to something that would slowly become a powerful social institution. Within a few years of the completion of the waterworks, in fact, new and enlarged departments were created within city government—departments that would play key roles in redefining life in Milwaukee.[56]

Preserving the Health of the Body Politic

The public waterworks was the first step taken by municipal government to provide for the well-being of Milwaukee's citizens. Other steps occurred almost simultaneously. In 1867, the Wisconsin State Legislature authorized the development of a new Board of Health. By 1880, the Board was composed of a health commissioner, an assistant commissioner, a meat inspector, and two other staff members, and it had an annual budget of $5,000.[57] The overall health of residents in the city was not particularly good, and as industries flourished and the number of residents increased, it worsened. In 1870, the death rate in Milwaukee was one of the highest among large cities in America.[58] Illnesses raged within the homes of many. Tuberculosis, typhoid fever, and scarlet fever were the leading causes of death. Moreover, certain diseases seemed to prevail especially among the city's newcomers. Germans, it was said, were especially prone to develop smallpox, primarily because they refused to get public vaccinations.[59]

The new Board of Health took it upon itself to prepare and to urge the public to become more attentive to their healthcare. The health commissioner required such measures as regular vaccinations for easily communicable diseases. By the early 1870s, such vaccinations were imperative for children who wished to attend public schools. The Common Council of Milwaukee also enacted new legislation in 1875 to authorize the Board of Health to establish garbage disposal for the city. Until then, the task had been left principally in the hands of young children who would scour the city streets, hoping to make small change by collecting residents' night soil and garbage.[60] The Board of Health also took an aggressive stand against the many abattoirs in the city, seeking to stem the flow of blood and intestines that found their way into Milwaukee's rivers and streams.[61]

The municipal government made more substantial investments in new facilities as time wore on. In 1878 the first public hospital in Milwaukee, South View Hospital, was erected on the city's south side to provide care for indigent patients. Previously, such care could only take place at one of the city's private hospitals.[62] But because of limited resources, South View Hospital rarely was used for the care of patients.[63] By 1892, a second public hospital, the Johnston Emergency Hospital, had been added. New ordinances also were enacted by the Common Council to govern the location and use of outdoor privies by city residents. The health commissioner set into motion public information programs: Vaccinations were urged for the public, among other things. The results soon became obvious. Over the course of the thirty-year period, the death rate in Milwaukee dropped sharply, from 23.2 per 1,000 in 1870 to 13.9 per 1,000 in 1900.[64] By 1910, the city was thought to be one of the leading urban centers for public healthcare and general well-being in America.[65]

Other efforts developed to provide care and to enhance the well-being of the growing numbers of Milwaukee citizens. A system of parks in the city had begun in 1889. By 1891, the municipal government had set aside a considerable sum of money, $547,000, simply for the purchase of new park lands.[66] A Board of Park Commissioners was appointed to oversee the parks and their development. Within the space of ten years, the city had developed a system of fourteen parks located throughout Milwaukee, a system assessed at a value of more than $2.5 million.[67] One of the parks, Washington Park, on the western edge of the city, also included a handsome zoo to which notable and affluent residents could make occasional donations—an elephant, a set of lions, and other similar wildlife. Many of the parks held outdoor concerts in the summer months; others possessed small lakes that offered visitors the chance to boat and to swim.[68] Other ventures also were taken by city officials to provide for the well-being of residents. Late in the 1890s, the city constructed the first public natatorium for those who enjoyed swimming during the cold weather months. Located on the south side of the city, it was close to the homes of working-class citizens and became a favorite spot of residents.

Altogether, then, Milwaukee's municipal government initiated a host of changes over the period, all of them designed to furnish better care for the endless flow of new residents. Most of the improvements arose simply because the needs of the population required them. Ever growing numbers of people required better public facilities; the very density of the population grew, more so than many other cities not constructed in such a small, compact area. The public health commissioner, among other city officials, often was the figure who strongly voiced the concerns for providing for the care of Milwaukee citizens; he was particularly concerned that the increased density of the population might easily foster the rapid and deadly transmission of disease.[69] Workers, themselves, possessed few means of transportation—certainly none of those that became available to the wealthier residents of the city by the end of the century.[70] And even though some industries would provide new kinds of health care and special attention for the workers, ultimately the major responsibility came to rest in the offices of city government.

Securing Order in the City

If the government of Milwaukee provided for the welfare of its citizens with the one hand, filling in where capitalist enterprises failed to do so, it also exacted its own heavy price with the other. Part of such costs were the obvious ones—the simple requirement of taxes or fees for the services it rendered to the public. The construction of new hospitals, for example, had been done on the basis of public bonds so that citizens, themselves, ultimately were responsible for paying off the debt. So, too, the innovations in healthcare exacted their own costs.

Yet there was another way in which the city government came to take its pound of flesh. It began to perform something of a dual role in the city, furnishing for the well-being of individual citizens, on the one hand, but attempting to secure public order in the city, on the other. In this latter respect, especially, Milwaukee city government acted very much the complement, one might even say handmaiden, to the emerging industrial empire of the city.

Three departments were approved for further expansion in Milwaukee's municipal government by the state legislature in the late 1860s. They were the fire department, the police department, and the public schools. The fire department initially garnered most of the funds from the city coffers. A host of fires to businesses had destroyed business property, and it was the concern of leading citizens that such destruction could prove fatal to the business fortunes of the city. In 1871, for example, the loss of property to fires in Milwaukee was more than $250,000; more than half of it was not covered by insurance.[71] Thus, every effort was made to enlarge the city fire department, by providing a new fire chief, fire equipment, and a host of hydrants positioned at strategic locations throughout the city. The creation of the new waterworks naturally had made possible the development of the hydrants. By 1874, the municipal government of Milwaukee, moreover, had begun the first fully paid fire department in its history.[72]

The destruction of the business property of capitalist enterprises was foremost on the minds of the fire officials, suggesting clearly how the fire department was intended to protect the business fortunes of the city—rather than, let us say, to save human lives. In his annual reports, the fire chief of Milwaukee would routinely begin his declarations with observations about the loss of business property, the amount of the loss, and the insurance coverage. Though residential fires, as a group, typically represented the largest number of fires in the city, it was the damage to business property that was of greatest significance to the chief. In 1881, for instance, the chief urged that "a steam engine be stationed near the Menomonie [sic] Valley [because] large and valuable buildings have been constructed of late in the western part of our city."[73] Only one year later, he repeated the same urgent appeal, observing that "within a few years the Menomonee Valley will become the great manufacturing center of the city."[74] Even when a major fire at Newhall House took the lives of 71 people in 1883, the chief's report almost casually dismissed the loss of life within a text that as usual began with his statement on the loss of business property in the city:

> The total loss for the past year aggregates $479,295. The total insurance loss involved was $1,140,000. The total loss on which there was no insurance was $132,000. The total value of property involved was $1,869,254. The most serious fire ... was the burning of the Newhall House, on the morning of January 10th, 1883, involving a loss of $146,277 and the sacrifice of seventy-one lives.[75]

Therein, of course, lay the real message—that the newly emerged fire department was intended precisely to help secure order and to protect the expanding sector of the capitalist enterprises of the city of Milwaukee.

Order also soon came to be the watchword of the police department. Developed somewhat later than the fire department, it grew largely in response to the need to secure public order in the city. In the 1870s, it was a relatively minor department. It consisted principally of a salaried police chief and a handful of detectives and patrolmen. It lacked the whole array of equipment available to the fire department for the protection of business property. By 1880, its budget had increased to $69,888, which compared favorably to the budget of the fire department at the time.[76] The dramatic expansion of the police department took place during the 1880s. The strikes of 1886 represented the key moment for the expansion of the police force. In 1885, the police force consisted of 93 men; one year after the strikes, in 1887, the force had expanded to 156 men, a larger absolute growth in numbers than would occur in any similar time span throughout the period.[77]

Over the course of the three-decade period (from 1870 to 1900), the police department came to display all the features associated with an agency that would become a major and significant force for establishing order within the city. Besides the sheer growth in absolute numbers of officials and foot soldiers on the streets, which grew to a force of 322 by 1900, the police department, like the fire department, evolved a set of regulations and criteria that proved the benchmark for creating a strict and regimented force.[78] In the 1880s, a set of examinations was introduced, the successful completion of which was required for membership on the force.[79] Uniforms also came to be the order of the day as the police chief insisted that this represented yet another sign of the professionalization of the force. Further, a clear and ranked hierarchy also emerged within the department; by the close of the century, it employed a long string of officials ranging in seniority and salary from the chief of police, at the top, to the patrolmen at the bottom.[80] Thus, within the space of thirty years, the department itself, like the city, had become fundamentally transformed—changed from a small, volunteer staff, run primarily by temporary recruits, to one that was highly professional.

Nevertheless, the clearest sign of how Milwaukee municipal government sought to establish and to regulate the expanding immigrant population of the city was evident in the schools. The state of Wisconsin encouraged all children, ages four through twenty, to attend some kind of school and made public schooling readily available to them. By the late 1860s, the state legislature had authorized the city to expand its programs.[81] Within a short space of time, the public schools had begun to flourish. In 1870, there were only 21 public schools, but by 1880 there were 38, and by 1900, 50.[82]

Many students were enrolled in private schools. In 1880, for instance, of the 21,289 students who attended school in Milwaukee, fully 35 percent of them attended private schools.[83] A number attended Catholic schools in the city, among them St. Hyacinth's, the most popular. The most notable of private schools was Peter Engelmann's German-English Academy, where the children of the affluent German families attended.[84] Nevertheless, the large majority of students attended the public schools; by 1900, the percentage of children who did attend actually remained at roughly two of every three pupils in the city.[85]

The public schools acted to do many things on the behalf of early industrial Milwaukee. They developed, among other things, programs designed to train students in the vocational arts. In the 1890s, a series of programs in manual training were developed, along with courses in such practical arts as that of cooking.[86] But, most of all, the schools were viewed as agencies that would enforce and establish the moral order of the expanding city. Just as the streets gave evidence of the filth of civilization, so, too, there seemed to many to be a moral decline in the population—one that grew as the number of immigrants grew increasingly in the city. In his annual address to the Milwaukee School Board in late 1895, the Board president remarked that "we have humane societies to ferret out and punish evil-doers against the brute creatures; health inspectors to guard against infractions of our health laws; police to arrest grown-up vagrants; but idle boys are allowed to lounge about streetcorners. This is a crime against the moral health of society."[87] He urged that officers be appointed by the School Board to get the boys off the streets and into the classrooms.

Frederick C. Lau, the first superintendent of Milwaukee Public Schools, laid out the grounds for public education and the school system with simple clarity. In 1871, as the schools were in the midst of an expansion, Lau insisted that "teachers should never lose sight of the fact that *order is not only Heaven's first law, but also the first and fundamental law of the successful management of a school.* To secure this important point must be the aim of every teacher."[88] Two years later, he restated the same point, insisting that the "*first requisite of the school is* order: *each pupil must be taught first and foremost to conform his behavior to a general standard.* Only thus can the school as a community exist and fulfill its functions. In the outset, therefore, a whole family of virtues are taught the pupil, and these are taught so thoroughly and so constantly that they become fixed in his character."[89]

The whole array of school regulations and laws regarding the discipline of students subsequently were directed toward precisely this end—maintaining order in society, inculcating direct and explicit conformity to the moral standards of the city. The rules of the Milwaukee public schools required that principals ensure that order occur throughout the schools, when students passed in hallways, for example, and that students help to maintain cleanliness on the school grounds.[90] Rule violation entailed stiff penalties for the miscreants who refused to obey their teachers and who comported themselves in ways that ran counter to the authority of the school. A series of articles were established in the early by-laws of the schools that allowed the principal to suspend students if they displayed any form of "pointed or open disobedience."[91]

In sum, then, these three major departments of Milwaukee municipal government—the fire and police departments, and the school system—were created and designed in ways that sought to implement a single explicit purpose in the construction of an urban society: to ensure that order came to be the watchword of the individual citizen and to do so in ways that eventually would promote order in the larger society. Both in explicit and in implicit respects, such purposes were pursued as a necessary complement to ensuring that the capitalist enterprises of the city could go about their daily business with few unnecessary interruptions—in short, to secure the certainty of the marketplace.

Creating Public Property

The municipal government of Milwaukee did not make the kind of stir that other city governments, run and staffed by party machines, did. Just south of the city, in that place so long regarded as Milwaukee's primary urban rival, a vast and powerful machine was being constructed—one that would soon take possession of Chicago. To all appearances, Milwaukee suffered none of the evils that had overtaken Chicago, or, for that matter, a host of other large urban centers.[92]

Appearances, however, can be deceiving. The changes that occurred in the public sector of Milwaukee over the course of the early industrial epoch were often so gradual and seemingly so inevitable that residents probably overlooked their long-term consequences. This is not to suggest that politics failed to grab the headlines in Milwaukee or that somehow the city was entirely free of the ills of corruption that beset so many other American cities. Milwaukee displayed its own brand of corruption, in the form of the fiery and colorful Judge David Rose, who occupied the office of mayor from 1898 to 1904 and again from 1906 to 1910. Furthermore, Milwaukee also possessed its own reform firebrands, in the manner of the Municipal Reform League. During the course of the 1890s, the League managed to call for and to implement fundamental changes in municipal government that served to streamline City Hall's operations.[93]

However, there was an immanent tendency to the emerging municipal government, one that escaped people's eyes but soon would cast its own spell broadly across the city. Over time, the municipal government had come to wield enormous power and authority over the local population. Although many laws and acts originated in Madison, eventually the authority lay in Milwaukee. Immigrant children were compelled to obey the law of Milwaukee public school authorities if they entered these classrooms; newcomers were compelled to obey the laws of the Milwaukee police force if they resided and worked anywhere within the city's boundaries; and new and booming businesses, if they wished to remain safe from the hazards of fires, eventually were required to submit to regular and detailed inspections by the Milwaukee fire department.

Ultimately, the public authority that was unleashed in Milwaukee became tangibly evident in the form of the property that municipal government controlled within the city limits. There was the new and spacious City Hall; a network of city parks; a broad array of new and excellent sewer facilities; and the many and widely dispersed materials of the fire department. Over the space of thirty years, from 1870 through 1900, the value of this property had increased enormously, more so than any other piece of private property. By 1900, in fact, the assessed value of public property in Milwaukee far outdistanced that of any single, indeed, of any combination of major pieces of private property. In 1870, the assessed worth of public city property in Milwaukee was just under $500,000, and that of all private property was $21 million.[94] Thirty years later, the comparative value of the two kinds of property had changed dramatically: City municipal property was now valued at an estimated $21 million, while all private property, including real estate and personal property, had a value of $158 million.[95] The ratio of the one to the other, in other words, had changed over the three decades from 1:42 to almost 1:7. No wonder that someone like Judge David Rose wished to control City Hall; in doing so, he would have had available more resources than anyone else in Milwaukee.

By the turn of the twentieth century, the municipal government of Milwaukee had undergone as much in the way of revolutionary transformation as had the Milwaukee marketplace: Municipal government now was poised to flex its muscles in ways that no one could have ever imagined.

Summary

Perhaps no era would prove so decisive to the creation of industrial Milwaukee as that from 1870 through 1900. Industry emerged from within the bowels of the city, and it began to redesign nature itself, remaking the land and the once beautiful rivers. The nature of work changed as well, becoming transformed from small, lively enterprises into large factories, where people tended more to the care of machines than to themselves. Physical and social distances came to merge with one another. Workers were compelled to live near the factories in the Menomonee Valley, close to their daily pursuits, whereas the wealthier citizens could afford to move out to the more rustic and less desecrated surroundings.

Industrial capitalism, in effect, had transformed Milwaukee and set into motion a host of forces, some of which it could control and others of which it could not—at least, not very easily. The labor strikes of the mid-1880s were an effort to seek to achieve more in the way of material rewards for the thousands of laborers in Milwaukee—but, for the period being discussed, at least, they made relatively little difference in the lives of workers. Nonetheless, the struggle between the effort to create growth and promote progress, at least in a technical sense, and the effort to fairly distribute the fruits of this process to workers grew more intense. The Social Democrats would begin to mobilize themselves more effectively in the city as the inequalities created by industrial capitalism grew ever more severe.

The larger institutions that developed in the immediate wake of industrial capitalism served to promote the interests of the capitalists at the expense of those of the working class and of urban residents, in general. This was especially true in the case of municipal government. In Milwaukee, as in so many other cities, municipal government became tailored to satisfy two major tasks. One was to provide for the many needs of local residents, such as good healthcare and bountiful parks, that the local capitalist enterprises simply failed to meet. The other was to create an array of local departments that served to secure order in the city, order that helped to ensure that the transactions of local capitalists could be done easily and efficiently. The priorities of Milwaukee's fire department, for instance, were clear: to protect and defend the property of local capitalism first and to worry about the loss of human life only afterward. Instruction in the public schools was intended to ensure that every child who proceeded through the school system was taught, first and foremost, to become a morally responsible citizen—that is, to acquire the moral standards of the larger urban order—standards intended to make people into cooperative and loyal members of the labor force.

Critical changes had taken place in the larger city—changes that would forever alter its earlier form. In the immediate future those changes also would have an impact—for they had fashioned a municipal government that would no longer serve merely as the plaything of wealthy local citizens, as it had done in an earlier time. While it provided security in the city, maintaining law and order, local government also had begun to gain a measure of its own strength. By 1900, it was on the verge of seeking power as an exercise of its own sovereignty and thus would change once more—from a mere complement to local capitalism to become one of its principal antagonists.

5

Mature Industrial Milwaukee: 1900–1930

The magnitude of the changes that swept across the city of Milwaukee in the final third of the nineteenth century was not to be duplicated in the first third of the twentieth. Instead, the city remained on the course it had begun in the 1870s. It grew into an even more powerful industrial urban presence, ranking by 1910 as the twelfth principal urban center of the United States in population and tenth in the value of its manufactured products.[1] Large plants, such as those of Allis-Chalmers and the Harnischfeger Company, expanded further.[2] New and ever larger numbers of entrepreneurs joined the effort to create a broader expanse of capitalist enterprises in the heart of the city. Meanwhile, the municipal government continued to expand, asserting its powers to corral territories that lay adjacent to the city proper.

There were distinctive hallmarks to this phase of the life of Milwaukee. Possibly the most visible was that the rapid growth of the late nineteenth century, which had sent the numbers of residents skyrocketing from 70,000 to almost 300,000 by 1900, had considerably diminished. Between 1900 and 1930, the city would just about double in size, reaching a population of close to 600,000. The revolutions that had marked the preceding era, both in industry and in urban government, had come to an end. The new institutions of the city now faced the more difficult task of achieving some degree of permanence and stability.

Indeed, this phase in the life of the city also became notable as a time of consolidation. Consolidation assumed many forms. Among the very wealthy Germans, for example, a set of relationships were developed that forged a substantial and powerful upper class in the city. The appearance of such a class itself was novel in the city's life. Although key leaders and entrepreneurs, such as Alexander Mitchell and a set of his allies, had previously been good friends and bound through close business associations, never before had there emerged such a cohesive and inclusive set of social relationships among the very rich. At the other end of the spectrum, too, a parallel alliance surfaced—one that gathered the leading dissident el-

View of Exposition Hall and housing in downtown Milwaukee ca. 1890

ements in the community and united them under the banner of the Social Democrats or, more commonly, the Socialists.

Milwaukee, in fact, had become home to the two chief social alliances of the industrial era, the wealthy owners of industry, on the one hand, and the political
representatives of the working classes, on the other. It was between these alliances
that the struggle over growth and equality would be fought. Moreover, efforts on
behalf of equality, as well as the fairer distribution of rewards to members of the
working class, gained more momentum in Milwaukee than in most other industrial cities in America. How that effort would transpire in Milwaukee, of course,
would cast much light on the ability of workers to mobilize themselves in other
cities.

However, social alliances tell only a part of the story of consolidation. The leading institutions also sought to achieve consolidation, and no institution pursued
this end more vigorously than municipal government. The city government of
Milwaukee, though heretofore something of a complement to the capitalist enterprises, now sought to consolidate its own sovereignty. This is a tale that, if not un-
told, certainly has been understated in recounting American urban history.[3] Citizens and scholars, alike, typically have spoken of the politics of this period in
terms of the new immigrants and their ugly political machines.[4] However, this
captures only the superficial details. Now, as we look back from the close of our
century to its opening, with the veil of contemporary rhetoric and struggle lifted,
we can see clearly that municipal government in Milwaukee, as in so many other
American cities, itself had ventured to become the author of its own authority.

Consolidation also became offset by division. Division and conflict, of course, were by no means new to the life of the city. From the moment of its birth, as we learned in Chapter 2, conflict paraded the streets of Milwaukee as though it were one of the daily pleasures of the urban rounds. But now, in its mature phase, the character of the conflict, like that of the city generally, had undergone a profound metamorphosis. What once had been almost exclusively a conflict between and among people, in particular, the allies of Byron Kilbourn against those of Solomon Juneau, had turned into a conflict of institutions, and the territorial establishments they represented.

Milwaukee had become transformed from a city of people into one of social institutions and social relationships. The very forms that now served to constitute its daily life, the institutions and the alliances, became the central actors in the struggles over who was to gain dominion in the city. Further, this transmutation would forever mark the subsequent history of the city.

The Powers of Municipal Government

Assertions of Sovereignty

From the moment that it received its first official charter in 1846, the government that represented the citizens of Milwaukee fought a constant battle to assert, and thereby to define, its authority. (See also Chapter 2.) It is in the very nature of the federal system that has evolved in the United States that there exist neither clear nor firm boundaries in the powers to be exercised by the federal government, the state, and the city, respectively. Such powers seem constantly to be in flux; in fact, federalism has turned from a legal structure into a process.[5] In every state during the course of the latter part of the nineteenth century, the demarcations of authority constantly had to be defined and redefined.[6] Though federalism had been established as a doctrine both to limit and to constrain the powers of the federal government over individual citizens, as time passed it was left up to the individual sovereign bodies—the federal government, the state, and the city—to wage battle over who could assert power, when, and where. In consequence, the city government became a limited sovereign power, and it sought to assert its authority in ways and at times that befit its changing material circumstances.

By the outset of the twentieth century, as in so many other localities in the United States, the power of sheer resources had shifted to the city of Milwaukee. By 1910, the city's population was 373,857, or fully 16 percent of the people in the state of Wisconsin; and only a decade later, the proportion of Wisconsin residents who lived in Milwaukee had climbed to 20 percent. Other resources also had become concentrated in the city. Of the net capital produced in the state in 1910, for instance, much of that capital was produced by industries located in and around the city of Milwaukee.[7] Accordingly, the city government began to take steps to bring its own capacity to be sovereign into harmony with the substantial resources it housed and with the services it delivered to the many local residents and industries.

It pursued several complementary lines of attack. One was an effort to extend its control over territories adjacent to the city proper. As time passed, this strategy would become an ever more visible part of the play of municipal and metropolitan politics in Milwaukee. Until 1893, annexation to the city of Milwaukee had taken place through a series of specific acts of the state legislature. Then, in 1893 the state legislature acted to give the city of Milwaukee greater control over its own affairs. The city government now was permitted to annex territory to itself through a two-stage process. The first stage consisted of a petition, signed by the majority of property-holders in a specific area, requesting that the area be annexed to the city proper. The second stage consisted of the approval of this petition by a majority of the members of the Milwaukee Common Council. The city government did not actively pursue this course of annexation until the turn of the century. By 1900, and then well into the first several decades, it actively worked to encourage the annexation of new territory and thus to extend its own sovereignty over adjacent areas. In this regard, it had become a strong force to help generate the continuing expansion of the city.[8]

A parallel line of attack was pursued simultaneously. Until the early twentieth century, the growth of new industry and new residents in Milwaukee County had taken place primarily within the confines of the city itself. By the early 1900s, however, a new movement occurred, one that produced an increasing number of new immigrants outside the city limits. For example, while the city population grew by 203 percent between 1900 and 1930, the population of the county, exclusive of the city, increased by 329 percent. The effects of this growth were obvious and immediate. County government, which had been a relatively minor political body for the greater part of the history of the city, now assumed much greater significance. It began to take on new and different responsibilities.[9] It also became something of a rival of city government as well. Thus, by the late 1920s, city officials began to urge a consolidation and merger of city and county governments, hoping, among other things, to offset a duplication of services.[10]

The Milwaukee city government also pursued a third strategy. It tried to bring the local electric railway company, The Milwaukee Electric Railway and Light Company (TMER&L), under its authority. TMER&L was run by two men, Henry Payne, the chief stockholder, and John Beggs, the manager.[11] Payne was a central figure both in Wisconsin politics and in local Milwaukee affairs. He pursued various business interests, held much Milwaukee real estate, and was a close associate of Charles Pfister, another leading capitalist in the city, and adopted son of Guido Pfister, the leather manufacturer. Payne and Beggs had managed to run TMER&L at considerable profit to themselves and to their shareholders—but not without substantial resistance. There were continuing controversies over the fares charged to residents, as well as over the efforts of the two men to control the development outside the city through the new routes they established.[12] By the beginning of the twentieth century, various city officials, in addition to a host of reform groups such as the Municipal Reform League, began to protest that the Railway acted improperly and unfairly with regard to its fares of Milwaukee citizens, and they, therefore, demanded that the Railway, like the water and sewerage systems, should be brought under the authority of the city government.

The last strategy exercised by the city government to assert its sovereignty was its pursuit of home rule. The doctrine of home rule, as it came to be first articulated both in California and in Missouri in the late nineteenth century, meant that the electorate of a city could create their own charter and thereby take more direct control of their own affairs.[13] It was this doctrine, in particular, that helped to define the limits of sovereignty between the city and the state. Heretofore in Wisconsin, such powers lay with the state legislature and with Milwaukee's representatives to the state legislature. However, now, in the first part of the twentieth century, city officials began to urge that, as part of the new powers sought by Milwaukee, home rule should be granted to the city. The Socialists, for example, made this plea a regular part of their party platform. They asserted that if the citizens were to enjoy their own sovereign status in the city, as residents, then the city, itself, needed to be in a position to define and to defend its constitutional rights.[14]

Each of these several strategies became part of the vigorous program by Milwaukee city government to define its powers in ways that would accord with its growing material prominence both in the Wisconsin polity and in the state's economy. Some of the strategies proved highly successful. For example, after years of pleading and cajoling by Milwaukee officials, the Wisconsin State Legislature, by virtue of a vote taken of the Wisconsin electorate, approved home rule for the city of Milwaukee in 1924. Yet other efforts to assert sovereignty, particularly the attempts to consolidate city and county governments, as well as to gain control over adjacent territories, would prove to be far different matters altogether.

Boundary Wars

Few issues disrupted or divided the Milwaukee metropolis quite so much in this period as the disputes that arose over the boundaries of the city and the authority of the city government. These were no trivial struggles. At issue was whether the municipal government, created originally to serve the interests of local capitalism, would now be able to act to serve the broader public of the city of Milwaukee. From plaything to handmaiden, municipal government now began to act to exercise its own sovereign powers and to thereby serve the interests of the urban public. In so doing, it also ran headlong into the power of that other major social force in the city—local wealth and capitalism.

The city government of Milwaukee constantly asserted its need, indeed its prerogative, to annex lands that lay adjacent to its boundaries. One regime after another, one set of city officials after another, regardless of political stripe or ideological bent, took it upon themselves to act as agents on behalf of the city's quest for new territory and greater authority.[15] But the city government also met a good deal of resistance in these efforts. Many people, particularly the vocal residents of adjacent lands, dismissed the pleas of the city as mere rhetoric, as nothing more than the simple quest for greater power.

In one fundamental respect, this counterclaim was quite accurate. The city government had grown quite full of itself. It now exercised control over a vast array of lands and of material equipment in the city. By 1910, for example, the assessed value of all of its properties was $45,743,193, or almost 20 percent of the assessed value of all private property—and improvements—in the city.[16] At the same time, its plea to expand, and particularly to annex, was not entirely illusion and pretext. In fact, the city government, having established its authority to meet a broad range of local residents' needs, from healthcare to parks to sewers to garbage service, required ever greater monies to fund such programs.[17] The productive and profitable plants, such as Allis-Chalmers, which had opened in previous decades on the outskirts of the city, could, under the authority of the law and taxes, provide additional monies to the city coffers and thus help to meet the needs of the growing body of citizens, many of whom, of course, also served as laborers in such plants.

There was another equally compelling reason that lay behind the city's effort to expand and to draw in adjacent lands and villages. By 1910, the city proper had a population of almost 400,000 people. These residents now were housed in an area as compactly and thickly populated as any in the United States, bar none. Consider the population size and the land areas of the major American cities at this time, as portrayed in Table 5.1. Of the sixteen largest cities in 1909—the time of the detailed study by the U.S. Census of American cities—only two cities, Boston and Baltimore, had higher population densities—numbers of people residing per acre (or by extension, per square mile)—than Milwaukee. In addition, Milwaukee possessed the smallest land base of any of the major American cities. Roughly ten years later, the situation had grown, if anything, far worse. Milwaukee now tied with Newark, New Jersey, for the most densely settled large city in America. In the interval, Baltimore, by striking contrast, had grown (in land base) by 172 percent, reducing the density of its population accordingly.

Saddled with an obvious problem, indeed, by common perception almost a crisis of space—one that was exacerbated by an antiquated legal statute of the state that limited the height of downtown buildings to no higher than 125 feet—the city government of Milwaukee set about making aggressive and unending efforts to annex new lands to itself.[18] Thus began a new, and decisive, phase in its evolution—one in which the *sine qua non* of its sovereignty became the effort to expand its own powers through the acquisition of new territories. Territorial issues became the political métier of the day, as they would in a host of other industrial cities.

Two camps stood in wait for the assaults, hoping to defend their own territorial rights. On the one hand, there were the capitalist industries, such as Allis-

TABLE 5.1   Population and Area of the Sixteen Largest American Cities, 1909

City	Population	Area (Acres)	Density (People/Acre)
New York	4,629,310	unreported	—
Chicago	2,142,156	117,793.1	18.18
Philadelphia	1,526,386	83,340.0	18.32
St. Louis	677,123	39,276.8	17.24
Boston	657,312	24,679.0	26.63
Baltimore	554,095	19,290.0	28.72
Cleveland	538,374	26,178.8	20.56
Pittsburgh	527,694	26,510.7	19.90
Detroit	447,484	26,102.6	17.14
Buffalo	415,314	24,791.0	16.75
San Francisco	410,343	29,760.0	13.80
Cincinnati	360,454	29,019.7	12.42
Milwaukee	**359,060**	**14,137.1**	**25.40**
Newark	355,949	14,826.0	24.01
New Orleans	334,470	125,440.0[a]	—
Washington, D.C.	326,430	38,408.4	8.50

[a]Area is a combination both of land and water.

SOURCE: U.S. Bureau of the Census, *Financial Statistics of Cities, 1909* (Washington, D.C., 1910). Table 1, "Date of Incorporation, Population, and Area of Cities Having an Estimated Population of Over 300,000 on June 1, 1909."

Chalmers, A. O. Smith, the Patrick Cudahy Company, and others, whom the city hoped to annex. The division that emerged in this period was significant in at least one exceptional respect. The city government of Milwaukee had, in the 1870s, taken on its own particular form, as a provider of welfare services and as an enforcer of the public order, to complement the activities of the capitalist enterprises of the city. Now, in a twist of some considerable irony, the municipality had turned on those very enterprises, themselves, and attempted to take them under its wing.

These particular battles broke out in several different quarters of the city. The chief battleground was that of West Allis, which lay just southwest of downtown Milwaukee. It was here that the Allis-Chalmers Company had been relocated in 1901. By 1922, this small village ranked as the fourth-largest industrial city in Wisconsin. According to some estimates, the per-capita income of residents in the area was the highest in the state.[19] There were a host of industrial corporations located elsewhere in the metropolitan area, too, all of which were located just outside the boundaries of the city proper. The city now sought to acquire these corporations through annexing the land on which they had been built. Eventually, deep antagonisms developed between the city and their industrial neighbors. Angry spokesmen for the territories, such as West Allis Mayor Delbert Miller, insisted that "we do not see where we will gain any advantage in annexation, and we believe it will result in higher taxes."[20] And there arose a very visible and popular image, at least in City Hall, that the city of Milwaukee had become encircled by, as

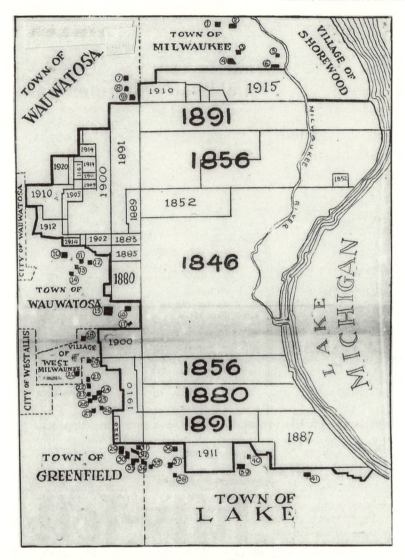

Map of Milwaukee city boundaries (1846–1920)

Commissioner of Public Works R. E. Stoelting phrased it, "an iron ring of industries."[21] A territorial line had been drawn—in steel.

The other major struggle also pitted the city government against wealth, but, in this case, it was the wealth of individual residents and families. Just as West Allis had grown to become a home and refuge to the Allis-Chalmers Company, likewise, many other areas of the city had become home to a set of new and wealthy residents. There was an array of such places, including Whitefish Bay and Shorewood on the northern shore of Lake Michigan. Whitefish Bay had been developed in the late nineteenth century as the site of the Pabst Resort. Located about six miles from downtown, travelers could get to the suburb by taking rail transportation and, later, with the completion of Lake Drive along the shore, by motor vehicle. Shorewood, which lay just south of Whitefish Bay, experienced a similar kind of growth boom, both in magnitude and in quality. Somewhat closer to downtown Milwaukee, it managed to attract numbers of fairly wealthy residents who could afford the trek outward and who also wished to escape the bleak decay of downtown Milwaukee. Eventually these two suburbs, along with others like Wauwatosa, which lay due west of downtown, came to be seen as prize attractions to city officials.

Over the course of the 1910s and 1920s, a series of battles erupted that pitted the city of Milwaukee against the suburbs and villages. The scenario of such disputes was always identical: The city government sought to drum up sentiment in favor of its efforts to annex the territory among local residents. City officials would employ a variety of arguments to attempt to induce cooperation, ranging from arguments on behalf of the benefits to be had through the availability of cheap and accessible city services, such as the water and sewerage, to arguments about the increased value of land that would come about in the annexed sections. Photographs in the local newspapers, such as the *Milwaukee Journal,* sought to depict how visibly improved an area could become as a result of annexation. Every possible device and step was taken, including public rallies and educational meetings at which city officials showed up to persuade voters to side with the city.[22]

Nevertheless, the resistance to the arguments of the city was considerable. Arguments against annexation often emphasized that the loss of local suburban control would lead to a decline in services to the suburb's residents.[23] Many suburban residents simply refused to become part of a city from which, in fact, they had so desperately sought an escape.[24]

Each and every battle, whether it be with a local corporate town, such as West Allis, or a wealthy suburb, such as Whitefish Bay, was fought on its own terms. The city did try periodically to gain the upper hand through the introduction of special legislation in Madison. In 1917, for example, a special bill, the Jennings Bill, was proposed that would have permitted the city of Milwaukee to annex areas outright, with no right of veto by the particular area in question. The villages and suburbs, however, acting through their assembled representatives in Madison, successfully lobbied to prevent the passage of that bill.[25]

When all was said and done, the city of Milwaukee had proven less than absolutely successful in its efforts to bring in adjacent towns and villages. Between 1900 and 1930, the city had doubled its territory from slightly more than 21 square miles to more than 42 square miles. A large part of the credit was owed to a very aggressive Department of Annexation, begun in 1923. Nevertheless, the city also had lost a sizable number of battles. The territories that it most treasured, such as West Allis, Whitefish Bay, and Wauwatosa, remained outside its jurisdiction. The

Wealthy Milwaukeean's mansion ca. 1890

Workers' homes in downtown Milwaukee ca. 1890

View of workers' homes and businesses in downtown Milwaukee ca. 1890

Stately homes on Prospect Avenue ca. 1890

ultimate consequence was the creation of a range and variety of municipalities within view of downtown Milwaukee. Balkanization had taken root in the metropolis, a design that subsequently would fragment the city, limit its possibilities for growth, and set the stage for historic divisions among its people. Further, it was a pattern to be found not only in Milwaukee but in a host of other cities, from Cleveland to Cincinnati and from St. Louis to Pittsburgh.[26]

Much has been made of the great divide that lies between suburbs and central cities in the United States.[27] Some observers have regarded the emergence of suburbia as the desire of Americans simply to move upward and outward—to the regions of the crabgrass frontier.[28] Yet others, especially those who work in the tradition of the human ecologists, take only the slightest notice of the historic creation of the difference between the two areas, at best remarking on the demographic movement of people from the center to the periphery—so long as they can afford the move.

Here, in turn-of-the-century Milwaukee, we learn in detail how suburbs came into existence and how they fought to resist merger with the central city. Wealth—that is, capitalism—lay at the root of it. This great social force, which had transformed Milwaukee during the era of rapid industrialization, also had now marked a great divide in what once had been common territory. Moreover, the divide gained permanence because it became reaffirmed through the creation of separate municipalities in the suburbs. *Wealth and territorial power eventually would serve to reinforce the impact of one another; social inequalities in urban space had become transmuted and overlain by territorial differences.*

The Operations of Government

During the first three decades of the twentieth century, the basic operations of the city government of Milwaukee continued in much the same form that they had taken originally. Municipal government provided a wide range of welfare services to local residents through, among other things, an extensive system of parks as well as a growing number of health services. Such services now included a new hospital and extensive public health programs in the local public schools. The city continued to rank among the leading municipalities in America in the quality of its healthcare. It also continued to furnish the basic instruments to establish order in the city. Both the fire and the police departments, for example, were extensively upgraded, adding to already substantial investments in personnel and equipment.

In addition, municipal government began to consolidate and to streamline the forces within the institution, itself. Its purpose was to create a city administration that was run efficiently and systematically.[29] In the boundary wars, for example, the city's new Department of Annexation was run by its head, Arthur Werba, with exemplary skill and effectiveness. Even though the department failed to gain the full success it had anticipated in its efforts to acquire new territories, Werba won praise from city officials for the thoroughness and intelligence of his actions.

No department better illustrated the themes of consolidation and efficiency than the Milwaukee Police Department. In 1921, a new chief of police, Jacob Laubenheimer, was appointed to the post by the mayor. He took over from a man who had run the department for more than two decades. With the outright encouragement of other city officials, the new chief set out to create a new and more rigorously formal department. A whole array of systematic procedures was developed to aid in police work.[30] A new Bureau of Detectives, for example, was added to the department to follow up on crime work. New investigative procedures for detecting criminal activities also were introduced. And, in perhaps the most important step, a program was set in motion to train new policemen for their service. Reflecting on his efforts, Laubenheimer remarked that "systems which eliminate waste time, unnecessary records, and duplication of work are most valued in any department, regardless of the nature of the work."[31]

These changes had almost immediate consequences for the civil order of the city. Consider simply the number of arrests credited to the Milwaukee police force. For the period from roughly 1910 through 1920, arrests in the city had been consistently in the range of about 10,000 per year. Yet once the new regime was put in place, these numbers changed dramatically. Table 5.2 presents the appropriate figures on arrests. Between 1922 and 1930, the number of arrests increased phenomenally—from 16,899 to 41,534. These increases covered the whole range of different crimes.[32]

Other departments soon followed suit. The fire department introduced its own training program, as well as new methods to keep account of fires in the city. The health department, which had been exemplary for its own procedures for some time, also introduced new methods for systematic recordkeeping. Throughout City Hall, in fact, new methods of administration were introduced, from more systematic techniques for recordkeeping to more efficient systems for handling the day-to-day procedures of each department.

Although the city government had emerged in so many respects to pursue its own destiny, its ties to local capitalist enterprises were not severed entirely. The school system, in particular, had expanded its offerings to devote considerable attention to the manual arts and to vocational training for students. In his report of 1912, the superintendent of the Milwaukee Public Schools noted that "the state must provide as a part of its educational system, for the training of your people in those useful arts and crafts by which they may be enabled to acquire greater usefulness to their employers and a greater earning power."[33] Accordingly, the school system opened two new schools in Milwaukee—a trade school for boys and a trade school for girls. New courses were given in such subjects as engineering and accounting. A new Board of Industrial Education was developed to oversee a series of courses on industrial training in the Milwaukee school system. Many of these new programs and curricular changes were developed with the explicit and enthusiastic approval of local business figures.

TABLE 5.2   Number of Arrests, Milwaukee Police Department, 1919–1930

Year	Total Number of Arrests
1919	9,138
1920	10,545
1921	Not Available
1922	16,899
1923	22,026
1924	23,443
1925	24,902
1926	32,636
1927	34,313
1928	36,324
1929	42,536
1930	41,534

SOURCE: Annual Reports of the City of Milwaukee Police Department, 1919–1930.

Still, when juxtaposed to the whole array of the government's other activities, the efforts of the school system disclose the full extent to which municipal government had set off on its own particular course by the first part of the twentieth century. Several dramatic achievements took place during this period. City government had properly come into its own and sought now to exercise authority in new and fundamentally different ways. It won some battles, such as that over home rule; and it lost others, such as a number of struggles with nearby industries and suburbs. As an institution, it also sought internal consolidation of a sort, creating a more formal and systematic set of procedures to guide its activities. Finally, it joined battle with the very capitalist enterprises that had first created it. In a paradox of no little consequence, it now fought to gain authority over those very industries that had fostered its powers originally as a way to regulate the civil order and the marketplace of the city.

Alliances of the Laboring and Upper Classes

The Socialists Take Power

The growth and developing resources of the municipal government of Milwaukee made it an increasingly attractive prize for those groups that sought to gain power. Political parties, which themselves were seeking a foothold in the new urban firmament, aggressively fought one another for public office. Individual candidates arose to battle one another for the fruits of political victory. Politics had come to be a game with its own rules, just as the institution of city government had helped to define the nature of its own boundaries.

The most well-known politician to occupy the office of mayor at the turn of the century was David Rose. Rose, a Democrat, was a magnificent stump orator who

managed to win elections often on the strength of his own personality. He was opposed by the standard Republican, who more often than not represented the established business interests of the local capitalists. Moreover, as the new century
unfolded, Rose and his associates soon came to be opposed by a new force that
had slowly grown from within the belly of Milwaukee, the Social Democrats.

The Social Democrats had firm and diverse roots in the city. The Germans who
composed the core of the party had migrated to Milwaukee in the mid-nineteenth
century, and they often came from radical backgrounds. Their presence in the city
signaled their unhappiness, sometimes outright forcible exile, from their birth-
place. Many had escaped Germany on the eve of the 1848 revolutions, victims to
the growing power of the state—a power that would reach full flower under Bis-
marck only decades later. They brought with them to Milwaukee a strong sense of
interest in politics, and, in particular, a desire to effect changes in their political
circumstances. The city, like America generally, was made to order for the radicals—a new, relatively undeveloped setting in which they could go about creating
a new social and political system almost from scratch. Originally many such migrants had organized themselves into the *Turnverein,* a club of German citizens
who met regularly to engage in debate, to participate in athletic contests, and,
generally, to enjoy one another's company. As the city grew increasingly industrialized at the end of the nineteenth century, the Turnverein, along with representatives of the fledgling labor movement in Milwaukee, especially the American
Federation of Labor, laid the foundations for a new political alliance, the Social
Democrats.

Several individuals assumed particularly prominent roles in the creation of this
new alliance—among them, especially, Victor Berger. Berger had been raised in
Nieder-Rehbach, a section of Austro-Hungary, and migrated to Milwaukee in
1881, taking up work in a variety of different pursuits. He was especially interested
in the life of the mind, and throughout his career as a public figure was commonly acknowledged as a man of deep learning and of a keen ability to use words,
particularly the written word.[34] Once in Milwaukee, it was not long before Berger
became involved with the radical politics of the working classes in the city; and
soon he took over as editor of the central organ of the radical movement on behalf
of the workers, the *Social Democratic Herald.*

The Social Democrats, constituted from the remnants of the Knights of Labor,
trade unionists, as well as Fabian Socialists, came into being in 1897, the collaborative result of work by Berger, Frederic Heath, Eugene Debs, and a host of
others.[35] From its beginnings, the political stance of the Social Democrats was different from that of competing labor and political alliances in Milwaukee. Although the Social Democrats acknowledged that ultimately, in the grand national
scheme of things, they must create a uniform doctrine that would bind individual
and autonomous organizations together, people like Victor Berger insisted on the
effort to create reforms tailored to each and every individual city. Besides this, the
Social Democrats of Milwaukee also came to believe very strongly in working

through municipal government in order to improve the welfare of the working class. In this regard, they took a different position than many of the labor organizations, all of which sought to extract benefits from capitalists in the workplace. The Social Democrats—in particular, Berger—argued that broad and deep changes, which would improve the welfare of the workers, should be effected through the local municipality.

In contrast to the Progressive party, a home-grown middle-class movement inspired by the charismatic leadership of Robert LaFollette, the Social Democrats believed that the beneficiaries of their efforts had to be the working classes of Milwaukee. This, they insisted, was also their natural constituency; and, as industry continued to grow in Milwaukee, so, too, did the size of this constituent base. By 1910, for example, fully 52 percent of all Milwaukee laborers were employed in manufacturing; by 1920, the proportion of men, alone, had grown to almost 60 percent.[36] The Social Democrats insisted that changes needed to be effected that would improve the lot of the workers—changes such as an increase in the public welfare benefits to families, improvements in the quality of public school education, and the municipal control of major public utilities, especially, in the case of Milwaukee, The Milwaukee Electric Railway and Light Company.[37]

By 1902, the Social Democrats of Milwaukee had become a sufficiently well-organized and powerful alliance, competing against the reigning capitalist powers and those of Mayor Rose, their favorite target, to be able to run a list of candidates for local office. In 1904, for example, they ran Berger for mayor, along with a handful of other men for positions as aldermen. Although Berger failed to win election, nine Social Democrats did win positions as aldermen, the first of their party to secure public office in Milwaukee.[38]

As the first decade of the twentieth century wore on, the efforts of the Milwaukee Socialists grew. In the election of 1908, for example, Emil Seidel, the Social Democrat, won 33 percent of the vote in the race for mayor, the largest percentage of the vote thus far tallied by the party. Moreover, the party retained key posts in the Milwaukee Common Council.[39] They now were poised to make a serious effort to take power in Milwaukee.

The Election of 1910. By 1910, the Social Democrats felt themselves to be on the verge of achieving a sizable victory in Milwaukee. The national party had committed itself to achieving victories in local contests. The problems of the continuing expansion of the city, particularly the density of the living conditions that had prompted the city government to make efforts to annex adjacent territories, created the real material foundations on which the Social Democrats could play out their themes. Moreover, the Social Democrats had by now become expert in the ways of political campaigns—in fact, far more effective at drumming up votes than the rival parties of the Democrats and the Republicans. Particularly notable were the "bundle brigades," groups of campaign workers so-called because of the bundles of campaign literature with which they flooded the wards of the city.

The Social Democrats, drawing on their diverse ethnic heritage, tailored their appeals to the linguistic diversity of the city. German had become the party's natural tongue, and English, of course, ran a close second. But the party also sought to capture the growing Polish electorate in the city by addressing them with papers and pamphlets written in their own language. Altogether, the party carried on its campaign in a total of seven different languages, thereby hoping to corral as much of the diverse ethnic mix as possible.[40] By 1910, there was no group nor party in Milwaukee politics that could run a campaign as effectively as the Social Democrats.[41]

Their organizational preparedness put them in a strategic position to take advantage of the missteps of their rivals—and missteps there were. Although Milwaukee, unlike its rival neighbor to the south, for example, did not possess the well-oiled political machine that could take advantage of the powerful resources of municipal government, David Rose and his cohorts, it was alleged, had engaged in their own bit of political skulduggery while holding office at City Hall. Beginning in 1904, in fact, a series of indictments were handed down by the Milwaukee grand jury against various public officeholders. When finally tallied, the complete count of such indictments came to 70. Rose himself seemed to have been a rather sharp and conniving politician. By 1910, word had it that corruption was to be found everywhere throughout city government.[42] The *Milwaukee Journal* claimed that "the city suffers under the reign of ward healers and cheap politicians."[43]

The campaign of 1910 proved to be a fierce one. The Social Democrats once again ran Emil Seidel for mayor. In addition, they ran a candidate for each one of the 35 aldermanic positions at stake. The newspapers, in particular, the *Milwaukee Journal,* took a strong position against Rose, while the *Milwaukee Leader,* the organ of the Social Democrats, strongly pushed Seidel and his fellow party members. When the results were finally assembled, Seidel had won the office of mayor, defeating his closest rival by a margin of more than 7,000 votes, the largest margin of victory in the city's history up to that time. The Social Democrats also managed to capture 21 of the 35 aldermanic positions; the post of city attorney; the post of city comptroller; the post of city treasurer; and fully one-fourth of the positions available on the Milwaukee School Board. The election was a complete rout in favor of the radicals.[44]

This was a historic moment. No other major American city ever had witnessed the election of a Social Democrat as mayor. Milwaukee now became the crown jewel for radical movements in America, and all eyes, both critical and sympathetic, turned to the city to see what changes the Social Democrats could effect.[45] Over the course of their two-year tenure in office, 1910–1912, Seidel and his allies were able to take a number of initiatives, some successful, some not. For instance, their central concern had been to secure home rule and thus sovereignty for the city's working class. In this effort they failed. On the other hand, they also hoped to bring TMER&L under municipal authority. Though they failed to gain control of the railway company, they did manage to win concessions for lower fares—a victory obviously for the workers.

All the while that the Social Democrats were in power, however, their enemies were biding their time, making plans to overthrow them. By the time of the 1912 election, a new amalgam, the Nonpartisans, had emerged to pose the major threat to the continuing dominance of the Socialists. The Nonpartisans simply reconstituted the Democrats and the Republicans into a single ticket. It was done precisely to provide the opportunity to defeat the Socialists at the polls. The 1912 campaign, like that of 1910, proved to be a heated one. But, at the end, Emil Seidel had been turned out of office, along with a number of his fellow Social Democrats as aldermen. The Nonpartisan strategy had worked to elect Gerhard Bading as mayor. Four years later, the Nonpartisans were behind the effort to enact a law that later enabled them to run Nonpartisan candidates routinely for office.

1912 and Beyond. The Social Democrats of Milwaukee would never again exercise so much power. They would manage, however, to retain their hold over the office of mayor. In 1916, Daniel Hoan, city attorney while Seidel held office as mayor, ran for the position and defeated the Nonpartisan candidate, Bading, by a margin of roughly 3,000 votes. While in office, Mayor Hoan proved enormously successful at bringing about efficient and effective politics in Milwaukee. Under his regime, the Milwaukee Social Democrats became known as the "sewer Socialists"—primarily because they were so effective at building a strong infrastructure for the city and also because they brought fiscal responsibility to city politics.

At the same time, they failed to create a strong and coherent program of the sort that first had won Hoan office. The Socialist party, in general, grew progressively weaker over time, and eventually in the late 1930s collapsed altogether. Hoan was returned over and over again to office primarily because he brought to the position a style of management that met the needs of the capitalist enterprises in the city—he brought order and certainty to the local marketplace that, of course, was just what the local businessmen required. In fact, he became the darling of the local conservative establishment, even gaining the occasional endorsement of such outlets of opinion as that of the *Milwaukee Journal*.

By 1930, the end of this era, the issue before Milwaukeeans was whether the Social Democrats—or, actually, Daniel Hoan—had made much of a difference both to the operations of the municipality and to life in the city. Had the leadership of Hoan made the city a better place for the working class, for example? Had it reduced the economic disparity between the very rich and the very poor? Had it created a municipality that, in effect, served the interests of the common man and woman rather than merely the affluent? In short, had the reign of the Social Democrats in office done much to achieve greater equity in the distribution of the fruits of manufacturing in the city—equity as opposed simply to further growth? In fact, on none of these counts could one conclude that the Social Democrats were especially effective, though in this respect they seemed to share much in common with virtually every other municipality in the United States where Social/Democrats had secured power.[46]

In one respect, however, the Social Democrats gave every appearance of having achieved great success in the city. Government seemed to be a little bit better run and more *honest* than in other American cities.[47] Nonetheless, the question remained whether this alliance of radical politicians had managed to move the city off the course on which it had been set—namely, to add to its sovereign powers over people and territory within the local area. In fact, the Social Democrats, if anything, had managed to expedite and to move the process of creating a powerful local institution even further along. It was, after all, under Daniel Hoan that the police department became the efficient, well-oiled machine that stood out, providing a model in Milwaukee city government for its other departments to emulate. Thus, one more irony emerged in this era: The party that sought to *empower the working class* actually had helped to *empower the city government*. This was a lesson learned throughout the world, and a lesson learned in Milwaukee owing to the very powers of the municipal institution, itself.[48]

Why did the Social Democrats fail, after all? Why did they fail in a place where they had mobilized themselves to run municipal government in a way that would benefit the large majority of residents in the city? Surely one major reason for their failure was that even when they gained a brief upper hand in the Milwaukee Common Council, exercising control over municipal government was no simple matter. Local government had established its own agenda and could no more easily be controlled by the Social Democrats than by the wealthy businessmen of the city. The Social Democrats, in effect, became a prisoner of the complicated operations of local government. Lacking the will to overturn government, all they could do was to make it run better. But there also was another reason for the failure of the Social Democrats to achieve equity for the working class of the city—the sheer power and dominance of the German upper class.

An Emergent Upper Class

While the Social Democrats rallied the laborers around the banner of promised improvements and benefits, the dominant elements of the city managed a consolidation all their own. The most distinctive trait of this emergent upper class was that, like the Social-Democratic alliance, it was composed almost exclusively of German families. Beyond that, it would prove as tightly knit and as cohesive as one could imagine.[49]

Several figures and families appeared as the key actors in the creation and consolidation of this particular alliance. There were, for example, Frederick Vogel, Sr., and his son, Fred, Jr., who, along with Guido Pfister, had created the extremely profitable company for the manufacture and marketing of leather goods, Pfister and Vogel Tanning Company. By the turn of the twentieth century, the firm had offices outside Milwaukee as well, in Buffalo, New York, and Philadelphia, Pennsylvania, and did business across the United States. There also was Charles Pfister, the adopted son of Guido and Louisa Pfister, who by the early 1880s had become a kingpin of Milwaukee and Wisconsin politics. Pfister was a leading figure of the Republican party and worked closely in a number of enterprises with Henry Payne, another major player in Wisconsin politics. Between the two of them, they held considerable wealth and exercised considerable influence over the fortunes of the city. Finally, there was the array of Uihlein brothers—Alfred, August, Charles, Edward, Henry, Gustave, and William—who, upon the death in 1875 of their uncle, Joseph Schlitz, had come into possession of the Schlitz Brewery Company of Milwaukee. By the early 1900s, they had made their company into one of the dominant breweries in America and had plants scattered across the land.

A central figure among these leading German players of the city was Otto Falk—General Otto Falk as he came to be known—the son of Franz Falk who had built one of Milwaukee's earliest breweries. Otto Falk consciously crafted a powerful and illustrious career in Wisconsin. In the late nineteenth century, after completing his schooling at Allen Academy, a military institute, he became a member of the Light Horse Squadron, a division of the Army's Fourth Battalion. His politics were fashioned early and decisively. He was in the leading contingent of soldiers that acted to bring the strikes by laborers at the Bay View Rolling Mills in 1886 to a conclusion. He ascended the ranks of the military rapidly and soon came to be regarded as a major military figure of great promise. Milwaukee's high society beckoned him as well, and he became one of the most visible members of the crowd of prominent young men and women in the city. Further, when political notables, such as the German ambassador, came to town, Falk usually was among those invited to attend their dinners and to escort them to various gatherings throughout the city. By the late 1890s, he also had come to be known as one of Milwaukee's most visible and eligible bachelors and was routinely invited to appear at the debutante balls and other gatherings of the leading lights in the city.

Thus, it probably came as little surprise to city notables that in 1904 Falk would take in marriage Elizabeth Vogel, the daughter of the wealthy manufacturer, Fred Vogel, Jr. The marriage helped create a pattern of intermarriage that had begun only years earlier as industry was taking root in the city. Fred Vogel, Jr., himself had married Louisa Pfister, the daughter of Guido, the partner of Fred's father in the tanning and leather business. Now it was Otto's turn, and he and his new wife soon became the parents of two children, Otto, Jr., and Elizabeth. The children's upbringing was a model of the time and a mirror of the German upper class. Like the children of all other wealthy German families of Milwaukee, they attended the very best private school in the city, the German-English Academy founded by Peter Engelmann. (Somewhat later, in the 1910s, the name of the school was changed to Milwaukee University School, to counter the anti-German sentiments that had been stirred up by World War I.) The academy maintained a strong curriculum and taught many of its courses in German. In fact, German was as often used by the members of the German upper class of Milwaukee as English. The two Falk children also traveled the standard circuit of parties, weddings, and clubs in town, regularly attending gatherings at the Milwaukee Club, the Town Club, and the Milwaukee Country Club.

All the while that his children were being raised to become members of the Milwaukee upper class, Falk himself remained at the very center of capitalist operations in the city. Once out of the Army, he had become involved in several different business enterprises. In the late 1890s, he had joined with his brothers, Clarence and Frank, to develop the Falk Corporation. It began as a small manufacturing firm, but within the space of a few years it had achieved great fame and financial success by the invention of a new technique to make metal rails. Soon the Falk Corporation was distributing its products to railway companies across the United States. By 1910, just as the Social Democrats had peaked in the budding strength of their political alliance, so, too, Otto Falk had risen to become a major presence in Milwaukee. He now was a major figure in the Merchants and Manufacturers Association in the city and had become one of the leading spokesmen for the capitalist point of view.

Falk's ideas about the growing industrialization of the city, as well as the growing number of laborers, matched the views of the other capitalists of the day. In a speech he gave to his fellow members of the Milwaukee Metal Trades and Founders Association in 1908, on his ascension to the presidency, Falk, for example, argued against trade unions in the city, noting that "we will give to labor its just reward and more, but [we] will not tolerate the domination of any class of banded labor, [for we] stand for freedom for employer and employee, first, last, and all the time."[50] Later, as president of the Merchants and Manufacturers Association in 1911, Falk attacked the Social-Democratic regime in City Hall, saying that they "have sought to cause defiance to law and order, threaten the courts, and implant prejudice and class hatred among the masses in Milwaukee."[51] Further, Falk went out of his way to anger the working classes of the city when demands were made to eliminate the stench and soot from the Menomonee Valley industrial district and to change the area into a setting of parks, in effect returning it to its natural state. Falk insisted that the Menomonee Valley was the heart of industry in Milwaukee and must remain so, regardless of efforts to promote the improvements for the large body of citizens.

Falk and his fellow Germans eventually came to dominate the whole spectrum of capitalist enterprises in Milwaukee. Charles Pfister, who by most accounts probably exercised more influence in Wisconsin than Falk, had by the beginning of the twentieth century come into ownership of the *Milwaukee Sentinel*. From then, until he relinquished the reins of control owing to poor health in 1924, the *Sentinel* became the voice of Republican interests in the city and the state. Among other things, the newspaper condemned the Social Democrats almost routinely and supported their opposition in both local and state electoral contests. But Pfister also held, or shared, control over a number of other enterprises, including the Pfister Hotel, a magnificent building on Wisconsin Avenue completed to honor the memory of his father; TMER&L, the local railway line; and a variety of real estate properties in the Milwaukee metropolitan region, including properties in Whitefish Bay and elsewhere.[52]

The various Uihlein brothers had become equally powerful and rich, though they tended to mind their business more than their politics. By the early part of the twentieth century, August was the chairman of the board of Schlitz, Henry was the president, and Joseph, August Uihlein's son, was the superintendent of the downtown plant. Edward, who had relocated to Chicago in 1875 in order to run the works of the company there, now insisted on calling himself a "U-line" rather than an "E-line." The various brothers accumulated enormous wealth and took care to develop properties and real estate outside the city of Milwaukee itself. For example, they jointly owned and ran properties in Florida and New Jersey, including a stable at which they bred and raised dozens of handsome horses. They also had assumed control of the Second Ward Savings Bank at the close of the nineteenth century. By the early 1910s it had become the second leading banking firm in Milwaukee.[53]

Others in this German group also grew to become very powerful and influential in Milwaukee. Fred Vogel, Jr., for example, took over as the head of the First National Bank in Milwaukee in 1905 and remained in the position until the consolidation of the bank with Second Ward Savings Bank in 1919. He also was active in the Northwestern Mutual Life Insurance Company of Milwaukee, a major insurance company in the United States. Further, like his friends and relatives, he served as a director on a host of boards in Milwaukee, including Allis-Chalmers, First Wisconsin Trust, and TMER&L, among others.[54]

Otto Falk, however, continued to exercise the greatest influence. By 1912, Allis-Chalmers was forced into bankruptcy, and Falk became receiver for the company. Roughly one year later, he became president of the newly reorganized company. Within the space of a couple of years, prosperity returned to the company. Word had it that the newly discovered profits could be attributed almost exclusively to the work of Falk, who was viewed as something of a savior. Though the claim was considerably more perception than fact, it had the effect of springboarding Falk to even greater national visibility. Newspapers and journals now regularly sought him out for his advice on how to run a good capitalist corporation.[55] He was seen as a kind taskmaster, urging cooperative problem-solving among his employees, and always intent on the bottom line.

Falk, moreover, became a regular spokesman and analyst for economic matters in Milwaukee. His friend Charles Pfister made him the year-end analyst of economic trends for the *Milwaukee Sentinel.* By the early 1920s, he had become Milwaukee's most notable citizen. He sat on the board of directors of virtually every major corporation in the city. The Republican party encouraged him to campaign for political office, but he declined. Nonetheless, as the president of Allis-Chalmers, now one of the major heavy-manufacturing corporations in the country, Falk's advice was regularly sought at the highest levels of government. He was on good terms with President Hoover and was invited occasionally for special dinners, of key business figures, to the White House. Otto Falk, as the leading representative of the Milwaukee upper class, now had transported the interests of the city itself, and its counsel, to play a central role in the markets and the political arenas that lay beyond Milwaukee.

The German upper class, propelled by the energies of Otto Falk and others, had managed to bridge and to solidify the distinct lines of capitalist industry in the city.[56] Perhaps the most arresting quality to their alliance, however, was the extent to which they had fostered family and kinship connections among themselves. The first marriage had linked the Vogels with the Pfisters; a second marriage had linked the Falks with the Vogels. But there were a host of other marriages that achieved the same result. Fred Vogel, Jr., and his wife, Louisa, had two daughters, Elizabeth, who had married Otto Falk, Sr., and Ilma, who became the wife of Joseph Uihlein, a son of August Uihlein. Further, one of their close relatives, Agnes Wahl, whose uncle was Franz Falk, the father of Otto Falk, Sr., had married Lucius W. Nieman. Nieman was the publisher of the *Milwaukee Journal,* which next to the *Milwaukee Sentinel,* was the other leading newspaper in the city. In other words, besides the breweries and the financial institutions and the heavy-manufacturing plants, the family alliance of Germans also controlled the two major media outlets in the city.

The pattern of upper-class intermarriage did not halt there. In fact, the tendency for intermarriage, if anything, increased by the time of the third generation of these families. Of the two children of Otto Falk, for example, each produced a marriage with another leading family. Elizabeth Falk, their daughter, married William Pabst, the son of Gustave Pabst; this marriage, though it produced one child, William Pabst, Jr., would last only five years, ending in 1929. Otto Falk, Jr., married Elizabeth Elser, the daughter of Albert and Mathilda Elser, the latter of whom was the daughter of Alfred Uihlein, one of the six original Uihlein brothers. Gustave Pabst, Jr., the son of Gustave Pabst, married Louise Uihlein, the daughter of Joseph Uihlein and Ilma Vogel. And on it continued.

By the late 1920s, the German upper class of Milwaukee had developed a powerful alliance. Families intermarried; their members attended the same schools; they gathered at the same parties; they went to the same weddings; they traveled abroad together; and they invariably sat across from one another on the very same boards of directors. All of this inevitably led them to try to mobilize their collective energies on behalf of the economic markets—markets that continued to fuel the expansion and growth of Milwaukee.

The Engine of Industrial Capitalism

While the German upper class of Milwaukee played a notable part in helping to guide the city's fortunes, it would be misleading to suggest that they exercised absolute control over those fortunes. They did not. Perhaps no upper class ever does. A market economy, anchored by manufacturing corporations, had taken root in the city by the end of the nineteenth century. It was the rich diversity and full productivity of that economy that helped to expand the fortunes of the city. And now, in the early twentieth century, that economy, as an institutional form itself, sought to develop even further.[57]

An important part of the story of the Milwaukee economy during this era is similar to that of city government and the leading alliances. Just as consolidation happened in these spheres, so, too, it took place in the economy. A number of notable mergers were crafted over the course of the mature industrial city. Allis-Chalmers represented one such merger. The thriving manufacturer had been created from the consolidation of several different companies—the original Reliance Iron Works of Edward P. Allis, the Fraser and Chalmers plant of Chicago, the Gates Iron Works of Chicago, and the Dickson plant of Scranton, Pennsylvania.[58] There were other notable mergers as well. The First Wisconsin National Bank was created in 1919, the merger of two key financial banking houses, the Wisconsin National Bank and the First National Bank of Milwaukee, the latter of which represented the interests of Fred Vogel, Jr., Charles Pfister, and John Beggs, of TMER&L. By 1921, the new bank ranked as the wealthiest financial corporation in the city, with a capital investment of $6 million.[59] And there were still further mergers, including one involving the merger of Cutler-Hammer, a firm that became a leading American enterprise in the manufacture of electrical equipment.[60]

Another part of the story of the industrial economy had to do with the leading lines of manufacturing. Those that had been among the most prominent in the preceding era tended to continue to be important in this one. The firms in iron and steel, especially, led the Milwaukee economy. Among them, besides Allis-Chalmers, were Harnischfeger, the Nordberg Manufacturing Company, A. O. Smith, the Falk Corporation, the Bucyrus Company, and a handful of others. By 1920, these corporations helped to make Milwaukee among the most prominent American cities in the production of heavy equipment and other metal goods, a role it would retain for at least another decade.[61] The city also continued to lead the nation in the manufacture of leather and tanned goods. Pfister and Vogel represented the major manufacturer of such products. In 1905, for example, it possessed a capital investment of $4.5 million, making it already one of the wealthiest corporate enterprises in the city.[62] Other such enterprises included the Albert Trostel Corporation and A. F. Gallun & Sons Corporation, but Pfister and Vogel produced more than half of the leather goods in the city.[63]

Two other lines of manufacturing also kept Milwaukee atop the heap of manufacturing cities in the country. Packaged meats had become a thriving industry in the city by the early part of the twentieth century, making the city into one of the leading producers of such goods, ranking behind Chicago. The chief firm was that of Patrick Cudahy who already had also established both a realty firm and a city for himself, Cudahy, bordering the Milwaukee city limits.[64] In addition, knit and woolen goods, which included an array of corporations as well as small cloth-iers throughout the city, ranked among the leading products of Milwaukee. The major manufacturers included companies such as the Friend Brothers Clothing Company, Fried-Ostermann, Phoenix Hosiery, Holeproof Hosiery, and a host of others. Among them, Phoenix Hosiery was the most substantial of the Milwaukee firms.

One line of industry did disappear, however, over the course of the first couple of decades of the twentieth century. Beer, which had made Milwaukee famous and had generated enormous profits for firms such as Schlitz, Pabst, and Blatz, be-came outlawed as a result of Prohibition. Some people saw this as a special attack of discrimination against the Germans of Milwaukee. Rabbi Samuel Hirschberg, a leading rabbi of the city, actually went on record in 1924 to state that Prohibition had been a "serious moral mistake for America," as well as a "disguised attack on the Germans in the American brewing industry."[65] Yet the very wealthy Germans, such as the Uihleins and the Pabsts, already had spread their wealth elsewhere into real estate and banks and had devoted capital to different lines of production. In any case, by the late 1920s, the brewing industry had virtually dried up in the city, and plants, which previously had employed more than 6,000 workers, now employed in the hundreds.

By the twenties, Milwaukee had become known worldwide for the quality and extent of its manufacturing. Its iron products, such as the tractors of Allis-Chalmers and the cranes of Pawling & Harnischfeger, ranked as the very best in the world. Through the efforts of figures such as Otto Falk but primarily through the energies of the city's firms, the markets for Milwaukee products now stretched across the country and penetrated other markets as well. Milwaukee products, particularly large cranes and other forms of heavy equipment, helped in the in-dustrial development of nations throughout the world. They were also to be found in such countries as Canada, Australia, and Japan, among others. Allis-Chalmers and Bucyrus were at the forefront of such pioneer efforts, but there were other plants as well, including both the Falk Corporation, which had be-come known now for special types of engine gears, and the A. O. Smith Com-pany.[66]

Profits rolled into the Milwaukee marketplace, as did a continuing supply of jobs for workers. Between 1900 and 1930, for example, the number of people em-ployed in manufacturing nearly doubled, from 48,328 to 94,873.[67] The value of products manufactured in the city went up even more substantially, from $59 mil-lion to $340 million by 1930. Moreover, new industries sprang up continuously in and around the city; in 1929 alone, it was reported, fifty new enterprises had been added to the Milwaukee marketplace.[68]

The picture of Milwaukee manufacturing, however, was not an entirely rosy one for a number of reasons. For one, Milwaukee, as a city, had long ago resigned itself to lying in the shadow of the Chicago marketplace. Chicago possessed clear advantages. It stood as the railroad hub of the Midwest, drawing in trainloads of products and passengers daily and shipping out equal numbers across the country. Milwaukee simply did not possess the financial resources nor the productive energy of Chicago and, therefore, could stand only as a rival to other, smaller cities, such as St. Louis or Pittsburgh. Its second-class status did not particularly bother Milwaukee citizens, though some, such as Daniel Hoan, were concerned about its long-term effects on the city. For another, there was a sense that perhaps Milwaukee had developed itself too exclusively as a manufacturing center. While many cities envied its position as the leading manufacturer of heavy equipment, the city also was not nearly so diversified as a number of other metropolitan areas. Of particular concern was the fact that such a large proportion of the Milwaukee workforce was employed in manufacturing.[69]

And yet a third problem loomed on the horizon. Although Milwaukee manufacturing companies remained extremely profitable over the course of the 1920s, there was a suspicion that the taxes imposed by city government, which helped to produce the fragmented metropolis, and the taxes imposed by the state, inspired by the reforms of the Progressives, eventually could lead to the loss of industry. In one of his annual columns for the *Milwaukee Sentinel,* Otto Falk had raised this question and suggested that if the markets did not continue to produce profits for Milwaukee's corporations, there would be substantial resistance to the city and the state taxes. Implicit in his assessment was the judgment that if Milwaukee did not remain an attractive suitor to corporations, then such corporations could take their business elsewhere—to other cities or even to other states. But he meant this, of course, as just a threat.[70]

None of these several matters, however, seemed to represent substantial drawbacks to the Milwaukee economy. Times and profits were booming during much of the period, with declines here and there owing to poor economic times throughout the nation. Everyone felt, however, that the prospects for Milwaukee's continuing prosperity—indeed, the continuing and seemingly endless expansion of the city—were high and that nothing could ever deter the city from becoming an even more serious rival to Chicago in the future. Or so they thought.

Summary

If the previous era became known as that of a great industrial revolution, one that benefited capitalism in Milwaukee, this era became known as one of consolidation—and of failed hopes. The power of the various institutions of the city became consolidated. Municipal government emerged from under the shadow of local capitalism and began to flex its muscles in new and aggressive ways. In some respects, moreover, it gained considerable success, particularly in securing home rule for Milwaukee and in annexing some lands to itself as a means of reducing the density of the population and gaining more revenues. Local capitalism became consolidated as well. The manufacturing enterprises of the city tended to merge with one another, and the engine of capitalism continued to produce great profits.

But this was also an era of sharp conflict and division, and it was a time in which the landscape of the city would be deeply etched by inequality. Municipal government sought to add new territories to itself, particularly the adjacent industrial and residential suburbs. To all appearances, such an act seemed very practical. Revenues for the city were based on taxes on local properties; as the population increased, demands to meet the needs for this population increased accordingly. Taxes could go up only so often. Thus, the city government's only option seemed to be that of gaining greater revenues both from local industries and from the wealthier residents.

Under this new form of pressure from the city government, the self-interest of capitalism came to be distinct from–indeed, at odds with—that of the common welfare of the community. However much the leading capitalists, such as Otto Falk, spoke of bringing new enterprise and new industry into the city, when it came time to share the profits, by providing more in the way of tax revenues to local government, Falk was unwilling to do so. And so, too, were the other leading capitalists of the city, those who had helped to establish the suburban municipalities in places such as Shorewood and Whitefish Bay. The *common good* proved only to mean *the good of industry,* not that of the local laborers.

This deep underlying conflict, which from one angle assumed a struggle between municipal government and the suburbs, from another angle assumed the struggle between the Social Democrats and the dominant upper class of the city—the German industrialists and their rich and layered networks with one another. Here, it seemed, the upper class possessed a decided advantage. Their industries continued to churn out profits, thereby providing employment for numbers of workers, and they were able to create a climate in the city that promoted business and resisted any effort to improve the lot of laborers at their plants.

The failed hopes of the Social Democrats and the working class in this period probably sprung, in part, from the same kind of divided energies remarked upon by Ira Katznelson, when he wrote of the division between residence and work that undermined the effort by the working class to secure more fruits for itself in New York City.[71] In Milwaukee, there was divided energy as well, but that energy was diffused between work and City Hall. The Social Democrats became convinced that they could acquire the reins of government and turn the institution to benefit the great majority of Milwaukee citizens. What they failed to appreciate is that by this time municipal government had become so complicated and powerful an institution, in its own right, that it would not easily submit to the pressures of its occupants, however well-meaning the Social Democrats might have been. Thus, in some sense, the Social Democrats became victimized by the very institution they hoped to dominate. Further, by making government more efficient, they also enhanced the overall operations of capitalism in Milwaukee. Perhaps, if they had directed more of their attention to mobilizing workers, rather than voters, they might have truly effected an improvement in the conditions of most Milwaukeeans. Perhaps—but we shall never know.

6

Reshaping Industrial Milwaukee: 1930–1950

The Industrial Revolution of the late nineteenth century transformed the city of Milwaukee in important ways. It created an array of productive industries, along with a large and vocal working class; gave birth to the forces and needs that would promote the creation of municipal government, changing what had been a largely voluntary activity into an institution that would assume professional dimensions and wide powers; and helped to promote the shift of the nature of the city from a setting of people into one of institutions and of relationships.

However, in this new era, two events—and one, in particular—largely external to the city itself, would set in motion changes of almost equal consequence: the Great Depression and World War II. Both led to a series of changes that would begin yet another transformation of the city and of its institutions, in particular. Yet, unlike the Industrial Revolution, the Great Depression and World War II did not completely remake the city of Milwaukee. The urban institutions and social alliances of the city had achieved a substantial degree of permanence in the period from 1900 through 1930. This was especially true for municipal government, which, as I discussed in the previous chapter, sought to exercise its authority in new and significant ways.

Instead, the events of the 1930s and 1940s essentially served to redefine the character of Milwaukee and its institutions. The events helped set the stage for a new relationship between the municipal government and the federal government, one that resulted in a far greater dependency of the former upon the latter. Municipal government effectively became less sovereign. The events also helped to reform the fortunes of the local economy and to mobilize unions and other alliances on behalf of the working classes. Most of all, the two historic developments helped to unleash a furious battle between the unions and the industries for survival in Milwaukee—a battle whose unintended consequence would be to create fewer rather than more jobs for the workers of the city. In the midst of the fury of the 1930s and

1940s, the murmurs of eventual decline could be heard on the streets of Milwaukee.

The Great Depression

Lost Jobs and Ruined Lives

The most immediate impact of the Depression on the citizens of Milwaukee was the loss of jobs. Milwaukee was hit hard by the upheaval in the economy—harder, in fact, than many other industrial cities.[1] The city had grown to depend heavily on its array of heavy industries, employing tens of thousands of workers at various tasks. Now many of those plants began to suffer. At Allis-Chalmers, for example, sales fell from a high of $45.3 million in 1929 to a low of $13.3 million in 1933.[2] Employment in Allis-Chalmers changed correspondingly, from 7,000 to fewer than 3,000 in the workforce.[3] Many Milwaukeeans now found themselves on breadlines, seeking sustenance for themselves and for their families.

Jobs began to disappear in large numbers shortly after 1930, though the city seemingly was slow to acknowledge the loss. Newspapers, such as the *Milwaukee Sentinel,* sought to put a bright face on the decline. Leading captains of industry, such as Otto Falk, tried also to soften the blow, claiming on the eve of 1931 that the new year would bring great opportunities for local citizens.[4] But the new year failed to do so. The overall number of workers unemployed grew rapidly over the years of 1930 through 1932, reaching its ebb by late 1932. By 1933, the number of employed wage-earners in the metropolitan area was 66,010, about 50,000 fewer than in 1929.[5]

The harsh realities of the Depression slowly began to set in. More and more men and women roamed the streets of the city, looking for work. Milwaukeeans suffered greatly. One woman wrote the *Sentinel,* informing the paper that "I am a mother of 9 children and am appealing to the Sentinel for some aid as work in evenings, as from 5 or 6 in the evening till midnight, or 1, 2, or even 3 in the morning. I have no time to run out in the day to look for a job . . . because I have small children at home. . . . I want to work to make a Christmas for my children because they never had a good Christmas yet, and for clothes which they never had."[6]

Years later another woman recalled that "it got so bad there was hardly anybody working. . . . There were so many people eating at our table, twelve in all . . . [mother] said she never lived through such times in her life. . . . The people did not have any alternatives when it came to survival. Either the family was supported by an earned income or they resorted to the county for aid."[7]

Even people who turned to the county for aid, the woman continued, found their needs curtailed. "What can you do?" she went on. "People went to the county; they got nothing but food and coal; they didn't pay any rent. People got cereal, oatmeal, flour, potatoes, meat, figs and herring. They did not get all these at once. If you got herring, you didn't get meat. Of course, if you got meat, then you didn't get herring. . . . They got cocoa for drinking. No coffee or milk either."[8]

The Depression turned Milwaukee from a place where people made a good living and raised happy families to a city where they could barely survive from one day to the next. The situation would get much worse before it improved.

Emergent Alliances and Labor Conflicts

Alliances of the discontented, social scientists tell us, can appear under any sorts of circumstances, whether they be good ones or bad. The central factor at work in the creation of such alliances seems to be the extent to which organizations, already mobilized for purposes of politics, can take advantage of the opportunities presented by the times.[9] The Depression, and the dislocation it created in the lives of Milwaukee residents, provided nascent labor and political alliances, along with specific organizations, with precisely such opportunities for mobilizing the discontented.[10]

Although the Social Democrats until now had represented the leading force in Milwaukee on behalf of the general interests of the working class, the Depression and the loss of jobs soon shifted the focus for remedies from that of local government to that of the workplace. The Social Democrats—Victor Berger, especially, but also Daniel Hoan, as mayor—had urged that the municipal government become the vehicle through which the needs and grievances of Milwaukee workers would be corrected. It was precisely for this reason that the Milwaukee trade unions had continued to support the efforts of Social Democrats to gain office in the city. But, apart from the period from 1910 through 1912, the Social Democrats had failed to achieve large enough majorities on the Common Council to effect much of anything. Now the widespread unemployment in the city made it abundantly clear that, if wrongs were to be righted in the city, they would have to be corrected primarily at the plant, not at City Hall.

The American Federation of Labor (AFL) was one of the oldest labor organizations, possessing a strong foothold in the city already. It had organized workers in a variety of craft jobs and by 1932 could proclaim a local membership of roughly 20,000 workers. Only four years later, that total would climb to more than 60,000 workers.[11] The Congress of Industrial Organizations (CIO) arrived on the scene much later, a rump effort to represent workers that had gone unrepresented by the AFL, those in the industrial unions. The CIO was officially organized in a national meeting in 1935 and finally made its way into the Milwaukee labor movement by 1938.[12] The two organizations did not always see eye-to-eye; in fact, it was their differences both in constituencies and in strategies that would provoke some of the most heated conflict in this era.[13]

But the AFL and, eventually, the CIO were only two of the alliances that would develop and take active roles on behalf of the working class in Milwaukee. The Social Democrats sought to take their own advantage of the economic decay and reached a peak in their popularity in 1932 when they again achieved a majority of seats on the Common Council. But they nevertheless proved far less successful than they hoped, and eventually they surrendered their role as the leading radical proponent for change in the city to the Communist party.

As in so many other industrial cities throughout the North, the Communists worked hard to gain support in Milwaukee. By 1930, the party was holding May Day parades in the city; by 1931, it was storming the Common Council chambers to urge that the city invoke higher taxes on the rich.[14] Eventually the party was able to recruit figures such as Meta Berger, wife of Victor Berger and former Socialist, to their cause.[15] At the same time, it would also prove to be a major thorn in the side of the Social Democrats and Progressives in the city, constantly attacking the Common Council for its inability to bring an end to the suffering of the city's workers.[16]

Together, these various alliances and organizations provided the necessary resources to mobilize and to channel the widespread unhappiness of the period in Milwaukee. The Communist party remained a fairly small band of activists throughout the 1930s, reaching a peak in their popularity by 1935; but the trade unions proved far more effective in corralling the discontented.

Before 1934, there had been only a handful of major strikes in Milwaukee, including one in 1916 at Allis-Chalmers. In 1934, alone, however, there were 42 strikes at different plants in Milwaukee, putting almost 14,000 workers on the picket lines.[17] And yet again in 1937, there were 76 strikes by Milwaukee workers, accounting for an average absence of 16 days of work per worker. The numbers of strikes in Milwaukee for the better part of this period are shown in Table 6.1.

Often the strikes were about the demands of unions to gain recognition for themselves in the bargaining process with employers. Between 1934 and 1935, for example, the number of unions located in Milwaukee increased from 92 to 165, many of them formed on the heels of successful labor strikes.[18] Work shutdowns took place at all manner of industries throughout the city, ranging from plants that produced auto bodies to those that produced clothing. Among the plants struck were the Phoenix Hosiery Company, at which about 1,500 workers left their jobs on September 23, 1931, and did not return until about one month later, when the company agreed to the demands of the American Federation of Full Fashioned Hosiery Workers to act as the bargaining agent for the employees. Holeproof Hosiery, a local competitor of Phoenix, signed its own contract with the union at the same time.[19] In 1935, the dairy industry of Milwaukee came under fire as the local unions struck three major dairies—Gridley Dairy, Gehl Dairy, and Blochowiak Dairy Company. In the course of the strike, milk wagons were overturned and horses unhitched, creating major havoc on the streets of the city.[20]

Some of the strikes proved very violent. One of the most violent was the walkout against The Milwaukee Electric Railway and Light Company (TMER&L). It resulted in the accidental death of a striker who was electrocuted at a power sta-

TABLE 6.1   Strikes of Local Origin in Milwaukee, 1929–1945

Year	Number of Strikes Beginning in Year	Number of Workers Involved
1928	2	365
1929	1	100
1930	4	182
1931	6	1,973
1932	1	100
1933	6	482
1934	42	13,980
1935	21	3,952
1936	24	4,512
1937	76	14,079
1938	40	10,053
1939	18	16,788
1940	17	1,135
1941	28	3,012
1942	8	887
1943	—	—
1944	37	11,017
1945	37	15,205

SOURCE: U.S. Bureau of Labor Statistics, 1945.

tion.[21] Many citizens were up in arms since the workers' action shut off electricity to much of the city and put the local streetcars, which transported many people to their jobs, completely out of service. There were massive assaults by one group of citizens against another, resulting in some gatherings that numbered, according to a local newspaper, on the order of 10,000 people.[22] There also were a host of arrests, prompting the chief of Milwaukee police, Jacob Laubenheimer, to demand the "maximum punishment for rioters."[23] The walkout proved so offensive to the powers-that-be that, on its conclusion, an editorial in the *Milwaukee Sentinel* reminded residents that "our city, one of the great cities of America, was in a state of virtual revolution."[24]

The main consequence of such strikes was to create a recognized voice for the interests of laborers at most of Milwaukee's plants and to make labor in the city, in general, a powerful new force to press the claims of the working class—the first time in the city that unions had gained such widespread power. But, of course, the unions did not carry their task forward without resistance, as subsequent events would show.

Municipal Government and Its Relationship to County and Federal Governments

Until the Great Depression, the city government of Milwaukee had acted as the principal public authority both to secure order in the city and to provide welfare to meet the needs of local residents. In effect, it could exercise considerable control over the local population because, in return for the order it required in the city and secured through its agents such as the schools and the police force, it provided an array of benefits—public parks and good hospitals, among others. From the early part of the twentieth century well through the 1940s, the municipal government of Milwaukee, for instance, continued to maintain the city's ranking as one of the healthiest and safest cities in all of America.[25] The *Sentinel* constantly was aglow with reports attesting to the quality of the city's government, noting that "Milwaukee is cited as a city free from crime . . . [and] that no other city has such a record."[26] Further, the *Sentinel,* which often proved the stubborn critic of Mayor Daniel Hoan and the Social Democrats, was equally quick to praise the municipal government when, in early 1932, it became known that it was one of the only municipal governments in the country to have recorded an actual surplus in its coffers at the end of 1931.[27] The municipal government, in other words, remained an institution noteworthy for its regimen of strong service on behalf of the citizens, an "efficient and economical" regime, much as it had been since the late nineteenth century.[28]

But the Depression produced a major impact on the city's capacity to perform as a provider of welfare to local residents (though it did not affect the city's capacity as an agent of public order). The Depression saddled the local government with a greatly expanded population of people in need, many of whom had been laid off from jobs or were the families of men and women who suffered thereby. At the same time, it also produced greatly reduced tax revenues with which the municipal government could handle the array of its tasks. More and more citizens had begun by 1932 to lag in their payments of taxes to the city—if not to default on them entirely. By the end of the year, roughly $24 million was owed the city in late taxes, more than the entire tax levy issued by the city for 1933.[29]

The municipal government of Milwaukee soon came to a virtual standstill. Despite its surplus of funds in 1931, it proved unable to handle the overwhelming needs of the population. By 1933, owing to its low cash reserves, it was even compelled to compensate its own employees in script. Private agencies in the city, such as the Family Welfare Association, Goodwill Industries, and the Salvation Army, among others, were financially unable to meet the demands of displaced workers and their families. Of the total relief expenditures in 1932 of roughly $9.5 million, for instance, only a small sum—$375,000—was contributed by the private relief groups in Milwaukee.[30] Obviously something had to be done.

Two major decisions took place that once again would further influence the character of the local government in Milwaukee, as had the earlier division between the suburbs and the city. The first was that the New Deal government of Franklin D. Roosevelt, inaugurated in 1933, began to take immediate steps to put people back to work and to provide them with an array of relief funds. Under the auspices of the Works Progress Administration (WPA) and the Public Works Administration (PWA), the federal government provided an array of funds for Milwaukee—and other cities—to rebuild their infrastructure and to put people back to work. It became part of the overall plan whereby the New Deal now fundamentally inserted itself more forcefully into the affairs of cities and into the lives of their residents, in particular.[31]

The New Deal spent millions of dollars furnishing aid to Milwaukee in the period after 1933. In 1934, for example, the superintendent of the Department of Outdoor Relief in Milwaukee County, Benjamin Glassberg, estimated that the federal government paid 70 percent of the relief costs in the county—which, at the time, amounted to roughly $10 million per year.[32] About five years later, the Milwaukee County auditor, Frank Bittner, would estimate that the relief efforts in the county had cost on the order of $110 million.[33] These monies were for the direct relief costs, such as the provision of food and clothing, as well as for the work relief programs.

Within the city of Milwaukee, itself, which composed the large majority of the county's population, the New Deal undertook massive programs of relief and public works. The programs involved efforts to improve park facilities, build new roads, and assist in work on the construction of a new public museum. In the early years of the WPA, the federal government paid for approximately 90 percent of the entire costs of public projects, the remaining amount paid for by city government; by 1942–1943, just before the WPA closed down its operations in Milwaukee, the federal government's share had dropped to just under 65 percent of the monies. Altogether, over the life span of the WPA, approximately $49 million had been spent on 268 public works projects in the city of Milwaukee.[34]

But it was not the federal government, alone, that took steps to deal with the needs of local Milwaukee residents. So, too, did the Milwaukee County government. In the early 1920s, the Milwaukee County government ran on a much more limited budget than that of the municipal government and operated such local agencies as the county infirmary, a county hospital, and an asylum for the mentally ill. It also operated a small Department of Outdoor Relief whose task was to provide for a small number of families in need of food and clothing.[35]

By the time the Depression hit the city, the Department of Outdoor Relief in Milwaukee County was the only local public agency in a position to meet the needs of the unemployed and their families. Its operations grew enormously over the 1929–1933 period. From a low of 30,000 families served by the Department in 1929, it reached a high of 140,000 families in 1933, the peak year of the Depression.[36] The numbers of families on relief provided by the county increased dramatically just between 1931 and 1932. In June 1931, for example, 9,474 families were on relief; one year later, that figure had climbed to 29,879.[37] Moreover, the monthly average number of families on relief jumped from 4,600 in 1928 to 42,877 in 1932.[38] At one point, in fact, it was estimated that fully 25 percent of the population in Milwaukee County was on relief provided by the Department of Outdoor Relief.[39]

The actions of both the federal government and the county government now would reshape the overall character of government in Milwaukee, itself. The effort of the federal government proved to be only the beginning of an attempt to assert its own powers more vigorously over the urban landscape. But even more significantly, the efforts of the county government did not themselves end. As a result of the Depression, the county government itself now grew into a far more powerful institution. The change in its authority was most noticeable between 1930 and 1940. In 1930, for example, of the total taxes levied on Milwaukee citizens, 72 percent went for city expenditures and only 16 percent went for county expenditures.[40] By 1940, the amount of tax monies provided to the county by levies on Milwaukee citizens had climbed to 33 percent of the total tax levy.[41] Moreover, by 1950 it still remained at roughly 30 percent of the total tax levy on Milwaukee residents.[42]

Just as in the case of the federal government, the County government had assumed more of the local responsibility for caring for the needs of Milwaukee citizens. In 1937, for example, a decision was reached to make Milwaukee County responsible for the care of city parks, thus bringing under one authority all the parks in the area. The county also continued to operate the public hospitals and to care for the mentally ill in its facilities in the Blue Mound Sanatorium. By 1950, in fact, the shift in responsibilities for the welfare needs of the local Milwaukee population was noticeably evident in the budgeted expenditures of the city. From a figure of approximately 10 percent for welfare expenditures in the city in 1920— for healthcare and the parks, among other things—that budget item had declined to 6.6 percent in 1950.

The resulting shift of responsibility for caring for the needs of the poor and indigent in the city helped to refashion Milwaukee's municipal government. Now the *principal* responsibility of the municipal government was to secure order over the local population. Observe, for example, in Table 6.2 that almost 56 percent of the city budget of Milwaukee in 1950 was for expenses of the schools, the courts, and the police and fire departments.

The long-term consequences of this reformation in the assignment of government responsibilities over local citizens in Milwaukee would be profound—as profound perhaps as any other event in the historic creation of local government. What, in effect, had happened was that the city's capacity to give with the one hand, in providing welfare to local residents, in order to take with the other, to secure order over the local population, now had become a single-edged sword. The city government of Milwaukee would still be responsible for securing the public order, especially through the police, fire, and court systems; but its ability to provide inducements for such order had become severely curtailed. The reassignment of functional responsibility would mean now that the county and the federal governments were the institutions primarily able to act to meet the needs of local residents, whereas the government most directly connected to the lives of the overwhelming number of citizens in the city was left the unenviable task of pun-

TABLE 6.2   Type of City Expenditure by Purpose, Milwaukee, 1920–1950 (percent of total budget)

	1920	*1930*	*1940*	*1950*
Officials/Boards	4.4	3.1	4.4	5.0
Public Order (schools; courts; police; and fire)	53.3	59.2	61.4	55.5
Welfare (health; parks; library; museum)	9.9	9.0	5.8	6.6
Infrastructure (public works; sanitation; utilities)	31.1	26.8	25.2	31.1
Miscellaneous	1.3	1.8	3.2	1.8
Total expenses	$13,218,072	$27,060,157	$23,467,589	$44,079,205
Total percent	100.0	99.9	100.0	100.0

SOURCE: City of Milwaukee Annual Reports, 1920–1950.

ishing the population with no rewards whatsoever. Municipal government in the city of Milwaukee had grown to become a misfigured and lopsided institution.

The other major local consequence would be that government in the metropolitan area of Milwaukee would become even more complicated and complex. Whereas the struggles to annex the suburbs had created a Balkanization of the region, prompting minor municipalities to arise here and there, now the city and the county governments were themselves further set apart. The complication inevitably would mean more administrative apparatus in the governance of local residents and a seemingly unnecessary duplication of taxing authorities within the metropolitan region. The lives of Milwaukeeans, in other words, would seem to suffer yet another blow at the hands of a public institution that they believed was constructed to serve their interests, not dictate them.

The Declining Fortunes of Local Industries

The Depression affected the fortunes of Milwaukee industries, as it did those of so many other industrial cities in America. But perhaps it affected them more so in Milwaukee. Milwaukee as a city had become heavily reliant on an array of heavy-manufacturing industries, in the areas of machines, tractors, and automobile equipment among others, all of which required skilled laborers. The proportion of the workforce involved in manufacturing in Milwaukee in 1930 was one of the highest of all major manufacturing centers in America—second only to Rochester, New York.[43] The economic decline of the 1930s put many of these workers out of their jobs.

But there were other, more tortured consequences for the industrial base of the city, as well as for its possibilities for promoting continued growth and expansion. The Depression, and the labor alliances and demands created thereby, brought home to the capitalist class of the city the need to provide better benefits for the laborers. Devastation reigned throughout the city; there was little question of it, and it was particularly evident by comparison with the prior years of industrial expansion. Now industries, and industrialists, were faced with demands to provide more to the needy working class.

However, many capitalists strongly resisted doing so. Claiming their rights to maintain profits, individual plants and operations began to refuse to deal with their workers and with the unions. Although the attitude of the capitalists was bred partly in the heat of the present disputes, it was a stance acquired years earlier. Industrialists like Otto Falk, head of the largest employer in the city, had long argued for the prominence of capitalism and industry over the interests of socialism and the worker. Recall, for example, that as head of the Milwaukee Metal Trades and Founders Association, Falk had been quite clear on his attitude toward unions:

> [W]e will give to labor its just reward and more, but *[we] will not tolerate the domination of any class of banded labor.* [This Association] stand[s] for freedom for employer and employee, first, last, and all the time.[44] (My emphasis.)

The upper-class alliance, fashioned in the late nineteenth century, stood firm in its refusal to concede to the demands of the unions. This same attitude continued to pervade the view of capitalists in the city during the course of the upheavals of the mid-1930s. During the four-day strike against TMER&L, for example, S. B. Way, the president of the company that once had been controlled by Frederick Vogel and Charles Pfister, was roundly criticized for his unwillingness to grant the unions a right to act as bargaining agent for the laborers. Even Mayor Hoan attacked him, arguing that his arrogance toward "your employees, our people, our city, our federal government" was likely to produce widespread rioting by strikers in the city.[45] The unprecedented violence that accompanied the strike against TMER&L ultimately forced Way to comply with the union's demands.

Soon individual enterprises began either to leave the city or to decide to build new plants at other sites. Both local newspapers, the *Milwaukee Journal* and the *Milwaukee Sentinel,* were quick to take note of the departures.[46] Just a year after their plant had been struck by the union, the Holeproof Hosiery Company announced that it would open new plants in Georgia.[47] Likewise, just six months after they were struck by a union, the Weyenberg Shoe Manufacturing Company reported that it planned to move one of its departments to Ludington, Michigan.[48] By early 1938, the departures of companies from the city had grown so large that the *Milwaukee Journal* ran a feature length article in which it reported that 31 industrial corporations, with a total employment of almost 14,000 people, had located plants elsewhere since the beginning of the decade.[49] The list of departures included a number of clothing and shoe manufacturers, along with some major manufacturers of heavy industrial goods such as Inland Steel Company.[50] These departures signaled the first dramatic loss of industry in the city's history. A number of them also revealed the first signs that companies were willing to move out of the Midwest altogether and to settle in states, such as Georgia, or other places in the South and elsewhere.

Of greatest significance, however, is that the decisions became framed in terms of two root causes, ones that both the *Sentinel* and the *Journal* would comment on—the choice to leave took place because the unions had demanded wages that were too high *or* because the taxes both in Milwaukee and in the state of Wisconsin were too costly (or even sometimes both). An article in the early 1930s in the *Sentinel* had gone into depth on the potential loss of industry to the city and the state. It noted, in particular, that "Southern states, seeking more industries and more employment for their residents, are encouraging manufacturers to locate there. In some instances plant sites are offered and taxes are waived or reduced to a minimum and no rigid labor or wage restrictions are placed upon the hosiery men. The manufacturers here say that this letting down of the bars in the Southern states brings about almost ruinous competition because the Southern mills can produce hosiery at low cost and sell it below the cost of manufacture in Wisconsin."[51] These arguments, that industries stood to lose profits by remaining in Milwaukee, would take on the character of an economic litany over the years and would be repeated time and again as local manufacturers elected to move their businesses elsewhere.[52]

In effect, then, the heightened union activity and strikes, coupled with the ability of some industries to move their operations elsewhere, had provided an opportunity for industries to depart the city. The exodus of capital should have come as no surprise to Milwaukee residents, however. For it was simply an extension of the great divide that long had loomed between industrial capitalists and the laborers of Milwaukee. That great divide had first become visible in the rupture that produced the industrial suburbs, such as West Allis; now it continued in the full and complete departure of industries not simply from the city but from the state. If capitalists could not succeed in Milwaukee, their actions said, they would simply pick up their marbles and move their game elsewhere.

World War II and Its Aftermath

World War II, and in particular, the effort to mobilize the productive capacities of industries and workers in America, proved a temporary salvation for the city of Milwaukee. The war effort had a particularly strong impact on the fortunes of the city. Many industries, such as Allis-Chalmers, already engaged in the manufacture of equipment vital to the machinery of war. It was only a small step to actually transform their production of goods for a market economy at peacetime to one at war.

The Resurgence of Industry

The war helped to spell the end of the unemployment and personal devastation of the Great Depression. Workers now were put back to work. In Milwaukee, the effects of the war, as well as the demand for equipment vital to the efforts of the Allied forces, began before the United States actually had entered the war. By 1939, a number of major firms in the city had begun to report business profits unlike any of those of the 1930s. Further, most were in the business of producing heavy machinery, such as tractors and trucks, as well as turbine equipment. Bucyrus-Erie reported a profit of $1.75 million in 1939, as compared to one of only $677,952 in 1938.[53] Weeks later, Allis-Chalmers reported a large profit of $3.7 million compared to one of only $2.5 million in 1938. The company already had begun to profit from the sales it made years earlier to the Navy for new steam turbine engines.[54] The Harnischfeger Corporation, another industry hit hard by the decline of the Depression, began to see a rise in its profits by 1940, as did the Heil Corporation.[55] In the case of the latter corporation, the *Journal* reported that the profit "increases were due to orders for national defense materials from the firm."[56]

By 1942, after the United States had entered the war, the rate of recovery and employment in the city picked up noticeably. Numbers of plants that produced heavy machinery and equipment quickly became mobilized for the war effort. Harnischfeger Corporation, for example, began to produce electric cranes and hoisting equipment exclusively for the Navy; the Falk plant received recognition, in the form of a Navy "E" (for excellence) citation, for the gears it produced for ships; the Nordberg Company gained a Navy "E" award, as well, for the torpedo tubes it produced.[57] A host of other firms joined the parade of defense contractors, including the Wisconsin Bridge and Iron Company, the Kearney-Trecker Company, the International Harvester Company, and the Chain Belt Company, all firms located in Milwaukee.[58]

The effects of the demand for goods from Milwaukee plants were substantial on the overall economy. By April 1941, before the United States entered the war, Milwaukee industries had received more than $100 million in contracts for defense equipment.[59] And by early 1944, the city had received major defense contracts totaling nearly $2.3 billion, roughly one-third of which were for ordnance items, such as combat vehicles.[60]

But the most important effects, of course, were on the employment of workers in the city. Employment, which at its ebb had numbered only about 60,000 workers, climbed to 110,000 in 1940 and swelled to about 200,000 people by 1943. The numbers included a large contingent of women in the city, about 60,000 according to one estimate.[61] Correspondingly, of course, people now were able to withdraw from the relief rolls of Milwaukee County. By May 1941, the number of families on relief numbered somewhat more than 11,000, or roughly one-quarter of what the monthly average had been in 1933.[62]

The city was put back to work, and the fortunes of local industry, which had been severely affected by the declines of the early 1930s, looked bright for the first time in nearly a decade. But the new profits would prove to be something of an illusion.

The Deepening Division Within Milwaukee: Labor Versus Capital

If the war effort spelled the end of the devastation of the Depression, it also furnished the opportunity for new strategies and designs of the various alliances developed by the working class of the city. Trade unions now pressed their demands even further to secure additional benefits for the workers. Strikes continued to happen at various plants. As late as 1945, there were still 37 strikes reported in the city, putting roughly 15,000 workers on the streets of Milwaukee.[63] Moreover, no company would suffer more greatly nor signal more visibly the power that had grown now among the trade unions in the city than Allis-Chalmers.

Allis-Chalmers had prided itself for years on its relations and its care for the needs of its employees. It had provided special group insurance plans for the employees and had furnished a limited pension plan as well.[64] However, the company—like most others in the city—did not furnish nearly enough in the way of benefits for its workers, especially during the tough years of the 1930s. As a result, the efforts to unionize workers had grown very intense during the depth of the Depression. Initially, local branches of the AFL had represented many of the Allis-Chalmers employees.[65] But many of the skilled workers at the plant were unhappy with representation by a union that dealt primarily with craft workers. Thus, when the efforts began to organize industrial workers, through the fledgling Congress of Industrial Organizations, there was immediate interest in forming as a local chapter of the new organization.

By 1937, a new local affiliate of the CIO, United Auto Workers Local 248, had been formed at Allis-Chalmers.[66] The creation of the new union signaled a split between moderate unionists, those in the AFL, and the more militant unionists, those in the CIO, and left hard feelings on both sides. Moreover, the decision to affiliate with the CIO had also helped to secure the leadership of key figures in the union at Allis-Chalmers, chief among them, Harold Christoffel. Christoffel, who had begun work at the plant in his teens, proved to be a superb organizer and effective strategist on behalf of the Allis-Chalmers employees, as well as a thorn in the side of company management.[67] Over the course of the late 1930s and well into the 1940s, Christoffel, as the head of Local 248, pressed forward with a number of the union's demands of the plant management. Altogether, there were almost 200 grievances that went to the Labor Advisory Committee at Allis-Chalmers (out of 2,500 filed), including, among them, detailed concerns about the work conditions on the shop floor, layoffs, wage scales, and a host of other issues.[68]

Unhappy with conditions of work at the plant, however, Christoffel and the union members voted by a margin of 5,958 to 758 to go on strike on January 21, 1941. The strike had been immediately precipitated by the refusal of two AFL workers to join Local 248 and by the willingness of management to support the refusal of the two workers. The more general concern of Local 248 was that the management of the company had failed to grant security to the union in its efforts to bargain on behalf of disgruntled workers.[69] Eventually the strike stretched out over two and one-half months. As the largest employer in the Milwaukee area, any strike against Allis-Chalmers proved to be newsworthy. However, other facts made this particular strike especially so. The company had received several contracts from the government to produce major goods for the war effort of Great Britain, an ally of the United States. With workers off the job, the production of such goods now came to a standstill. When word of the strike reached Washington, federal officials sought to intervene and demanded both that the strike be resolved and that the workers return to their jobs. Both parties were called to Washington to negotiate the dispute. An agreement was reached, but it eventually failed to create a permanent settlement of the issues.

The conflict turned very heated and very nasty. People who attempted to cross the picket lines at the plants were stoned, and cars in the nearby areas were overturned. Thousands of people gathered regularly at the company gates and rushed guards placed there for protection by the company. A number of clashes broke out between the warring AFL and CIO factions, adding fuel to the anger directed at the company. Management and Local 248 also traded their own insults, the former insisting, among other things, that the Local had rigged the election on behalf of a strike, whereas the latter claimed that management simply was reluctant to permit workers legitimate representation by the union. Eventually the strike was settled, and Local 248 was granted new rights. The settlement produced a substantial victory for the union and for Christoffel, in particular. Among other things, the union now gained greater authority to act as the bargaining agent for the workers. It was a clear victory for labor.

This, however, did not turn out to be the end of the siege against Allis-Chalmers. Another more serious strike was called on April 29, 1946. This particular action was overwhelmingly approved by more than 8,000 workers.[70] By this time, Harold Christoffel had been called into military service, and the union was under new leadership. The strike produced both a plantwide walkout of thousands of workers and the complete shutdown of production at the West Allis factory. As the union and the company were unable to negotiate a settlement acceptable to both sides, the strike lingered on for weeks, then for months. By the fall, both the *Journal* and the *Sentinel* turned their full firepower against the unions and the strikers. In a series of articles run in the papers, claims were made that Local 248, in fact, was dominated by Communist leaders.[71] Among other things, it was claimed that Harold Christoffel was a member of the Communist party. It was further insinuated that other union officials also were Communists, for a number of them, it was alleged, had signed petitions in support of Sigmund Eisensher, a one-time Communist candidate for governor of Wisconsin.

The imbroglio played itself out over successive months. The papers, it turned out, had acquired much of their information on the alleged Communist activities of union officials by materials furnished directly from the management of Allis-Chalmers. The document that showed that union officials had supported the Communist candidate for governor, for example, came directly out of a pamphlet prepared by the Public Relations Bureau of Allis-Chalmers and distributed earlier to workers in an effort to discredit Local 248.[72] A labor committee of the U.S. House of Representatives got wind of the allegations of Communist activities within the union, through word from Allis-Chalmers officials, and got both union and company officials to testify at hearings held in Washington. New allegations also now came to light. Louis Budenz, editor of the *Communist Daily Worker* and a former Communist who had subsequently embraced the Catholic Church with deep fervor, now alleged that Harold Christoffel had been a member of the party and that the strike in 1941 actually had been planned in advance, with the help of Eugene Dennis, then head of the party in Wisconsin.[73]

Ultimately, Christoffel was sent to prison on the charge that he had perjured himself to the committee when he failed to admit that he was a member of the Communist party. By the time it was over, the conflict had generated widespread publicity both in Milwaukee and across the nation. It also helped in an indirect way to fuel the state support that brought Joseph McCarthy to office. But its most lasting impact was to drive deeper the wedge between the industrialists of the city and the unions that sought to represent the working class. Although Allis-Chalmers officials claimed to be pleased with the eventual settlement fashioned by Walter Reuther—one that, in fact, removed Christoffel and another 90 officials from the union—the fracture created within the city, coupled with strong union leadership at other companies, made Milwaukee appear to be a city inhospitable for new industries and new capitalists.

Summary

By 1950, much of the political and economic institutional architecture that can be recognized today as the city of Milwaukee had been put into place. There was the municipal government, possessed of its limited powers; the Balkanization of the metropolitan region; the division between the city and the county governments; an array of capitalist enterprises; and a deep division between the classes, signaled in this period by alliances of unions on behalf of workers and the alliances of the industrial capitalists. The industrial decline of the city that would pick up speed only a decade or so later, in hindsight, should not have been in the least unexpected. Both the actors and their goals already had been formed; their actions now would prove to be virtually inescapable.

7

The Decline of Industrial Milwaukee: 1950–1990

The decline happened rather swiftly after the end of the war. The facts were unequivocal: Between 1960 and 1990, the city of Milwaukee lost almost 150,000 residents.[1] By 1990, it had a total population of about 600,000 people, slightly more than sixty years earlier. The land area of the city had doubled from 48 square miles to 96 square miles between 1948 and 1960, under the reign of Mayor Frank Zeidler, but thereafter the city would gain no more land.[2] Moreover, in the 1970s and 1980s, when cities like Atlanta and San Diego, or Dallas and Miami, were gaining countless new jobs, Milwaukee displayed a dramatic dip in job opportunities, most of them in the historically important sector of manufacturing.

The changes in Milwaukee were part of a general transformation of the economies of many northern industrial centers that occurred from about 1960 through 1990.[3] A massive restructuring of the national economy took manufacturing jobs away from the central cities of major northern metropolises and relocated many of them either in cities of the South and West—where profits could be higher owing to an absence of unions and few, if any, local taxes—or abroad, in foreign countries.[4] Various forces were involved in this era of decline, most of them outside the control of cities such as Milwaukee. Cities in the South and West began to boom in the post–World War II period, partly the result of federal policies that produced a disproportionate share of federal—in particular defense—monies in these areas.[5] Such cities also became very aggressive in seeking to corral new industries for themselves, peddling their tax advantages to the industries of northern cities, such as Milwaukee. Atlanta and Dallas expanded precisely because cities like Detroit and Milwaukee were unable to retain some of their oldest enterprises.[6] The situation was reminiscent of the manner in which extra-local forces had impinged upon Milwaukee affairs during the 1930s and 1940s.

Nevertheless, the tale of Milwaukee's change from a mecca of opportunity to a center struggling to survive is not a story of any simple kind of determinism, by any means. Human agency and historical contingency might have intervened to save the fortunes of the city. If, for example, the needs of the local population in the city had not escalated so sharply, as they did beginning in the 1960s, it is entirely possible that the municipal government of the city could have remained a viable institution. Alternatively, if the local residents of great wealth had not continued to flee the city in large numbers to the outer regions of the metropolis, both the quality and the economic vitality of the city might have remained unimpaired.

There were two moments, in fact, when the citizens of Milwaukee might have seized the opportunity that chance afforded them, and sought to prevent the harm that the growing decline was doing to the metropolitan area, as a whole. Both would have required that they pay at least as much attention to issues of equity as to issues of growth. The first took place at the end of the 1950s, when Mayor Zeidler convened a commission to study the problems of the Inner Core of Milwaukee.[7] The purpose of the commission was to address the problems of the decline in the central city area. As it turned out, the commission did a far better job of describing the full dimensions of the decline than of taking steps to remedy it. The second occasion happened at roughly the same time, when an effort was made to develop some overarching metropolitan government that could, among other things, help to redistribute the public revenues available to the various municipal districts in and around Milwaukee. This effort, too, failed.

In this chapter, I will examine the full dimensions of Milwaukee's decline and why the efforts to limit its harm, especially to the minority residents of the Inner Core, proved so futile. Answers to these issues may help shed light not only on the particular evolution of Milwaukee but also on how to solve the tough questions that its decline and growing inequality pose to the residents of all older industrial cities.

The Decline of the City

Milwaukee's decline as a major urban center first attracted public attention in the early 1940s. Numbers of different people, but mainly local officials, began to take note of the decay and obsolescence that had overwhelmed the downtown area, in particular. As early as 1943, city officials began to complain about the disrepair of downtown buildings and to criticize the sad state of local properties.[8] Some even speculated that such poor conditions could hold serious ramifications for the future state of the city. City Tax Commissioner Thomas Byrne, for instance, drafted a report detailing the problems to Acting Mayor John Bohn. "The city is getting older," Byrne wrote, "and the oldest sections are downtown. Age does not improve buildings as it does improve wines. ... Older buildings become less safe, less sanitary, less convenient. ... The very expansion of the city has produced a process of decay in the center."[9] Five years later, the story remained the same. The Redevelopment Coordinating Committee, a group of local officials created at Byrne's insistence, decried the state of local buildings and the decay of the downtown properties.[10] In terms that set the tone for all future discussions, they spoke of the conditions of "urban blight and decay" in the central city and argued that such blight was like a human disease that, if not eradicated, would gradually poison every cell of the city's body politic.

In a few short years, the city's state of disrepair made headlines in the *Milwaukee Journal.* William Manly, real estate editor of the paper, was commissioned to write a series of articles that spelled out the nature of decline in the city.[11] His reports covered the entire waterfront of the city, from the crumbling exteriors of major downtown buildings to the conditions of those residents who were condemned to live within them. Manly, like so many others before him, insisted that if the conditions of property in the downtown area were substantially better, then local government also could count on much higher revenues to fund its services.

Thus, by the early 1950s Milwaukeeans had become intensely conscious of the decay that now ate away at the very heart of the city.[12] Some of the decline was inevitable, the natural product of the aging and obsolescence of buildings and properties originally created in the last decades of the nineteenth century. However, much of the decline simply provided physical testimony to the deeper problems that now faced the city, problems whose roots, in part, lay in the imperfections of its own institutions.

The Imperfections of Municipal Government

There were two respects in which the government of Milwaukee displayed its flaws in this period of decline. One had to do with the legacy created much earlier in the century—the territorial feuds that had grown up between the city and the suburbs. The other had to do with problems of the city government's own operations.

Boundary Disputes. One cannot easily dispense with certain legacies of the past. So it was with the boundary divisions and disputes between the city and its neighbors. Through an aggressive program of annexation, the municipal government of Milwaukee had been able to extend its powers over adjacent areas. But not without great resistance.

Shortly after the end of World War II, the effort to expand the city's boundaries outward had taken up where it left off prior to the Great Depression. Arthur Werba, the longtime head of the city's Department of Annexation, urged expansion of the city's boundaries into regions adjacent to the city (see Chapter 5).[13] It was his belief that the city needed to add such territories in order to maintain its control over the new housing and industry that was being developed in the region. Both major Milwaukee newspapers, the *Journal* and the *Sentinel,* provided strong support for the program as both seemed to acknowledge the need to increase the city of Milwaukee's tax revenues.[14] Eventually, however, only the *Sentinel* remained a strong advocate of the efforts, devoting the columns of its reporter, William Norris, to extensive coverage of the annexation programs.[15]

Werba continued over the course of the late 1940s and early 1950s to press for the annexation of adjoining properties to the city, arguing that Milwaukee needed to expand by at least 75 square miles "if it is to grow normally in the next few decades."[16] Frank Zeidler, a Socialist who assumed office in 1948, was a full and enthusiastic supporter of the activity and made various trips to the state legislature in Madison to urge the solons to endorse Milwaukee's programs.[17] But Milwaukee's government met a growing resistance from both the villages it sought to annex and from suburban residents who tried on principle to prevent the city's policy of territorial expansion.[18] Many of these suburbanites were recent emigrants from the city proper, themselves, and they wanted little more to do with its government and its peoples.

A central actor in the process to settle the legal claims on the annexation of adjacent territories was the Wisconsin Supreme Court. Throughout the earlier period of annexations, the state supreme court had generally ruled in favor of the city in its programs to add new lands. Now, however, the tide turned, and the court began to favor the efforts of villages and townships to block annexation to the city. In early April 1951, the court handed down a major ruling—one that disallowed an important annexation of a strip of land in Waukesha County on the grounds that the city possessed an unfair advantage over lesser municipalities in the methods it used for annexation.[19] Since 1898 the city of Milwaukee, unlike any other municipalities in Wisconsin, had been able to circulate a petition for annexation among residents without posting any notice, whereas all other municipalities had to post a notice thirty days in advance of circulating such a petition. The court invalidated that advantage and, in one fell swoop, reduced Milwaukee's powers to those of adjoining towns and villages. The effect was to make more difficult the methods the city now used to take in new lands, and to give its neighbors new powers. Areas of Waukesha County that adjoined Milwaukee County, as well as those laden with new residential developments and industries, that once looked ripe for acquisition, now seemed far out of reach.

Nevertheless, the battle, which had occupied the greater part of half a century, continued. Pressed to find new lands and new revenues for its operations, over the next five years the city government proved enormously successful at further annexations, taking in large amounts of land in the adjacent Granville and Greenfield areas, as well as nine and one-half square miles in the town of Lake. Some of the lands held new factories and plants that had prospered in the post-war bloom and that would now provide revenues to compensate, in part, for those industries that fell short in the downtown areas. Within the space of a few short years, the city had doubled in size.[20] But the aggressive effort of local government, and the irregular manner in which it annexed lands, were increasingly questioned. Because of its territorial boundaries, Milwaukee had been forced to annex irregular slices of territory, creating a city that seemed to lack form and shape. In 1954, the *Municipal Yearbook*, a handbook for city officials, called the annexations done by Milwaukee "overly stringent and tortuous," the result of "antiquated state annexation laws."[21]

Even William Norris, who had become the great champion of the city in the pages of the *Sentinel*, began to question some of the city's decisions. Land, he noted, was now added on to the city mainly, it seemed, to suit the needs of "speculative builders and real estate men."[22] He stressed that while the annexation policy of the city was intended to reduce the tax liabilities to city taxpayers, by adding to the local government's own revenues, in fact, the city seemed to be subsidizing the residential developments of real estate figures through the provision of low-cost streets and sewer lines.[23]

By the mid-1950s, the effort by opposition forces to prevent Milwaukee from further territorial expansion was capped by a crowning success. Attempts to halt the city's programs produced a bill in the Wisconsin State Legislature in 1955 that would effectively block further annexations. The bill, known as the Oak Creek Bill and so named because of the township that had brought issue with the City of Milwaukee, permitted fourth class townships to incorporate themselves as a means of preventing annexation to the city.[24] Accordingly, limited municipalities now were given greater autonomy to set their own futures—much as had happened with the Wisconsin Supreme Court ruling of 1951. Thereafter, areas of Waukesha, Ozaukee, and Washington Counties, the several counties that abutted Milwaukee on its western and northern boundaries, would have little to fear. Now the city proper had effectively become landlocked, bordered to its east by Lake Michigan and everywhere else by hostile neighbors.[25]

State law and the Wisconsin State Legislature thus brought to a close the attempt by Milwaukee's municipal government to extend its own sovereign powers outward, into other territories. Further, every knowledgeable citizen seemed well aware of the portents that these decisions would have for the future vitality of the city, itself. With decay eating away at its central portions and with boundaries now fixed seemingly forever, the city of Milwaukee and its citizens had become trapped into a future that seemed bleak at best. "The fragmentation of local government in metropolitan Milwaukee," the *Sentinel* wrote in 1966, "has thwarted solutions to our area's common problems—in transportation, housing, pollution, police protection [and] industrial development."[26] The effects would prove as inexorable as the drive by enterprises to secure profits. By 1990, Milwaukee County had become thoroughly overlain with competing and often uncooperative jurisdictional forces: Nineteen different municipal governments existed, roughly half of which were counted as cities like Milwaukee, and the other half as villages. Balkanization understated the dimensions of this political quagmire. But other problems remained for the city government as well.

Order and Expense. The city government of Milwaukee had been created in the late nineteenth century to complement the work of capitalist enterprises, securing public order in the city and meeting the needs of local citizens—needs not otherwise met by capitalism itself. The Depression years had complicated matters. Municipal government had been left with the task of meeting the needs to secure public order, through its police force, fire department, and school system, whereas both the federal and the Milwaukee County governments now met most of the welfare needs of local residents.

In this period of decline, the city government confronted tasks of enormous proportions. Its revenues were now becoming depleted, owing, among other things, to the decline of downtown properties. Yet, by its very nature, it was required to maintain the public order of the city. One would suppose, therefore, that the local government would have made every effort to become an even more efficient and streamlined operation, continuing the exemplary service it had provided and for which it had been amply recognized by various awards in the past. Paradoxically, however, it now turned from a very efficient institution into one that grew increasingly unwieldy—one that gave every sign that it had become too large and too complex to easily satisfy those needs in the local political arena for which it had originally become fashioned.

There were a number of notable examples of these difficulties. The tax rates of the city continued to climb from the 1950s through the mid-1970s, when the city government introduced a new method of property valuation that made it appear as though the tax rate had been reduced. In 1960, the city tax rate was $41.11 per $1,000 of assessed property; by 1972, it had climbed to $76.38, almost double the figure of 1960. In 1974, the tax valuation code was revised to increase the ratio of assessed value to full value from about 50 percent in the city to almost 100 percent.[27] With nearby suburbs, however, offering their residents far better property at considerably lower tax rates, everything conspired to work to the disadvantage of the city, itself, and to drive its more affluent residents away.

Some of the most obvious costs occurred in the school system of the city. A separate taxing authority of the city, these difficulties grew ever more obvious over time, especially when they were juxtaposed with the growing evidence of a declining quality of education in the Milwaukee Public Schools. As test scores, for example, went down in Milwaukee schools, the costs seemed to rise.[28] The problems of the system were clear just in terms of the sheer numbers of students in public schools, as well as the number of staff required to train them. Between 1950 and 1970, the number of students in Milwaukee public schools doubled from 66,544 to 130,617; simultaneously, the size of the school staff more than doubled from 2,468 to 5,556.[29] But in the next twenty years, the size of the student body changed dramatically, declining by 30,000 students. Yet the size of the faculty and the number of principals actually increased over this same period by about 250 people.[30] In other words, it now appeared that more staff was furnishing instruction of an increasingly poorer quality.

Yet, far and away the clearest indication of the growing problems that faced the school system lay in the sheer costs of public education. Over time in Milwaukee these costs had risen dramatically. Between 1950 and 1990, the cost of per-pupil education in the city had climbed from $284.27 to $5,570.00, a twentyfold increase.[31] Moreover, the increase took place at a rate far faster than post-war inflation in America; the rise was four times the rise in consumer prices over the very same period.[32] The sharpest increase took place from 1960 to 1980. While the Consumer Price Index rose slightly less than threefold over this span, the cost of educating a pupil in the Milwaukee Public Schools increased tenfold, from $396.65 to $3,618.00.[33] The cost in 1980 for educating a student in the Milwaukee Public Schools was roughly $900 higher than for the state as a whole, and about $1,300 higher than that for the nation.[34] No wonder then that by the early 1990s, Milwaukee citizens were up in arms about public education in the city.

The plummeting fortunes of local government, in general, were best conveyed by the value of properties it controlled as compared to those of private enterprises and persons in Milwaukee. In the early 1940s, the city government held properties valued at roughly 40 percent of those of the private sector in Milwaukee. Yet, by 1980, a comparison of the two sets of properties showed that the city held property valued at only about 13 percent of that of private property in the city, a dramatic indication of its diminishing strength as an institution.[35]

Once an institution that had proved effective enough to seek to exercise power over local capitalist enterprises, the city government had become barely able to keep afloat on its own resources, caught between suburbs that limited its designs on their sovereignty and by the complexities and costs of its own making.

Dependence on Federal and State Governments. With its revenues depleted and diminishing even more, the city government of Milwaukee was compelled to turn to other sources of funds. And now the general tendencies that had taken hold during the crisis years of the Depression would make the federal and state governments far more powerful actors in governing the city.

Over the course of the forty-year period from 1950 to 1990, both the federal and state governments came to be major sources of funds for city operations. The federal government's role grew substantially between the 1950s and the 1970s; by 1977, it provided fully 12 percent of the city's revenues.[36] The state of Wisconsin, through its system of returning revenues to localities based upon population size, provided almost one-third of the city government's total revenues over the entire four-decade period. In 1977 alone, the federal and state governments furnished more than 45 percent of the revenues available to the city for the expenses of its own operations.[37]

The growing dependency of local government on the state of Wisconsin became fully evident in the form of revenues provided to the local public schools in Milwaukee. Here a marked and dramatic change took place in the monies devoted to public education. In 1960, of a total school budget in Milwaukee of almost $39 million, $5 million came from state funds, or about 13 percent of the city's total school budget.[38] By 1990, however, of the more than $545 million now dedicated to schools in the annual budget, approximately $300 million, or about 55 percent, were derived from state appropriations.[39] The city schools, in other words, had become the fiscal child of the state.

Dollars, however, represented only the tip of the iceberg and revealed only minimally the extent to which the municipal government of the city of Milwaukee had become dependent for its own operations on outside governmental authorities. The federal government, in particular, had in post-war America become a very prominent actor in the lives of urban residents.[40] One of its principal domains was that of urban renewal. Beginning with the Federal Housing Act of 1949 and continuing through the legislative policies of the Lyndon Johnson era, the federal government took steps to help places like Milwaukee renovate their downtown properties. Obviously, in light of the city's own history, such steps were perceived as very critical to the life of the city.

A number of urban-renewal projects were developed in Milwaukee.[41] Some, through the provision of new public housing, enhanced the living conditions of many longtime residents.[42] But others had profoundly unexpected effects, contravening the very noble purposes for which they had been fashioned.[43] The renovation of the old Third Ward in downtown, for instance, effectively wiped out the center of the Italian community.[44] The Blessed Virgin of Pompeii Congregation, with a long history in the community, was removed as part of the renovation effort; the losses produced thereby eventually far outweighed whatever gains the city achieved in fashioning a piece of property unencumbered with people and buildings.[45] Indeed, possibly the only persons truly to gain from these kinds of federal renewal efforts in Milwaukee were those who drove cars, especially in and out of the city.[46] For the blight, once removed, frequently was replaced by new expressways and, when not expressways, new parking lots.[47]

Local Capitalist Enterprises

There are those observers, such as Ann Markusen, who would argue that the decline of industrial Milwaukee, like that of so many other industrial cities, is solely and exclusively the product of the decline of industry.[48] Such an *eco-centric* explanation, while no doubt of comfort to economists, is off the mark. If the iron ring of municipalities had not grown up around the city, and if the wealthy residents had not departed for the suburbs—if, in fact, the city government were more sovereign than it has become, the fortunes of the city of Milwaukee might look considerably more promising. Nonetheless, one cannot gainsay those who point to the fate of local capitalist enterprises as responsible for the city's decline over the past half century. Decline happened when industries began to leave and to take their jobs with them.

Many of the problems for the local capitalist economy sprang from the continuing divide that lay between capital and labor in this heavily industrialized city.

Labor strikes—and the efforts by the social alliances of unions to press for higher wages—did not conclude with the settlement of the Allis-Chalmers strike in the late 1940s. Instead, by the early 1950s labor strikes had become a regular part of the labor landscape of Milwaukee. In March 1952, a major strike occurred at International Harvester, a leading city enterprise, and it led to a walkout by almost 9,000 workers.[49] Soon employees and unions were striking at a whole range of Milwaukee plants, from Wisconsin Bell Telephone, to major truckers, to the major Milwaukee firm, Albert Trostel & Sons Tannery.[50] By mid-July, almost 15,000 steel workers were off their jobs in the city. One month later, the number of unemployed laborers reached 23,000—the highest count in more than two years.[51]

The strikes and industrial discord continued throughout the year. By early 1953, another pivotal set of strikes took place, called by the CIO brewery workers in Milwaukee. The strikes closed operations at all of the breweries in the city, including Schlitz, Blatz, and Pabst, among others.[52] Although intended to be of short duration, the strikes against the brewers continued over the course of the next two months. Charges and countercharges were hurled between management and labor. Eventually the walkout came to an end, but only after a period of more than two months.[53]

The strike against the brewers left a very bitter residue behind. The breweries claimed that the unions had cost them millions of dollars in sales. Blatz Brewery, the firm begun by Valentine Blatz in mid-nineteenth-century Milwaukee, ran a special advertisement in local papers at the end of the strike, claiming that the walkout had "cost us millions of dollars" and that it would take the firm months, if not years, to recover.[54] It soon became evident that the strikes against the brewers had led the firms, themselves, to reconsider the wisdom of remaining in Milwaukee.[55]

The discord between capital and labor in the city continued to poison the city's economic atmosphere. Milwaukee, as a city, was viewed by many as an inhospitable place to prosperous capitalist enterprises. By the early 1960s, the situation of industrial Milwaukee was viewed with considerable alarm by local residents. Harvey Hohl, a researcher at Marquette University, a respected Catholic institution in the city, noted that Milwaukee had begun to suffer a pronounced decline in its manufacturing employment, suffering a loss of 15,000 jobs just between the years of 1958 and 1962.[56] This loss from the very foundations of the industrial market, he added, meant that the city required a very vigorous and aggressive leadership to restore its economic fortunes.

Communities elsewhere, particularly in the newly developing centers of the South and Southwest, began to sense that the industries of Milwaukee were ripe for the picking. The city of Jonesboro, Arkansas, for example, no metropolis by comparison to Milwaukee, nevertheless was successful in recruiting the Hytrol Conveyor Company from the city. Moreover, it did so with the promise that it would issue $250,000 in bonds to build the company a new plant.[57] Once again, as in the 1930s, the reasons advanced by the company for its departure were the high taxes imposed by the city and state governments, and the wage rates demanded by local unions.[58] But the Hytrol Company would prove to be only the first of many to leave.

Over the next two decades, the city of Milwaukee hemorrhaged at its industrial lifelines. Cutler-Hammer, Inc., a longtime occupant of the city, announced in March 1964 that it would move a major manufacturing operation to Bowling Green, Kentucky.[59] Other plants soon followed suit. Schlitz Brewery, for example, informed Milwaukee that it would open a new production plant in the Dallas–Fort Worth area of Texas; Harnischfeger, the longtime German manufacturing firm, moved one of its major subsidiary plants to Indiana; and a tool-and-die plant located in the city proudly announced that it would move its quarters to Cedarburg, a small town outside Milwaukee.[60] When, at the end of the 1960s, the Albert Trostel & Sons Tannery shut down its operations after over a century of making leather on the banks of the Milwaukee River, citing "increasing competition from imports and leather substitutes," it was the final sign that the local economy was in a state of virtually bottomless despair.[61]

And yet the losses continued. Square-D, another important local manufacturer of tools and machinery, moved in late summer 1971, followed by the departure of International Harvester.[62] Sensing the need to take some kind of decisive action, Henry Maier, the man who assumed the office of mayor on the departure of Frank Zeidler, had created a novel program in the early 1960s, an industrial land-bank program.[63] It was designed so that the municipal government could purchase prime parcels of land in Milwaukee that then would be sold to industries that wished to locate in the city. Obviously, it was a way of luring new enterprises into the city—and along with them the jobs they would furnish and the taxes they would pay.[64] Maier also had helped to create the Department of Economic Development in city government, designed to find ways to improve economic conditions in Milwaukee. In fact, Maier rather quickly came to be viewed as a friend of business in the city—as someone, quite unlike Zeidler, who would go out of his way to attract new industries or to retain old ones.[65]

Nevertheless, when all was said and done, none of these efforts proved successful, underscoring not only the loss of capital but also the inability of local government officials to do much about it. The total loss of jobs in the city began to add up quickly. Between 1960 and 1973, it was estimated that the city had suffered the loss of 42,000 jobs in manufacturing alone; over the period from roughly 1950 through 1990, the proportion of manufacturing jobs in the city had been cut almost in half, from 42 percent to 23 percent.[66] Further, the culprits were rightly perceived to be not only other regions of the country, such as the South, but also cities that bordered Milwaukee. City of Milwaukee aldermen refused to cooperate on joint ventures with suburban officials because they suspected the suburbs intended to attract new industries to their own quarters.[67] Moreover, the aldermen were often right. James Parks, a reporter for the *Milwaukee Journal,* observed that the "industrial jobs (in the metropolitan region of Milwaukee) have grown rapidly in the three (counties adjacent to the city)—Waukesha, Ozaukee, and Washington," but not in the city itself.[68]

The alarms about the city's economy continued to be signaled well into the 1980s. Representative Henry Reuss, a Democrat and Chairman of the Joint Economic Committee of the United States Congress, convened a major hearing in the early 1980s, devoted to documenting the troubles of metropolitan Milwaukee.[69] There it was further revealed that a string of plants had either left the state entirely or had plans to close down their operations. The plants included the most famous and significant in the city's history—Schlitz, Allis-Chalmers, and A. O. Smith.[70] But the hearings did little else other than to acknowledge the full dimensions of the economic travail.

The departure of so many industries and jobs was due, in part, to the great division between capital and labor in Milwaukee. Yet, from another angle, it appeared to happen simply because the capitalist enterprises were mobile in a way labor—the working class, in other words—could never be. Frank Zeidler framed it best when he observed that "capital can move anywhere it wants ... to where the wage level is the lowest."[71] Capitalist enterprises, owing to the very purposes for which they had been created—the search for profit—eventually no longer saw any reason to remain in Milwaukee. In their eyes, unions simply existed to drive up wages. City and state governments, they believed, had no *raison d'être* other than to levy high taxes. Both conditions were anathema to their own interests.[72] Thus, industrial enterprises inevitably sought out markets where the potential for their own profits could be maximized.

The Changing Face of the City

The decline that happened to the central city of Milwaukee came about, in part, because of certain flaws in local institutions. No flaw was more serious perhaps than the one that enabled a host of separate and independent municipalities to continue to exist side-by-side, struggling over the uneven—and ever diminishing—distribution of public revenues. These disparities would soon grow even worse. The municipal institutions of the city of Milwaukee sought to govern in an environment that made increasing demands on them, an environment in which the needs of the population escalated while the institutions' own resources were increasingly diminished—a situation vastly different from that of the late nineteenth century. All of this eventually came to represent a challenge of the highest order to the integrity and to the history of Milwaukee.

Modes of Transportation

The nature of transportation in Milwaukee, as in so many other places, had played a major part in helping to shape the physical geography of the city. It was not so much a matter of technological determinism, in which the vehicles of transport determine the layout of the city, as it was the case that the social influences that lay behind the transportation routes and modes played a role in deciding how and where the city would expand.[73] Thus, for example, when the street railways, controlled by Charles Pfister and Henry Payne, began to expand in the late nineteenth and early twentieth centuries, they moved to areas where Pfister and Payne, among others, held property.[74] In effect, the owners of the street railways could use their own instruments as a means of developing the outlying suburban regions of the city.

Once again, at mid-twentieth century, transportation would come to play a critical part in the nature of Milwaukee's physical layout. The key actors were no longer individual developers, but rather the larger institutional forces, particularly the federal government, that had already come to intrude so markedly on the affairs of Milwaukeeans. In the bloom of the post-war years, the federal government had initiated a wide array of programs. One of the most significant was the plan to create great pathways across the American landscape, linking regions and cities to one another and providing for the further development of cities.

Milwaukeeans were not unaware of the need for new forms of transportation. In work done as part of the many "master plans" for the city, many citizens had decried the density of downtown traffic and had called specifically for new parking facilities.[75] The downtown, as that of so many other industrial cities, had become dense with cars and soot; those who worked in the area found it not only difficult to walk unharmed but also impossible to park. Plans called for, among other things, an effort to create certain one-way streets in the center of Milwaukee to help alleviate the flood of traffic and to ease the burden on both pedestrians and cars.[76]

The program to create a system of expressways, led by federal authorities, thus came about at a time when local citizens, themselves, were concerned about problems of transportation. The federal authorities began in 1945 to put together funds in Washington that would become available for cities and states to use to create new expressway systems. By the late 1940s, many millions of dollars in funds, some requiring matching grants from states, had become available for the asking. But Milwaukee did not ask—at least not initially.[77] A number of problems arose. One was that people differed over the wisdom of introducing expressways compared simply to repaving downtown streets. Elmer Krieger, the head of the City Land Commission, vested with the authority to make resources available for major plans for downtown development, insisted that improvements to downtown streets were preferable to the introduction of expressways.[78] Eventually he relented, and he agreed to support an expressway program, but not without retaining a basic skepticism—and not without suffering the loss of some available federal monies.

Another issue arose simply because of the fragmentation of political authority in the greater metropolitan region of Milwaukee. With so many governments and so little cooperation among them, it was not clear who would exercise authority for the construction of the expressways, nor how agreements could be negotiated among different parties. The officials of the Milwaukee city government wished to control the system, since the city was proposed to lie at the center of it. Yet, the projections for the system foresaw that it would cut across county lines as well as other adjacent political entities, and thus Milwaukee City Hall was not viewed as the proper authority to fund and to manage the expressway system.[79]

The control of the expressways eventually became a source of heated debate in the Common Council of Milwaukee. Several aldermen opposed the construction of the system, maintaining that it would not aid the city in its attempts to improve the lives of local citizens. Still others argued that in the attempt to revive the downtown sections of Milwaukee, the expressways could play a very key role, indeed. It was said, for example, that the expressways would help to revive the sagging fortunes of downtown by bringing new shoppers and customers into the area and thus increasing business opportunities for a broad range of enterprises.

This particular debate soon became symptomatic of the larger issue of the division and fragmentation of the metropolis. Eventually, the only way it could be settled was to remove the authority from any single power and to place it instead in the hands of a more general body. Thus, by December 1953, Wisconsin Governor Walter Kohler became persuaded that this course of action was best, and he appointed a committee of five men to become members of a new County Expressway Commission.[80] The commission was charged with the task of overseeing the funding and plans for expressways in the Milwaukee metropolitan area. Members of the commission included some of the most prominent business figures in the city—men who also would figure in a host of other revival efforts at the time—among them, Eliot Fitch, president of the Marine National Bank located in the heart of Milwaukee.

By the 1960s, a vast system of expressways was well under way in Milwaukee, connecting the central city to outlying areas. Proposed to the city by the federal government and the state of Wisconsin, through the availability of easy monies, the expressways ultimately were sold to the Common Council by those who insisted that the fortunes of downtown—and of the city in general—could be revived through a system of roads that connected the expanding outlying regions of the metropolitan district to downtown Milwaukee.[81] At a luncheon to celebrate the beginning of expressway construction in 1952, Mayor Frank Zeidler proclaimed that the expressways are "being done in the interest of the industrial and economic life of Milwaukee. This Clybourn-Blue Mound expressway [in particular] will be a citizen highway. ... It will help overcome blight and congestion. It will restore property values that are now depressed by the [automobile] traffic."[82]

Yet, nothing would prove further from the truth, at least as far as the city of Milwaukee was concerned. Just as the federal program for urban renewal often benefited those who drove cars, rather than the residents of areas that were stripped bare of housing, so the program of expressways failed to revive the fortunes of downtown, at least to any appreciable degree. Instead, the expressways permitted the residents of wealth to escape more easily to the outlying regions of Waukesha, Ozaukee, and Washington Counties. In this regard, the system simply sustained a fundamental tendency in the city's history—the bent that had allowed those who could afford to live outside the city to do so, while those who could not remained prisoners within its walls.

The Changing Demography of the City

Unlike many of its urban counterparts, such as Detroit or Cleveland, the city of Milwaukee had harbored a very small minority population well into the twentieth century. There was no apparent reason why this should be so. Milwaukee housed as much heavy industry as a city like Detroit and thus should have benefited from the great flow of migrants that moved north into that city at the time of World War I. But it did not. Even as late as 1950, only about 4 percent of the Milwaukee population could be classified as nonwhite.[83] The city had remained a place largely populated by Americans who could trace their origins to Europe—particularly to Germany and to Poland.

That peculiar homogeneity may have helped the city to avoid many of the struggles that other cities had experienced. Places such as Chicago, for example, had suffered through a series of terrible racial battles that had left people dead and the city deeply scarred. Yet by the 1960s, the number of people of color in Milwaukee had begun to climb noticeably and, by 1970, the nonwhite population had grown to 16 percent of the city's total population, a fourfold increase over 1950.[84] The change in social composition now would have a major hand in reshaping the city's future.

Black migrants, in particular, had begun in the 1940s to move to the inner portions of Milwaukee.[85] It was, of course, within many of these very same areas that city officials had uncovered the "blight and decay" of downtown. In reports issued as early as 1943, members of the Land Commission had noted that such areas were in desperate need of improvement.[86] Buildings were in a state of disrepair; many homes simply were falling apart. The streets were filled with soot and garbage. There was physical evidence of decline everywhere. Still, new migrants took refuge therein because these areas represented the only affordable one for them in the city.

A report on Milwaukee's black community by the Citizen's Governmental Research Bureau in 1946 observed that "67.7% of the dwellings occupied by Negroes in ... Milwaukee [are] in need of major repairs or [are] unfit for use, compared with 6.5% of the dwelling units occupied by the city's white population."[87] This proportion, the document continued, was substantially higher than that of cities like Chicago and Detroit. The report also concluded that the black population of the city was compelled to live in these sections because of racial covenants established by property-owners—covenants that restricted where black migrants could take up residence.[88] Landlords, many of whom lived in the wealthier sections of Milwaukee, rented their properties at low rates and did little to provide for the upkeep of the properties. Even the city government of Milwaukee lost out in the process, for it could not charge reasonable tax assessments on properties that bore so little economic value.

The Zeidler Commission Report. Many local citizens were aware of the problems that had rapidly accumulated in these sections of Milwaukee as well as of the rapidly growing nonwhite population in the city. Yet most chose to ignore the problems. However, Frank Zeidler, mayor of Milwaukee, was acutely sensitive to the needs of the new population. Zeidler, whose brother Carl had once held the same office, was a man of strong social conscience and convictions—a man acutely aware, too, of the possibilities for power that lay within local government.[89] Accordingly, using the special authority of the office of mayor, he commissioned a group of Milwaukee citizens to study the central city and to propose ways to remedy the many problems. In 1960, the commission published a lengthy series of reports and recommendations.[90] The study laid out in considerable detail the full dimensions of the decline of Milwaukee's central city and pointed to the many problems that now faced both the city and its new residents.

The Zeidler Commission's report furnished dramatic proof of how broad the issues facing Milwaukee had become, as well as of the great needs of the local nonwhite population, especially. The "Inner Core," as the area would become known, was a stretch of land that composed 26 different census tracts. It began one block north of downtown Milwaukee, ran westward to 20th Street, and was boarded on the east side by the Milwaukee River.[91] It housed about 100,000 people, of whom almost 20 percent were nonwhite as compared to only 4 percent nonwhite elsewhere in the city.[92] The conditions in which the residents lived were disgraceful by any standard, their poverty absolute. Of the thousands of residents, more than half received Aid to Dependent Children from the federal government.[93] Many had families that were extremely large, and they were confined to living quarters that barely could house them. Local public schools were viewed as insufficient to meet their needs. Recreational resources, which lay in abundance in outlying suburbs such as Whitefish Bay, were virtually nowhere to be found in the Inner Core.

Long before it had become popular to speak about slum landlords, the report of the Zeidler Commission claimed that the landlords who held property in the Inner Core had let it fall into a condition of disgrace and that they charged unconscionable rents. The conditions, thus, were not seen by the commission as the fault of residents; instead, the blame was placed at the doorsteps of the men and women who owned the buildings and left them in such a state of disrepair. The report also was candid in noting that other sections of Milwaukee, to which the new migrants might have moved, simply were off limits. Finally, it was observed that people who wanted to purchase homes in the area, with an eye to improving them, could not for very few "savings and loan companies will come into the area on any conditions with conventional loans, and those willing [to do so] can get no funds for the financing."[94]

Members of the Zeidler Commission were very farsighted in making its policy recommendations. One such recommendation called for creating a stronger bond between the police department and local communities. It urged the creation of community police teams consisting of men and women who had been trained to know the nature of the local beats they roamed and who had become familiar to the members of local neighborhoods. The commission also recommended that every effort be made to work closely and intensively with the new migrants in an attempt to alert them to the educational and occupational opportunities afforded by the city of Milwaukee. The mayor's group further insisted that a special commission be created that would implement the various recommendations of the Zeidler Commission and periodically review the progress that had been made.

Unfortunately, neither Milwaukee city government nor citizens' groups were quick to act on the problems. Indeed, no one seemed especially aggrieved by the misfortunes of the residents of the Inner Core. Businessmen in the city, for example, had far more to say about the importance of restoring the value of properties in the Inner Core than about the need to enhance the lives of the area's impoverished people. Most striking of all was the general attitude that those who drafted the report assumed with regard to the city's recent residents. These newcomers, the commission asserted, must be made over into good Milwaukeeans, just like everyone else who resided in the city. It was not an issue of living in a multicultural universe, nor even in a melting pot for that matter; in effect, the attitude was simply that people of the Inner Core must become "just like us." As the mayoral study group would conclude, "it appears that the great problem of all newcomers to the core area of the city is orientation and acculturation to the life of a highly industrialized urban community."[95]

The Post-Zeidler Era. The problems of the Inner Core and of poverty among nonwhites were later helped, in part, by programs undertaken by the administration of Mayor Henry Maier, who had succeeded Zeidler in office. Maier proved very adept at attracting and using federal monies, available in abundance, particularly during the Johnson years, to aid in the renewal of areas like the Inner Core. But, the position of City Hall appeared to be one that, itself, displayed less genuine sympathy for the needs of residents and more concern simply for removing the decay of the infrastructure.

During the 1960s, the effort to extend equality to members of the minority community of Milwaukee intensified, much as such efforts in other parts of the nation. In the early part of the decade, a series of boycotts of segregated public schools took place, led by Lloyd Barbee, a lawyer who worked with the National Association for the Advancement of Colored People (NAACP). The boycotts extended over a period of three years, from 1964 through 1967, and helped to focus attention on the problems of the Inner Core, and of segregation, generally, in Milwaukee.[96] Some of those who became involved with the boycotts were local priests. A number took an active role in street demonstrations and other actions designed to make visible the plight of people of color in the city. By the late 1960s, this movement, led by Father James Groppi, produced a number of dramatic marches in the city. In fact, at one point marches and other demonstrations stretched over a period of 200 consecutive days.[97] The call of the participants, many of whom were young devotees of the controversial Father Groppi, was to demand open housing in the city. By 1968, Mayor Maier and the Common Council had acceded to the wishes of the protesters, but only after President Lyndon Johnson had put a federal open housing law into effect. A number of municipalities throughout the Milwaukee metropolitan area eventually adopted such ordinances.

Nevertheless, these efforts, while extraordinarily visible and vociferous at the time, did little to reverse the plight of the people of color in the Inner Core. Many continued to languish in poverty, housing continued to be inadequate, and the crime rates increased dramatically. By 1990, the Inner Core actually had become enlarged. The boundaries of the area settled primarily by people of color now had moved outward, so that the western edge lay at the 4300 block of Sherman Boulevard. The northern edge of the area reached out to Silver Spring Drive, touching highly affluent sections of the city, and the southern edge reached to Juneau Street.[98] Milwaukee, moreover, had grown to become *the most segregated city in America.*

The struggles of the population increased as well. Those who lived in the Inner Core changed into a group that was primarily young and consisted mainly of single mothers and their children. It was in this area, too, that the rates of crime would rise dramatically by the early 1990s.[99] In general, the overall face of Milwaukee had changed markedly in this period of its industrial decline. Between 1960 and 1985, the size of the African-American population grew from 62,458 to 145,832; but, at the same time, the size of the white population had declined substantially, from 668,351 to 411,287.[100] Blacks now were, in effect, rapidly replacing the whites who had fled the city.

Perhaps the greatest tragedy for the city as a whole was that many migrants came to settle in Milwaukee at just that moment in history when businesses had begun to shut their doors. Most of the breweries, which might have provided employment at one time, had ceased their operations. Many of the other industries located in the central city, which also might have furnished jobs, especially for workers with limited skills, also had departed.[101] These losses, coupled with the increasing poverty of the new immigrants, effectively rendered Milwaukee city government unable to deal with the needs of the local population in terms of providing revenues and other forms of aid. Indeed, of course, as a result of the reshaping of its own purposes during the Depression, at best Milwaukee government only could do what it had done for decades—seek through agencies such as the police force, the schools, and the local courts to enforce order and restraint among the population.

Why, then, did the effort to promote equality among Milwaukeeans fail? In part, the program fell short because of the sheer magnitude of the economic decline and the areas of the city that it ravaged. But surely this was not the only reason. Politics had something to do with it as well—or, perhaps, the *absence* of politics. What one might have hoped for was an effort by prominent citizens to call on Milwaukeeans to lay down their arms, in effect, and to make peace with one another. Such a move would have been heroic, of course, but not out of the the question—for it had happened in other cities, such as Atlanta.[102] One can easily imagine that former Mayor Frank Zeidler, who had urged the careful study of the Inner Core in the first place, might have taken the lead in this effort.[103] But Mayor Henry Maier was no Frank Zeidler. Indeed, he was a very cautious and conservative politician who had no desire to move forward to promote greater equality for all Milwaukee residents. In this regard, Maier simply reflected the general abilities and attitude of leading figures in Milwaukee: good at finances and efficient in keeping the machine running, but reluctant to take heroic action. Moreover, none were willing to seriously address issues of fairness and justice in the city.

The outcome of the effort to promote equity for people of color in Milwaukee proved no different than the outcome to improve conditions for the working class decades earlier. In large part, it seemed to result from a major failure of political leadership in the city. As an eminent Wisconsin historian, William Thompson, would remark, "most of the elected and civic leadership of the city simply refused to admit that a serious racial problem existed."[104]

Newly Emergent Alliances: Of Bankers and Barricades

Reviving the Fortunes of Downtown

The contemporary era in Milwaukee has witnessed an explosion of different kinds of social alliances, more so than at any other time. However, these alliances did not arise out of thin air. The leading German families of the city remained in power for a long while, maintaining their influence over newspapers and industries, among other things. By the 1950s, however, they had begun to age and to move out to other cities. New figures and new alliances now arose—some of which had been fashioned in the course of the city's own celebrations of itself.

Chief among the alliances of the leading figures was that of the Greater Milwaukee Committee (GMC).[105] This group was created from a small number of individuals who had been assembled shortly after the end of World War II to commemorate the centennial anniversary of the city's founding—a group called the 1948 Corporation. The *Sentinel* of December 2, 1949, reported that Richard Herzfeld, president of the Boston Store and one of the founders of the 1948 Corporation, had just become head of the GMC. The central purpose of this committee, it was reported, was to provide directions for the city's future and, in particular, to furnish specific plans on how to restore the fortunes of downtown enterprises in Milwaukee.[106]

Now for the first time in its history, a new social alliance had emerged that would seek to exercise power over Milwaukee in ways in which the German families never had. The Germans had sat atop the profits of local companies and had provided a close-knit control over the institutions of capitalism. So important was their control that it never proved necessary—nor did they seem to desire—to reshape the larger purposes of the city, itself. They sat as a somewhat self-satisfied elite and let others engage in the day-to-day affairs of the city.

But as the fortunes of the central city and of its businesses took a decided turn for the worse, and as the various enterprises of the old German families became almost exclusively business operations, the need to foster directions for the city, above and beyond those provided by local government, arose. Moreover, the vitality of downtown Milwaukee had suffered so greatly that many citizens seemed to sense a need to do something—anything—to improve the situation. Hence, the alliance of leaders came to exercise power over the city in a way that was unprecedented.

The GMC made a number of key decisions early in its history that helped to create the perception that it wielded great influence. The committee, for example, played a part in forming the Committee of 21, a group that was to take a role in helping to negotiate the construction of expressways through metropolitan Milwaukee, and in helping, in particular, to shepherd the construction of Milwaukee's North-South Expressway.[107] There were a host of such projects that the GMC helped to fashion in one way or another.[108] The new public arena, built in 1950 along Kilbourn Avenue in downtown Milwaukee, grew out of GMC's deliberations. So, too, did Milwaukee County Stadium, which became home to the Milwaukee Braves in 1954, and the War Memorial Museum, a stunning architectural monument that straddles Lincoln Memorial Drive and overlooks Lake Michigan. The GMC, in other words, became a central vehicle for remaking and restoring much of the vitality of downtown Milwaukee.

The composition of the GMC was testimony in large part to the new diversity of the capitalist enterprises of the city and to the diminishing influence of the German families. One of the central figures to serve on the committee was Edmund Fitzgerald, president of Northwestern Mutual Life Insurance Company. An enterprise that had been founded in the nineteenth century, Northwestern Mutual Life grew to become one of the leading insurance companies in the United States.[109] In its wealth and in its influence, it also rivaled that of many other companies, such as Allis-Chalmers or the First Wisconsin National Bank, in which the influence of the German families had been so profound. Fitzgerald became a key figure in the workings of the GMC and, when he departed, his successor at Northwestern Mutual Life, Frances Ferguson, came to play an equally significant role.[110] The influence of both men was further testimony not simply to their energies but to the way in which the institutional enterprises of the city, rather than the energies of single entrepreneurs, had grown to become the leading participants in decisions taken to determine the city's destiny.

This new alliance, which would come to exercise historic influence in helping to set policies for the city, was almost exclusively populated by white males. Moreover, its members tended to be extremely wealthy and to socialize at many of the same popular clubs (the very same as those that once served as the stomping grounds of the German families) as, for example, the Milwaukee Club. The GMC also represented a body of Milwaukee citizens many of whom, themselves, had abandoned residence in the city for life in the suburbs. In this respect, of course, it represented nothing new; but it did mean that such citizens, like their forbears such as the Uihlein families, possessed less-direct attachment to the city, itself, and thus would not be entirely reliable advocates for the city when their own fortunes were so indirectly bound to it.[111]

Possibly it was this central fact, of the residence of members of the GMC in the suburbs, that eventually handicapped the group's efforts to promote further change in the city. And possibly it was this very fact as well that made the committee an ineffective instrument for preventing the fortunes of the city from dropping so precipitously. By the 1970s and 1980s, the GMC showed little ability to prevent the departure of mass numbers of enterprises from Milwaukee.[112] It showed no influence in being able to revive the full dimensions of economic enterprise in downtown Milwaukee. Though the GMC deserved considerable credit for helping to negotiate the financial arrangements for Milwaukee's new downtown Grand Avenue Mall in the 1980s, even this major project, done to retrieve some of the grandeur of nineteenth-century Milwaukee, did not restore the former financial vigor of downtown enterprises.[113]

But the greatest flaw in this alliance was that it seemed to have a blind spot for social issues. Those projects that the GMC undertook, with considerable initiative and strong political will during the 1950s and 1960s, they managed to make happen. But they appeared to have little interest in helping to overcome the vast social divisions that had grown up in the city; the composition of their own membership testified to their impatience with social differences. Thus, it was no surprise when, in July 1988, the report of a broad public commission in Milwaukee, which included some members of the GMC, observed that an intense effort in the 1980s to achieve certain goals in helping minority affairs in the city had been a virtual failure.[114] Accordingly, it also was no surprise that those left out of the decision-making powers in Milwaukee had come to feel it incumbent on themselves to develop their own alliances and organizations.

Defending the Neighborhood

A major shift has occurred in the character of the American city that has little, if anything, to do with the capacity of the major institutions to generate expansion or to prevent decline. The shift can be put simply: Over time people have changed their attention from the workplace as a source of pride and of well-being to that of the home and the neighborhood. Lifestyle has been added as a key element to the social stratification and social nexus of Americans, a lifestyle centered primarily on the realm of neighborhood.[115]

The explanation for the shift from the workplace to the neighborhood as the central element to define the status, and, in some cases, even the identity, of people is complex. In large part, it probably has much to do with the time that people in America spend at work today, as compared with the time they have available for other activities. With greater leisure time on their hands, they can devote themselves more fully to activities in the larger community and to those centered about the home. Moreover, as the density of population has grown in certain areas and as land has become more valuable to people—as it also has become scarcer—their attention moves more clearly to ways in which they can protect the land immediately around them.

Neighborhood, thus, becomes the vehicle around which people today can be mobilized. In Milwaukee, as elsewhere, many organizations, representing neighborhoods, have been formed to carry the concerns of residents before political bodies. In Milwaukee, such organizations grew up especially in the 1960s and early 1970s. Apparently the first neighborhood organization of any consequence, the Community Beautification and Stabilization Committee, Inc., took root in 1956.[116] Thereafter, several other groups appeared in the 1960s, including those representing the Mid-Town section of downtown Milwaukee, and the West Side. By 1963, only eight such organizations existed. However, by 1969, following on the heels of riots that tore away at the city's white and black communities, it was estimated that thirty-three groups were in existence in the city, and all were to be found in the central portions of Milwaukee.[117]

Most of all, these new neighborhood alliances, which replaced unions as the critical device for organizing those without power in Milwaukee, represented a way for voicing concerns that were otherwise unrepresented in the city, at City Hall, or in the councils of the GMC. Some alliances and organizations proved to be very powerful ones. For instance, over the course of the race riots that broke out in 1967, several groups played leading roles.[118] Moreover, in more recent times, neighborhood groups have sought to provide avenues through which the revitalization of their own domains could take place.

And yet, for all their display and glory, neighborhood alliances, along with other voluntary groups such as the Urban League, were unable to prevent the overall decline in the economic vitality of Milwaukee. They were not able to prevent the departure of industries to other areas, nor did they provide the means for recruiting new ones. They also were unable to shift the attention of local government in dramatic fashion to improve the quality of life for the residents of Milwaukee. In her careful 1969 study on the impact of neighborhood groups on Milwaukee politics, political scientist Miriam Palay observed that "most officials ... explained that citizen group activity most often reinforced their own viewpoints [and that] ... public officials as a whole admitted to little, if any, change in positions on issues."[119] And twenty years later, the massive citizen effort, Goals 2000, designed to involve Milwaukeeans in the effort to improve their own city, would conclude that this citizens' mobilization had made people aware of local problems but had done little to stem the flow of wealth elsewhere.[120]

In the end, as in the case of most such groups, these alliances would prove to be important outlets for citizen opinion; but they also would prove unable to alter the fortunes of Milwaukee, fortunes that depended on the play of larger institutional forces and circumstances over which collections of individuals seem to have had little control.

Milwaukee Today: A Deeply Divided Metropolis

Milwaukee today is like so many other major metropolitan areas in America. A deeply divided metropolis, it shows its main face in the form of deep divisions between the suburban areas—such as those in Waukesha County, which seem to grow ever more distant from the central city—and the central city, itself. These territorial divisions have received the legitimation of the highest courts in the state, and they have become calcified into legal boundaries that divide people from one another. Moreover, the social divisions that exist among the larger population are, in effect, poured into these territorial entities, serving to reinforce division rather than to create unity.

If there are important lessons to be learned here, it is that the history of this political fragmentation and division began many decades ago and has by now acquired an aura of permanence for residents. But the decisions that put such barricades in place have not gone uncontested or unquestioned. Time and again, Milwaukeeans have sought to consolidate and to overcome division. And the most active time for this effort took place in the 1950s, when the population still represented a vigorous and energetic community.

The opportunity for those living in the greater metropolitan Milwaukee area to overcome their petty territorial tyrannies took place at roughly the same time as the Zeidler Commission convened to examine the problems of the Inner Core.[121] A committee of leading business figures from the suburbs and the city, the Metropolitan Study Commission, was created by Republican Governor Walter Kohler, and signed into law by his successor, Vernon Thomson, in 1957. The overall purpose of the commission was to examine ways in which the city and its suburbs could work together to solve their common problems, among them, adequate water supply. This particular issue was a recurrent one, and it lay at the root of city-suburban controversies dating back to the 1920s.

At the beginning, it appeared that the commission would be able to effect some real change. Everyone in the metropolitan area, it seemed, could gain from cooperative efforts, especially those who lived in the declining areas of the city, where public revenues to support governmental services continued to evaporate. As the commission pursued its work, two things became increasingly evident: The residents of the metropolitan area could gain some real benefits from the introduction of some form of metropolitan government; yet neither city nor suburban officials seemed the least bit interested in working in some cooperative fashion.

In a document prepared in December 1958 to draw certain conclusions from its studies, the commission quoted the officials of various municipalities, virtually all of whom saw no particular gain in any kind of metropolitan governance. Officials of Cudahy, for instance, went on record to say "that more can be accomplished ... through the mutual co-operation of neighboring communities than through the creation of a metropolitan agency, functional consolidation or governmental consolidation."[122] Echoing these sentiments were the officials of the city of Glendale, who affirmed their belief "in the City form of government and are reluctant to surrender our prerogative to either accept or reject any services that would be made available to our City through a Metropolitan form of government."[123] Similar sentiments were voiced by officials of a number of municipalities, while Milwaukee officials went on record to urge the development of a metropolitan government and to argue that municipalities that could not function effectively on their own should consolidate with the city.

As its work continued, the momentum on behalf of metropolitan government among members of the Milwaukee Study Commission waned. Conflicts and disagreements broke out among different members, leading to departures and further delays. Even when the leadership of the commission was turned over to J. Martin Klotsche, provost of the University of Wisconsin at Milwaukee and a much-admired civic leader, little could be done to restore the original enthusiasm for metropolitan governance.

Eventually the efforts of the Commission came to nought. At best, its discussions led to a series of extended reflections on its failure and how such failure might be overcome in the future. Of course, Milwaukee was not alone in this regard. Other cities, such as Cleveland, also had considered forms of metropolitan government in the same period, but their efforts, too, produced no material change.

Thirty years later, the problems of Milwaukee and of her citizens are no different. On the one hand, suburbs continue to offer their residents an array of wonderful public benefits, chief among them, a set of richly endowed educational institutions. On the other hand, the residents of the central city, particularly the Inner Core, suffer not only the humiliation of inferior private housing but are provided with a public education that is second-rate at best. The divisions that Milwaukee has known for almost a century have not disappeared; nor have citizens, even the leading lights of the city, succeeded in overcoming them.

The territorial separations, coupled with the social ones, unquestionably sap the economic and social vitality of the city and its residents. They leave a mark on the community; and they represent further reasons why both people and industry wish to depart it. They represent both the barricades behind which the wealthy can take refuge as well as the obstacles for furnishing some real care and concern for the poor who dominate the neighborhoods of the Inner Core. It is these barriers that the city as a whole must seek to tear down—much as the Wall situated between East and West Berlin was torn down by the German people. It is these barriers that *must be overcome* if the city is to continue to thrive. To do anything less would be to forever abandon the fortunes of Milwaukee.

8

An Analytic Summary
of Milwaukee

Like many cities, Milwaukee changed over the course of its more than 150-year history. One way to mark that change is to note the stages the city went through as it evolved from a fledgling town into a mature industrial metropolis and then into an industrial city in decline. At each of the major stages of its development, the forces that brought about the growth, or the decline, of the city changed. The pre-industrial city was a city in which the forces that generated expansion, in terms of the size of the population, the land base, and the net capital, were those of a group of economic entrepreneurs who risked their own fortunes on those of the city. Land lay at the heart of the enterprise, of course, but, somewhat later, so, too, did traffic in grain sales. The growth of the city was primarily driven by economic concerns and economic motivations, and thus neatly fit a rather simplified Marxist conception of the world, in which profit drives the life of a community. Politics was something of an afterthought in the city—the activity of the economic leaders who were intent on securing the best opportunities for their own economic gains.

The early industrial city of Milwaukee, which emerged in the 1870s, proved to be a very different kind of city than that of pre-industrial Milwaukee. Industries, which specialized in the manufacture of heavy machinery, began to replace both finance capital and grain trade as the predominant forms in the economic marketplace. Many such industries were the brainchildren of new economic entrepreneurs, such as Edward P. Allis, whose own creation would become Allis-Chalmers, a major industrial enterprise in America. The economic growth of the city, through the plentiful new jobs that were generated, then helped to spur the growth of the city as a whole. Rapid expansion of people and of capital resulted accordingly, leading Milwaukee to become the twelfth-largest city in America by 1900. Simultaneously, the shape of city government changed, from a largely volunteer organization to an increasingly professionalized one—consisting of a variety of different departments and agencies.

By 1900, and the onset of what I have called the mature industrial city, the nature of the city changed once again. City government took the lead for the expansion of the city and, in the form of aggressive efforts to annex land, basically doubled the size of the city, from 22 square miles to 45 square miles, by 1930. Although the city increased in size, diminishing the density of its population per square mile, the net effect of its efforts to expand was to create a sharp barrier between itself and that of adjacent villages and suburbs. An "iron ring" of suburbs now grew up around the city, an array of sites that became the haven of those wealthy Milwaukeeans who sought to escape the city, itself. A political *and* a class barrier emerged, in effect, between the city proper and its environs, one that would play a major role in the tensions and conflicts of later years.

The city government also made efforts to streamline itself, becoming increasingly a more efficient and disciplined institution. Moreover, as an extension of its own effort to expand its authority, it even sought to annex those industrial suburbs, such as West Allis, wherein there lay enterprises, and their officials, that had stood behind the growth of the city, itself. This represented one of the great ironies of this period, namely that the municipal government, to which capitalism had given birth, now became its principal antagonist in the city. During this period, business in the city became consolidated. Mergers took place, creating larger and more substantial businesses, such as banks, breweries, and heavy-manufacturing industries.

At the same time, new and vigorous social and political alliances occurred. The most obvious was that of the Social-Democratic party, the Socialists, who had made Milwaukee their home for several decades. The Socialists gained limited control of city government in Milwaukee, but it was not sufficient enough to alter the direction on which the government had been set, namely, continued expansion and the growth of its own authority. The other alliance to emerge was that among the leading German families of the city, those such as the Uihleins and the Falks, who came to control many of the most substantial economic enterprises. This alliance became so extensive that it produced intermarriages among the leading families, such as the Falks and the Pabsts. Yet, again, it was not the alliance, *per se,* that generated the expansion of the city; rather it was the deeper institutional forces, both of capitalism and of local government.

The decline of the city, and of local institutions, began in 1930. The Depression had a profound impact on the city of Milwaukee inasmuch as the city was so heavily based on an industrial economy. Thousands of people were put out of work, families were put in distress, and the needs of the local population effectively overwhelmed the capacity of local government to meet those needs. Consequently, both the federal and the county governments became more active institutional participants in the life of the city. The county assumed much more active authority over the administration of the welfare services of the city, leaving the city government, itself, essentially to protect the social order of Milwaukee. In addition, new divisions developed between the unions and the capitalist enterprises of the city, and the city became the site of a large number of labor strikes. By the mid-1930s, there was already evidence of the departure of some early industries, the beginnings of a movement of capital out of the city that would years later decimate the labor force.

Between 1950 and 1990, the major decline of the city set in. In this period, which I simply refer to as the period of the decline of the industrial city, the city lost substantial numbers of people and substantial numbers of jobs, both to the suburbs and to other cities. It also became landlocked, so that it was unable to accrue benefits from further annexation of new territories. Essentially both the local government and the local capitalist enterprises were now unable to generate any further expansion of the city proper, and it changed from a place that was growing to one that was in decline.

The sources of the actual decline could be found, in part, in massive economic restructuring that occurred throughout the United States. Older industrial cities like Milwaukee suffered decline because many of its industries decided to relocate either in other regions of the United States or in foreign countries, both sites where their profits were likely to be substantially greater. Local capitalist enterprises, many of which had been run by local families, now were taken over by outside corporations, firms that had no particular commitment to the city, itself. City government was unable to generate much new expansion in the city, except for efforts to renovate portions of the central city. Local alliances were effective for a time, particularly in the 1950s, in generating new public projects, but by the 1970s and 1980s they were unable to counteract the broader institutional forces.

There were other events that conspired to make things even worse. The city almost overnight became home to a large population of people of color, many of whom were unprepared and untrained for jobs in the city. Many arrived at about the same time that a number of city enterprises were closing their doors and leaving the city. This new population increased the demands for services on local government, but, like so many, Milwaukee's local government was now caught in a bind, with growing demands and fewer revenues with which to fund them. And the metropolitan region had become even further Balkanized, as the new system of expressways, constructed with help from the federal government in this period, provided the escape route for the largely white, middle-class population that now ringed the city and represented the largest growth of the metropolitan region.

Periodically, efforts have been made in the course of the city's history to remedy the inequalities among Milwaukee's residents. They generally had little lasting impact. The Socialists made a valiant attempt in the early part of the twentieth century to improve conditions for the city's working class, but their main accomplishment was simply to make municipal government run more efficiently. In the 1960s, various figures fought to make things better for the people of color who resided in the Inner Core. But, once again, they left little of lasting value in changes. And the one major effort to redress the territorial and social inequalities, the Metropolitan Study Commission, came to nothing by the end of its tenure in the early 1960s.

This string of historic failures is by no means unique among American cities. But the insight that we gain from our understanding of Milwaukee history suggests that, at root, these failures are mainly those of ineffective, often conservative political leadership. Had Milwaukee officials and business leaders somehow been able to overcome their differences, many of which seem petty by comparison with the major problems that confront many of their impoverished fellow citizens, they could have made a difference. *They may not have prevented the departure of major industries to other locations, but they might have been able to make life considerably better for those Milwaukee residents left behind.* We shall return to this theme, and to steps for practical action, in the concluding chapter.

Over the span of the 150 years, then, Milwaukee changed form in many dramatic ways. The nature of the forces that generated the growth of the city changed, as did the *configuration* of those forces. Where once the economy had the upper hand, for example, and drove the city to expand, by the early part of the twentieth century the municipal government had become dominant and attempted to bring the entire city, including capitalist enterprises, under its authority. The differing configuration of forces, as between the economic and political ones, clearly suggests that any theory, or model, which posits *either* the political or economic forces as central in the expansion or decline of a place is far too simplistic to be of much help in understanding the nature and evolution of the American city. In addition, over time the forces that would serve to generate the expansion of the city changed form as well, from a group of individual entrepreneurs, principally motivated by economic gain, to a set of key economic and political institutions, each driven by its own internal logic. Further, by the period of its decline, in numbers and in capital, it was, in part, the flaws of those very same institutions—the focus of capital exclusively on profit, the failure of local families to restore their enterprises, and, in general, the duplication and Balkanization of local governments—that would attenuate the energies and enthusiasms of local residents.

But now we must wonder: Is the course that Milwaukee traveled over its 150 years of development a unique one? Do other American cities develop in terms of a set of stages? Do the agents responsible for the growth—or decline—of the city change form, as in Milwaukee? And do the political institutions develop as they did in the city, with, among other things, the notable Balkanization and territorial rivalries?

To learn about the extent to which the experience of growth and decline in Milwaukee is either unique *or* permits some degree of generalization, we now turn to a set of comparative historical studies. We shall compare Milwaukee with Cleveland, a similar Midwestern industrial city, to see whether the course of growth and decline of Cleveland took the same form, by stages and in terms of the rivalries and configurations of different institutions. Next, we shall compare Milwaukee with a newer city, that of Austin, Texas, a city of somewhat similar size but whose growth has taken place at a much different point in historical time. Here we shall try to discover whether there are certain structural parallels to the stages in Milwaukee and whether the institutional forces show the same configuration as they did in the latter city. Finally, we shall turn to compare the history of Milwaukee's city-building with that of Minneapolis, Minnesota, one of the places in the Midwest that has experienced a somewhat more successful past several decades than the city of Milwaukee. Here we shall try to learn why Minneapolis–St. Paul has been so successful in recent decades, and why decline has happened to Milwaukee.

PART THREE

Three Comparative Histories

Introduction

The chief advantage of studying a single city in depth is that it permits one to gain a better understanding of the intricate dynamics that have promoted the growth or the decline (or both) of that city. In contrast to those methods, popular among demographers that call for quantitative evidence on a great mass of cases, the study of a single case demands intensive exploration of detail along with the potential for understanding qualitative shifts not amenable, or discoverable, by quantitative methods. It is unlikely, for example, that we could have ferreted out the distinct qualitative shifts in the nature of Milwaukee's pattern of growth had we relied simply on an array of quantitative data amassed over time.

Yet, though the study of single cases permits intensive exploration of detail and a discovery of qualitative patterns of change, it fails to permit easy generalization. For this we need to turn to other cases to learn whether the patterns we found in Milwaukee can be extended in any manner to other cities; and, if so, in what manner such extension can occur. But which cases shall we select? And by what criteria? Frankly, there is not much of a literature on this matter in the social sciences, and there is not much on the study of single cases generally.[1] Most students have chosen either to study the single case or to study a massive number of cases. Very few scholars have chosen to examine a handful of cases for their similarities and their differences.

In the following three chapters, I examine, for its its instructive value, whether the patterns we uncovered in Milwaukee—in particular, the character of the several stages in the life of the city, and of the changing configuration of forces that promoted the growth of the city—find their parallels in other cities as well. To do so, we need to undertake two types of comparisons to discover whether the Milwaukee patterns are, indeed, capable of generalization. The first type of comparison is to look for other cities that are similar to Milwaukee in terms of the nature of their growth and decline, and to try to learn whether parallel events occurred in those cities. Did industrialization, for instance, have the same impact on the building of such cities? And what brought about the decline in the population and wealth of those cities?

On the face of it, there are any number of cities that could fit the bill. St. Louis and Detroit are among the handful of major urban centers in the Midwest, all of which developed roughly at the same time as Milwaukee and show parallel patterns of decline. Any one of these cities would provide useful comparative evidence. I have chosen to compare Cleveland to Milwaukee. First, it shows many of the similar patterns as Milwaukee—the same trajectory of growth and decline as Milwaukee. Second, there is available a good set of recent works that examine the history of Cleveland. These works provide a body of data that can easily be used to make comparisons and to draw out the essential similarities and differences between the two cities. Thus, we shall find out the extent to which we can generalize from Milwaukee to other such cities.

Suppose that we find that there are many similarities between Cleveland and Milwaukee, especially in terms of the development of urban institutions such as municipal government? Such a finding, while undoubtedly important, would not let us know whether the discovery is due to some general influences that swept across all American society, such as the impact of industrialization across all society, or whether there are some very specific happenings that accompany the growth of cities in America. Indeed, this is the conceptual problem that faces many of the urban histories of American cities that have been done—they fail to tell us whether the discoveries they make are discoveries about changes *in* cities, or whether they are changes *of* cities.

This distinction is an important one. If there is something to the notion that cities are critical features of societies and that they take on a life all their own, then we must wonder about the nature of changes that happen to them—to their institutions and to the way such institutions are constructed. Thus, our comparative analysis here calls for more than simply locating other cities that show parallel developments to Milwaukee. We must, in fact, look at the development of other cities that show growth or decline (or both) at an entirely different point in historical time, and learn what we can about the nature of city-building under different historical conditions in America.

It is obvious that if we seek to learn here, then, about the changing structure of cities and of their institutions in America, we need to examine the growth of cities at a more recent time period. Those of the Sunbelt fit the bill precisely. Many of these cities, though founded as early as some of the Midwestern industrial cities in America, did not, in fact, flourish until after World War II. It becomes of great interest to learn whether, in fact, their growth shares any similarities to that of Milwaukee—or whether they represent entirely different patterns in the construction of urban institutions. The discovery of parallels here is more than academic; it may be instructive to know precisely in order to avoid some of the pitfalls that have led to the decline of cities like Milwaukee.

Any number of cities would again provide satisfactory comparisons, ranging from cities such as Phoenix, Arizona, to Tampa, Florida, all of which are Sunbelt cities and have literally exploded in numbers and wealth since World War II. My own choice here of a city to compare to Milwaukee is that of Austin, Texas. The choice is dictated by, among other things, a great deal of previous research that I have done on Austin. Knowing this city in detail enables me to undertake a comparative analysis that is both systematic and taps the fundamental features of both Milwaukee and Austin. But, clearly, any number of cities could qualify for such comparisons; and presumably they would tend to show whatever parallels might exist between their patterns of growth and those of Milwaukee.

Finally, there is one comparison that will be useful to make here to move beyond the single case of Milwaukee. We need to know whether the problems that led to the decline of Milwaukee, from its transformation from the twelfth-largest to the eighteenth-largest city in the nation, were prompted by certain structural features of the city or even by the inability of alliances in the city to be more effective. To discover such possibilities, we need to compare Milwaukee with another city in the Midwest, one that is similar to Milwaukee but that has been more successful in avoiding the ravages of urban decline over the past several decades. There are several cities that again could qualify, such as Indianapolis, Indiana, or Columbus, Ohio.

I have chosen Minneapolis–St. Paul to compare to Milwaukee primarily because the Twin Cities developed at roughly the same time as Milwaukee and because they seem to share many parallels in the nature of industrial growth with Milwaukee. Yet, in contrast, the Twin Cities have been far more successful in avoiding the ravages of decline. The decline of both central cities has not been nearly so dramatic as that of Milwaukee. This comparison, then, should permit us to understand more about what has promoted the decline of cities like Milwaukee, as well as how such a decline might have been avoided. One added advantage is that it can help better inform us on ways to overcome the problems brought about by the inequitable distribution of public resources and private opportunities, as in Milwaukee. One of the most distinctive features of the Twin Cities is that they managed to create a metropolitan governance structure almost two decades ago, one that helps to avoid some of the major inequalities that handicap a city such as Milwaukee.

Thus, in sum, these three comparative histories will permit us to move beyond simply the lessons taught us by tracing the history of Milwaukee, Wisconsin. In particular, we shall be in a position to learn three additional key lessons: (1) the extent to which the findings for Milwaukee, on such matters as the several stages of its growth and decline, occurred in other cities, such as Cleveland, which developed at the same time in history; (2) the extent to which the city-building process evident in Milwaukee is evident in other cities, newer cities that have grown up since World War II; and (3) the extent to which a city like Milwaukee, which has suffered sharp declines, differs from cities such as Minneapolis–St. Paul, which seem to have survived recent decades in far better shape than Milwaukee; and whether those differences are at all instructive for what might have prevented the decline of Milwaukee.

Finally, while these cases will permit us comparisons, and thus the capacity to discover the degree to which we might generalize from our findings about Milwaukee, they also will permit us to discover variation. Indeed, the sheer beauty of having traced the course of Milwaukee's history is that it permits us to learn how and why cities differ from one another. It represents, in short, the beginnings of a framework that will permit one to build upon it and to learn more precisely of the elements that make cities in America both similar to and different from one another.

9

The Rise and Fall of
Industrial Cleveland

In the last decade of the late eighteenth century, a group of some forty people was dispatched from Connecticut to the western frontier of the United States. Led by a young man, Moses Cleavland, the group was commissioned to chart the new territory that had come into the possession of the Connecticut Land Company. The territory, known as the Western Reserve, was intended by the New Englanders to be a place where they could seek new homes and establish new lives for themselves.[1]

The Western Reserve numbered more than three million acres of land; it now constitutes the northeastern sector of Ohio. Like so much else on the frontier of America, its only inhabitants in the late eighteenth century were Indians. One of the first tasks of the company of Moses Cleavland was to settle the proprietary rights of the New England group to the lands with the Indians. Once accomplished, in 1795, the Connecticut Land Company set about creating the beginnings of a settlement, including the design of a public square fashioned much along the lines of the squares in New England villages. The company's chores were by no means easy ones. Much of the land could not be easily inhabited. There were countless swamps, filled with the overflowing waters of Lake Erie. Often they were so infested with deadly mosquitoes that many early settlers had to combat disease and illness as much as the rough terrain.

Much of the business of the early settlers in Cleveland, and in Ohio City, a hamlet that came to lie opposite it on the western bank of the Cuyahoga River, was in the category of land and of land speculation.[2] Some of the earliest pioneers in the small village of Cleveland gained their riches and fortunes from such land speculation and from the role the pioneers would play in laying out the territory.[3] Those who succeeded in the earliest of commercial and mercantile enterprises, men such as Horace Perry, Daniel Kelly, and Leonard Case, also were the same people who would be called on to hold local office and to take up the affairs of the village in the first two or three decades of the nineteenth century.[4]

The site that would become Cleveland—uniting the village of Cleveland with Ohio City in 1854—developed at a pace roughly two to three decades earlier than that of Milwaukee, partly because Cleveland was settled decades earlier than Milwaukee and partly because it lay so close to the eastern edges of business and political influence in colonial America. Commerce picked up steam in the city by the 1820s (by contrast, Milwaukee was just begining to take shape in 1818). Growing numbers of immigrants reached its shores by the 1830s; by the mid-1840s, Cleveland had attained some 12,000 individuals, and it appeared that its fortunes would prosper in the same way as had those of such great eastern U.S. ports as New York and Baltimore.[5]

The development of the Ohio and Erie Canal in a time when canals furnished the principal means for the growth and development of new American settlements profoundly affected the fortunes of Cleveland. The canal was completed in 1832, and very soon thereafter goods made their way easily between the outpost of Cleveland and eastern markets. Cleveland would import goods such as tailored merchandise, and, in return, ship raw materials and produce back to the East. At the same time, water transportation on Lake Erie became a prominent source of enterprise and initiative in the city. By the 1840s, Cleveland had become as prominent a port city as Buffalo, New York, only miles to the east, accounting for tons of goods in ship traffic annually.

Railroads also came to have a beneficial impact on the fledgling town. Owing again to its nearness to the areas of great population and enterprise in the eastern United States, Cleveland became home to several key railroads by the 1850s. Among them were the Cleveland, Columbus and Cincinnati Railroad. By 1860, there was a total of five such lines in the city, connecting it to such important eastern centers as New York and Philadelphia.[6] In this respect, as in so many others, the city gained a key advantage on its neighbors to the west, and, for a time, it seemed likely that of the many new frontier settlements, Cleveland was apt to count among the most successful. "On the eve of the Civil War, Cleveland had become one of the major rail centers of the country," write Miller and Wheeler.[7] In 1860, for example, just as the Industrial Revolution was about to sweep across the city, the population numbered more than 40,000 residents, ranking Cleveland ahead of more western outposts such as Milwaukee and Chicago.

From within, the city also took on a specific and special social tone. Settled initially by men and women from Connecticut, it had originally been fashioned to mimic many of those small New England towns and hamlets. The first of the prominent families had names such as Mather and Stone, affirming the city's connections to its New England roots. Indeed, by the end of the nineteenth century, a powerful and wealthy upper class of white Anglo-Saxon Protestants had surfaced in Cleveland, a cluster of people who believed themselves to be the leaders of their community and who, in the years ahead, would come to feel deeply threatened by the second and third great waves of migration that would bring other European immigrants to the city. However, for a time—for several decades, in fact—this group of Protestant families sat atop the fortunes of the city, making their voices and ideas felt in capitalist enterprises as well as in the social circles of great cultural events and activities.

Many such families achieved prominence in Cleveland in the period during which industry cut a wide swath across the city—industry that would leave as deep and permanent a mark on this place as it had on Milwaukee. The Industrial Revolution happened about ten years earlier in Cleveland, but its form would be in most respects the same.[8] Both capital and invention became focused in the new industries of iron and of steel. For example, the invention of a mechanical hoist by Alexander Brown happened in 1880, and new creations also took place in an array of related enterprises. With the ease of connection both to the lake port and to the railroads, the products of these new enterprises now could be easily transported to and from the city, promoting its opportunities even further.

The new industrial enterprises shook the settlement to its very foundations, with reverberations felt far and wide. Men who previously had been successful leaders in the city, owing to their commercial acumen, now gave way to both men and to enterprises that were the leaders in the great Industrial Revolution.[9] Names such as Grasselli and Glidden overtook others like Perry and Case. Moreover, the city also helped nurture some figures who would eventually exercise a profound influence across the entire American economy. Perhaps the most prominent in this regard was John D. Rockefeller who arrived in Cleveland in 1853 with his family. Initially a bookkeeper, by the 1870s Rockefeller had made the city into the home for his petroleum refineries. Moreover, owing to the success of his enterprises, he gained control of refineries across America, creating the Standard Oil Company. By the late 1880s, he, indeed, had become so successful that he shifted his own base of operations to New York City. Among other things, Rockefeller would make substantial contributions to the local charities of Cleveland.

The boom and success of Cleveland continued throughout the latter quarter of the nineteenth century. By 1910, the number of residents had reached roughly 550,000 people, making it into the sixth-largest city in the United States.[10] The wealth of local citizens proved to be equally enormous: The value added by manufacturing ranked the city seventh among all urban centers, and the value of private property in the city ran as high as $200 million.[11] In these respects, Cleveland amassed both more power and more financial wealth than many other cities, circumstances that unquestionably helped to foster an array of fine cultural institutions and a capacity to fund widespread philanthropic efforts designed to aid many of the poorer citizens of the city. By the 1890s, for example, the city of Cleveland already was home to the Bethel Associated Charities (formerly Bethel Union), an alliance of charitable groups throughout the city.[12] Moreover, there also was an emerging array of settlement houses destined to aid the thousands of new immigrants that began to pour into the city annually. The leading citizens of Cleveland clearly were intent on fashioning a broad array of philanthropic enterprises to help meet the expanding needs of the less fortunate citizens within the community.[13]

Political institutions expanded, too, in the wake of the economic revolution in the city. The municipal government of Cleveland gradually assumed a set of specific departments in order to meet the demands of the new citizens of Cleveland, but, until the turn of the twentieth century, it would remain a minor player on the scene. Various men paraded in and out of office, and by the 1890s, several of them were regarded as being as corrupt as those in many other cities at the time. Public schools also were expanded to handle the needs of educating the new citizens. Specific new schools were fashioned in areas such as industrial education, schools designed to train workers for the booming industrial plants of the city.[14]

At roughly the turn of the century, just as reforms were being introduced in Milwaukee (and so many other places during what we know as the Progressive Era), a highly successful businessman won office as mayor of Cleveland. Tom Johnson fashioned himself as a champion of the common folk and took his efforts to the people in the form of streetside performances and tent-filled congregations.[15] He tried to make local government into a more powerful and effective force for the great bulk of local Clevelanders—and, in this sense, he shared much in common with the Social Democrats of Milwaukee. Johnson believed, among other things, that private utilities should be owned by municipalities in order to help local residents by charging only minimal costs. He also came to adhere to the principles of Henry George, believing that a single tax on land would provide the most just treatment of urban residents. For these and other reasons, in his eight years in office he attracted both a devoted following of local residents in Cleveland and made bitter enemies of wealthy businessmen. Johnson left a deep imprint on the city of Cleveland, traces of which remain to this very day. For example, the area northeast of the original Public Square was, under Johnson's administration, envisioned as a large open space, to be lined with a variety of public and official buildings. Today that area, giving the impression of wide-open and spacious grandeur, houses the federal and county courthouses as well as the public library and the Cleveland City Hall.

And yet, for all that Johnson would attempt, and for all the enterprises that grew, and for all the numbers of people that came to settle in Cleveland, by the third decade of the twentieth century there were clear signs that the city sat on the same precipice of decline and decay as Milwaukee. Though the wartime efforts of industry in the 1940s would mask the structural changes taking place both in the local economy and in the realm of government, the problems were readily apparent much earlier. For one thing, a number of the central manufacturing enterprises of Cleveland, such as those in iron and steel as well as in shipbuilding, had previously changed hands from ownership by local families to control by business alliances and corporations outside the city, itself. A host of such transactions and changes had taken place over the course of the first decades of the twentieth century, and their effect, among other things, would be to make the leaders of such industries far less committed to Cleveland than to the profits they could reap through Cleveland-based business.[16] As Harold Livesay put it, "(n)ow, cost sheets—not family roots or tradition or civic pride—played the decisive role in determining whether Cleveland's businesses expanded or shut down, stayed in town or moved away."[17]

But it was not merely that enterprises were being shifted to people other than those that resided in the city. Cleveland was well on its way to becoming a deeply fragmented social and political metropolis. Owing to the great enterprise of two bachelor brothers, Oris and Mantis Van Sweringen, a widely heralded suburban development, Shaker Heights, came into being in the 1920s.[18] Shaker Heights was a carefully constructed community in many respects, not the least of which were a series of special ordinances that originally fashioned it as a white middle- and up-per-class setting.[19] Soon it became home to many people who wished to leave be-hind the filth and soot of downtown Cleveland. In this regard, it was symptomatic of the shift of population from the central city to suburban and rural areas of sur-rounding Cuyahoga County, a shift that would take wealth away from the city gradually, creating a kind of decaying inner core that was matched in its squalor by a similar core in cities like Detroit and Milwaukee.[20]

Alongside this shift of a white wealthy population into the surrounding cities and suburbs, each protected by its own ordinances and each determined not to become part of the city of Cleveland, a new wave of migration, prompted by the job-rich boom of World War I, began to alter the social composition of Cleveland, itself. The Great Migration, as it has become known in the lore of Cleveland, pro-duced an ever greater number of black Americans in the city.[21] More so than Mil-waukee—indeed, than many cities—Cleveland would change within a relatively short space of time from a city of white working- and middle-class citizens to a city housing a predominantly black population.

By the 1960s, these general shifts, accompanying the various forms of fragmen-tation, would produce the same losses and despair in central Cleveland as they had in Milwaukee. Businesses moved to other places, some outside the city, hop-ing to escape such matters as heavy property taxes. Although the conflicts be-tween unions and management were not as pronounced in Cleveland as in Mil-waukee, the loss of business would prove to be as great, if not greater. Indeed, the story of Cleveland became one of even more dramatic and precipitous decline. Once the fifth-largest and surely one of the most vital and prosperous of Ameri-can cities, by the latter part of the twentieth century Cleveland had become the eighteenth-largest city in the United States, ranking even below that of Milwau-kee. The numbers of people declined swiftly, from 914,808 in 1950 to 505,616 in 1990.[22]

Efforts to overcome these problems began in the 1960s. As in so many other places, the federal government entered Cleveland to help at the public level, pro-viding funds for urban renewal and for such heralded projects as Erieview, a high-rise public housing project overlooking the lake. Moreover, Cleveland became the first major American city to elect an African American as mayor. Carl Stokes came into office hoping to improve conditions for the city, and for many of the poor black citizens living therein. But nothing that he did could turn the tide, largely because the institutional momentum had become so great—both in terms of the fragmentation and division among local governments, and in terms of the loss of local industries. By the late 1970s, when Dennis Kucinich, a self-proclaimed populist in the image of Tom Johnson, became mayor, little could be done to save a municipal government now burdened with heavy income and property taxes yet dwindling revenues. On December 5, 1978, the city of Cleveland became the first municipal government to default on the repayment of loans since the Great Depression. Dennis Kucinich lasted in office for only two years.

By 1980, Cleveland probably had reached the depths of its decline. While cities in the Sunbelt now were booming, showing much evidence of new industries coming in from the North, capital continued to abandon Cleveland. Local property at the time was assessed at roughly $3.5 billion—only twice the assessment of such property in 1920.[23] Recognizing the problems, even local institutions began in some sense to abandon the city for a broader outreach that went beyond the city's borders. The Cleveland Chamber of Commerce, long a key local alliance of businessmen intent on protecting their profits in the city, changed its name in 1965 to the Greater Cleveland Growth Association, hoping to capture more growth and to represent more of the dynamism of the region, itself. This act—however carefully crafted to secure industry for the region—provided little immediate help to those who had become trapped in the decaying inner core of the central city.

Ten years later, many people insisted that all was no longer hopeless for the city of Cleveland. Although its broad patterns mirrored those of many older industrial cities, there were important new efforts to revive industry and culture in the city. New buildings and malls were constructed in the downtown area, including the magnificent Cleveland Playhouse. And new monies were raised to build a new Cleveland Stadium as well as to construct the Rock and Roll Hall of Fame.

Like Milwaukee, the question that remains for Cleveland today is whether it can recover, and even restore, some of its turn-of-the-century beauty and vitality; or whether it now is positioned to remain on the periphery of American society, merely serving as a witness to the changes that are transforming formerly small villages elsewhere into today's metropolitan empires.

City-Building in Cleveland and Milwaukee: A Comparative Analysis

With only slight variations, the nature and sequence of major events in the growth and development of Cleveland are virtually identical to those of Milwaukee. We turn now to consider the parallels as well as some differences. We shall rely here on the same stages as those we used in the case of Milwaukee—a classification both that proves useful to narrating the story of Cleveland and that reveals the changing configuration of economic and political forces that promoted the growth and decline of the city.[24]

Pre-Industrial Cleveland: 1796–1860

Cleveland was at its origins settled much differently than Milwaukee. A land company, composed of a specific group of Connecticut residents, established its rights to the territory in the Western Reserve and proceeded to develop various parts of the Reserve for settlement. Nonetheless, entrepreneurs, particularly land-based entrepreneurs, became those who dominated the early life of the city. Thereafter it changed into a city dominated by small commercial enterprises. The names of key figures in the city's early life were people such as John Allen, T. P. May, and David Worley, about whom a "brief analysis . . . shows that virtually all were wealthy businessmen, and many were deeply involved in the land speculations of the mid-1830s."[25] Moreover, there was an equal emphasis on the element of vision in creating the future city. Local newspapers, such as the *Leader*, began to emphasize the significance of manufacturing as the key to promote the future growth and expansion of Cleveland.[26]

Municipal government, as the economy, tended to develop some ten to fifteen years earlier than in Milwaukee. The first fire department was developed in the 1830s, followed shortly thereafter by the establishment of a police department. A sinking fund, among other things, was established in the 1840s to handle the accumulating debt of the city. But like Milwaukee at a similar stage in its development, the assets of the early municipality were only minimal, and the operations of government services were chiefly maintained by a force of volunteers. The assets of the municipal government in 1866, for example, were estimated to be about $1.7 million, consisting of the waterworks, schools, and the fire engine houses, among other things.[27] Municipal property represented only about 6 percent of the value of private property at the time.[28]

Early Industrial Cleveland: 1860–1900

Industry swept over the city of Cleveland. There were certain key industrialists and key inventors who would help turn the tide for the city. They included men such as Charles Brush who played a major role in the development of the electrical industry in America. Between 1860 and 1900, manufacturing took over as the major economic force driving the expansion of the city. The main lines of manufacturing were in iron and steel and were aided, of course, by the city's location astride Lake Erie and by the canal links to the Ohio River. Manufacturing industries also benefited from a vast network of railroads that connected the city to such distant ports as Philadelphia, making it into a central transportation hub.

Tens of thousands of new residents, most from European countries, poured into the city within a short space of time. A population of needy immigrants, in turn, created new demands of the city. Many such needs, as those for clothing and for healthcare, were met by municipal government. Moreover, during the course of the 1870s through the 1890s, the departments that would work to secure *order* in the city—that is, the police and fire departments—grew substantially.[29] By the turn of the century, the strength of local government had expanded markedly compared to the private sector as municipal resources had now grown to represent one-quarter of the resources of private property in the city.[30]

But Cleveland also displayed some critical differences from Milwaukee. Possibly because of its greater wealth—it was ranked fifth in population and had an annual value-added figure of more than $100 million from manufacturing by 1890—Cleveland was able to develop and to sustain a host of settlement houses and philanthropic organizations that aided new immigrants in settling in the city. Such agencies helped to provide important benefits to the new residents, aiding them in their accommodation to the new urban environment. Nonetheless, these agencies did not completely quiet the sense of oppression experienced by many new workers, leading Cleveland to suffer labor strife in the 1880s.

Economic institutions represented the central fact of life and of expansion in Cleveland's early industrial era. But municipal government would expand in power and find its own sense of energy in the next era.

Mature Industrial Cleveland: 1900–1930

All the essential facts uncovered in my previous study of Milwaukee during this same thirty-year period are to be found in Cleveland as well. Municipal government now assumed a key role, seeking to extend its sovereignty over the area.

For one thing, the resources of municipal government grew to represent approximately one-third of those of the private sector in Cleveland—a level at which they have remained up to the present.[31] The municipal government now included a wider range of properties and resources, among them, two city hospitals as well as a city infirmary. Home rule also was secured by local government in this period—in 1912. The effect would be to make it possible for reform politicians such as Tom Johnson to exercise authority in a way no previous mayor could; he enjoyed the luxury of resources and a scope of power unavailable to former officeholders. Though many of the reforms sought by Johnson would in time disappear, the strength of local government would continue unabated for a number of years. Moreover, a tendency for a twin emphasis on rationalization and efficiency took over in the operations of a number of departments of local government during this period.[32] This was evident in, among others, the police department. There was an initial increase in the number of arrests made by the department, especially in the early years of the twentieth century; later, this became modified somewhat, through the application of the so-called Golden Rule, a policy designed to limit the number of minor arrests in the city. In addition, numbers of new systems and procedures were introduced, all of which were designed to make the operations of local government considerably more efficient and precise.[33]

Merger also took place in Cleveland during this era, an effort to consolidate power in the economy in the same way as had happened in local government. The effect was to take control of the local industries out of the city and thus lead to a de-emphasis on retaining ties to the city. Cleveland also was dominated by a Protestant upper class, and had been since the late nineteenth century. This class had helped to create local institutions, such as the Western Reserve Historical Society, and sought to oversee the city's larger affairs.

Finally, a division between the central city and suburb, between the working class and upper class, took shape now, and it became centrally played out in the nature of the city's space. The upper class, benefiting from, among other things, local streetcar lines, sought refuge in the new outlying suburban developments such as Shaker Heights. They left the city to the working class, who were confined to living near their places of employment. Efforts also arose in this period to attempt some kind of metropolitan government, much like the one planned for Milwaukee. But the experience in Cleveland, now and later, duplicated that of Milwaukee in its complete lack of success.

Local government in Cleveland sought in a determined way to offset this tendency; the size of the city was doubled from 34 square miles in 1898 to 69 square miles by 1930 through an aggressive program of annexation.[34] But many suburbs, created as a haven for the upper class, simply refused to become part of the city of Cleveland, thus setting the tone for city-suburb relations for years to come—relations that eventually would undermine the capacity of the city to meet the growing needs of its impoverished citizens. Writing of this period in *The Encyclopedia of Cleveland History,* Ronald Weiner observes what could also have been claimed about Milwaukee at this time: "With the city now strangled by a surrounding ring of suburbs, it could not add to the tax duplicate (rolls) substantially through new construction. . . . Many of Cleveland's higher-income people, who were now living in the suburbs, were also members of the civic organizations advocating higher taxes that residents of Cleveland would have to pay."[35]

Decline of Industrial Cleveland: 1930–1990

The decline of Cleveland has been dated from 1930 by local historians. Even though the decline was not immediately evident in the sheer numbers of people living in the city, the drop would be far more precipitous and deep than in Milwaukee. While Milwaukee's population dropped by approximately 150,000 between 1960 and 1990, the city of Cleveland, which once had been the fifth-largest city in America, by 1980 actually had fallen to rank beneath that of Milwaukee.

Even its annual output of manufactured goods had declined dramatically as it made the shift to a service economy.

The main trends evident in the prior period in Cleveland continued. More and more people sought to take up residence in the suburbs of Cleveland, leaving the city to the poor population of color. The place was actually left quite devastated: Old streets of the mainline Protestants, such as Euclid Avenue, once home to very fashionable residences at the turn of the century, came to resemble nothing so much as a war zone. The black population continued to expand and to take over much of the central city. But it was a population left much in poverty, in large part because the industries had begun to depart the city by the 1930s.

At the same time, the municipal government proved unable to cope with the new demands placed upon it. The city, of course, went into default in 1978; perhaps this state of affairs could have been avoided, but it was a scenario that in basic respects all but occurred to a host of other cities. City governments became strapped for funds and had to turn to new sources to maintain their revenues. The municipal government of Cleveland, for example, introduced a local income tax; by 1990, that tax provided 60 percent of the annual revenues of the city compared to only 12 percent provided by property taxes.[36]

In addition, there was a growing fragmentation of local governance, creating new conflicts and disappointments. The government of Cuyahoga County assumed many of the welfare operations for the city in the 1930s, in large part because the city government proved financially incapable of doing so. At the same time, the twin needs, of *welfare* and *order,* provided for in Cleveland as they once had been in Milwaukee, now shifted in priority so that Cleveland's municipal government became primarily a force for sustaining *order* in the city, not for meeting the needs of local residents. For example, between 1943 and 1990 there was a dramatic shift in the service priorities of municipal government in Cleveland. In 1943, local government had spent 21 percent of its revenues on welfare operations for residents and 44 percent on the police and fire departments—agencies to secure order in the city. By 1990, the city only spent 3 percent of its revenues on welfare operations, while 59 percent of its monies now were spent on the police and fire departments.[37] In other words, six of every ten city dollars were spent simply to prevent crime and to halt fires.

It is also true, however, that Cleveland as a community struggled to provide for the needs of its local residents through its third sector, that of the nonprofit and voluntary agencies. During the recent era, for example, philanthropy has continued to be important. The administration of the man who succeeded Dennis Kucinich as mayor, George Voinovich (now governor of Ohio), managed to create a viable coalition with the business community to ensure that new structures and monies continued to flow into downtown Cleveland. But just as the new structures of downtown Milwaukee seem to be a virtual facade, covering deep problems within the city, so, too, there is a sense in which the wonderful architecture and great rebirth of the built environment of Cleveland seem intended to deflect attention away from the fragile foundations on which they rest.

Summary

In all essential respects, the story of the city of Cleveland—its development, institutions, leaders, and alliances—is pretty much the same as the story of Milwaukee. The specific nature of the stages of city growth as they occurred in Cleveland; the deep and permanent marks that industry left on the social and geographic landscapes of the city; the location of power in the hands of an upper class (Protestant but not exclusively German as in Milwaukee); the departure of industries beginning in the 1930s; and the great divide that separated the institutions of the city from those of the suburbs—these stories are virtually identical in time and in nature to the stories of Milwaukee.

One is led, therefore, to the inescapable conclusion that our discoveries about the course of events in Milwaukee history do not pertain to that place, alone, but evidently hold true for places like Cleveland—and, in all probability, for a host of other such cities as well. But there is something even more instructive that our detailed comparison between Milwaukee and Cleveland has yielded. It suggests that *the capacity of social alliances*—whether classes or Chambers of Commerce—*to control the destiny of their cities in American society may be limited at best.* Recall, for example, that the residents of Milwaukee lay their industrial decline at the doorstep of the leading families of the city, such as the Uihleins, about whom it was said that they retained control over their enterprises too long, thus diminishing the productive growth of those industries and, with it, the growth of the city. Yet in Cleveland, just the opposite happened. Prominent industrial families relinquished control of their enterprises as early as the 1890s, leading observers to claim that the industrial decline of that city was due to the diminished interests of absentee owners in the city, itself.

One cannot have it both ways. In fact, the existence of family-owned enterprises in Milwaukee and absentee-ownership of industries in Cleveland, together with industrial decline in both cities, suggests that *the pattern of ownership may have nothing to do with urban decline.* Instead, what seems clear is that broad local and extra-local forces and events took over both in Milwaukee and Cleveland, ones over which alliances of individuals could exercise little control, but ones that destined both cities to undergo major transformations. If such an inference is, indeed, correct, it suggests that it will take a far greater effort than that which can be mustered by groups of individuals, alone, to reverse the current fortunes of these two cities. Indeed, in all likelihood it will take major changes, probably in the very nature of local institutions, themselves, to fundamentally improve the future prospects for all the residents of Cleveland and Milwaukee, as for those who now live in many other older industrial places in the United States.

10

The Rise of a
Post-Industrial City:
Austin, Texas

Austin, Texas, with a population today of almost half a million people, is a key example of a city that has grown up in the great wake of the post–World War II boom in American society.[1] Aided substantially in its expansion by the uneven flow of federal funds into southern and western regions, Austin has reaped the considerable benefits of these monies. More than that, it represents the kind of city that, unlike either Cleveland or Milwaukee, has developed in the post-industrial age in America. Like most other such cities, its economic fortunes depend heavily on the success of its electronic and high-technology industries. By the mid-1980s, Austin was being referred to as the next great high-technology center of America, destined to rival that of the Silicon Valley in northern California and given its own name—Silicon Hills.

Austin was founded, like Milwaukee, in the 1830s.[2] Discovered by a group of explorers, who had been sent by Mirabeau Lamar to locate a site for the capital of the new Republic of Texas, the town that would become Austin—Waterloo—was located along the Colorado River in the midst of hills and flowering trees. That first group of white men who discovered the site recorded its wild and beautiful setting, noting that "the imagination of even the romantic will not be disappointed on viewing the valley of the Colorado, and the fertile and gracefully undulating woodlands and luxuriant prairies at a distance from it."[3] In this regard, Austin, too, was like the other frontier settlements of America in the nineteenth century, a peculiarly wild and uncivilized setting—one that remained for the white settlers to further discover and to settle. The early city was laid out most carefully, through a series of plots of land centered about the dominant hilltop, which would later become the site of the State Capitol.

Few records, of course, remain of these early years. Further, unlike Milwaukee, which was situated closer to the great routes for the migration both of people and of industrial enterprise, the growth of Austin occurred ever so slowly. Its numbers had reached only 4,428 in 1870, climbing to just a little more than 20,000 by the turn of the century.[4] Moreover, its choice as the state capital was not firmly settled until 1872 when, after a series of battles between those who wanted the site to be Houston and those who favored Austin, the final decision was made for the capital to remain in Austin. Gradually, more and more people made their way to Austin and to other sites in the "Hill Country" of central Texas. It remained a largely rural and agrarian countryside, one whose enterprises were mainly in crops such as cotton and corn. Migrants to the area came either from nearby southern states, such as Alabama or Tennessee, or were themselves the product of the great European revolutions in lands such as Prussia—the very same lands whose people would help to populate early Milwaukee. At mid-nineteenth century, for example, a host of German refugees made their way eventually to the Gulf of Mexico and thence to the port of Houston, where they disembarked and made their way north, settling in new sites that they named after their homelands, such as New Braunfels and Fredericksburg.[5]

Even with the influx of such new migrant populations, the growth of the region continued incrementally. Houston, the nearby local port, itself remained very small and undeveloped even by comparison to areas both to the north and to the northeast of Texas. By 1900, Houston had a population of 44,000 and was notable only as a small town on the Gulf of Mexico.[6] Austin, likewise, had a population of only half that of Houston. Thus, though the great waves of European immigration had carried hundreds of thousands of people to places in the New World, such as New York and Philadelphia, Chicago and Cleveland, and Milwaukee and Pittsburgh, Austin had not yet become a beneficiary of these vast new numbers of Americans. Because of its location in Texas and in the South, it remained far from accessible or even desirable to those new Americans searching for their fortunes in the new lands. The absence of easy means of transportation, in the form of railroads, for instance, also condemned Austin for decades to remain a frontier outpost in the United States, caught somewhere between the savage wilds of Texas and the hills, and the effort to become part of an advancing and progressive civilization.

The town also faced a number of other critical hardships. Perhaps the most obvious was that though its location along the Colorado River clearly seemed to promise greatness for it as a trade route, it simply was too far removed from other places, such as St. Louis or Buffalo, each of which, like Austin, lay along a breakpoint of water and land but were within far easier access to the major markets of the world and of America. There were a host of rather fruitless efforts to take advantage of this location and to try to make Austin a great inner seaport, something like St. Louis. One hope had been to take advantage of the river's ease of access to Houston, and to use this route as a means of transporting a host of goods, like cotton, down to the Gulf and thence to ports such as those in Great Britain.[7] But the costs proved prohibitive. Besides, there were a host of other ports, such as those in Savannah, Georgia, and elsewhere along the Atlantic Ocean that proved to have both the same goods and were within far shorter distances of the world's great markets.

The Colorado River would continue to play a major role both in the hopes for and in the actual destiny of Austin, as of much of the rest of the Hill Country of central Texas. When the effort to create a great market failed, other efforts were made to use the Colorado River as a means both of entertainment and the transportation of passengers, much as had occurred in Milwaukee. But these adventures, though surely exciting for local residents, would be but a sideshow for the settlement. By the turn of the century, when the fortunes of places like Milwaukee and Cleveland were flourishing, making these northern sites into the great urban empires of the new land, Austin's fortunes remained simply a dream for many of those most committed to its expansion.

Just as the destiny of Milwaukee came to rest on the shoulders of a few men at its outset, so, too, the destiny of Austin came to rest on the shoulders of a few men. There were, of course, the classic figures, such as the outlaw/marshal Ben Thompson. These men gave birth to the image of a reckless and wild frontier setting. Thompson had once been the local marshal in Austin, well-known for taking on and conquering any men who stood in his path. Then, as the city grew into a more settled site, he turned into the local gunslinger and a memorable gambler, one who continued to ride roughshod over his foes.

But Ben Thompson was only the most visible symbol of the faint line that lay between law and order. Those who gained the upper hand and were far more intent on creating a place were figures such as Alexander Wooldridge.[8] Wooldridge, raised in Louisiana and Kentucky, was a man of immense education and ambition for the city. Pursuing a career first as a lawyer, he moved on to become a businessman and a banker, and eventually served as the president of the Texas Bankers Association. Wooldridge personified the effort to create progress and industry in Austin and articulated many of the same elements of vision and of dreams as his counterparts in places like Milwaukee. Wooldridge was particularly intent on securing new industry in Austin, a place that by the turn of the century had at most a handful of small local firms and whose economy continued to rest on the profits of cotton and corn.

The story of Wooldridge, and of Austin, eventually became one with the story of the Colorado River. Wooldridge, as perspicacious and effective a businessman as anyone in town, urged that efforts be made to construct a dam in Austin on the Colorado. He thought that such a dam could help to control the fortunes of the city—fortunes that vacillated with the ebb and flow of periodic droughts and flooding of the river. Some years the river would overrun its banks, not only in Austin but across its entire course, running all the way to the Gulf of Mexico. In doing so, it destroyed crops and decimated the lives of thousands of Texas farmers. Other years there would be great droughts, and they, too, would produce considerable misfortune for local residents. Unlike the urban settlements to the north, like Milwaukee, there was too little wealth and too few residents to create the water systems necessary for sustaining the local population over a long period of time.

By 1893, in fact, a dam had risen in Austin. Yet a massive flood in 1900 destroyed much of the dam, and another one merely fifteen years later left the local citizens once again prey to the vagaries of nature. This situation continued well into the late 1920s when, as a result of the efforts of a number of people, and many local Chambers of Commerce, the private empire of Samuel and Martin Insull agreed to take on the construction of dams on the Colorado.[9] But, once more misfortune set in, for just as the Insulls were making headway in dam construction, their own financial empire collapsed under the weight of the Great Depression. All the while, then, Austin residents continued to lack many of the basic resources of an industrializing society, such as were readily available to Milwaukee residents. Not only did Austinites lack such things as drinking and bathing water, but they were also far more prone to disease. They also lacked that most basic resource of an industrializing society, widespread and easily available electricity.

A clear turning point in the fortunes of Austin citizens came about in the 1930s. The New Deal government of Franklin Delano Roosevelt was intent on helping to drag the country out of the depths of the Great Depression and chose the course of seeking to fund a vast array of new projects. Austin, as well as politicians from its nearby regions, was particularly well-situated to garner some of these funds. Congressman James Buchanan, for example, the representative of the Tenth Congressional District, sat as the chairman of the House Appropriations Committee, and Congressman J. J. Mansfield headed up the Rivers and Harbors Commission. Prodded by local figures and members of the Austin Chamber of Commerce, an effort was begun to secure federal funds to furnish the dams along the Colorado River. Eventually, through an intriguing series of political acts and conferences, an enabling act was created to establish a Colorado River Authority, with headquarters in Austin.[10] Once secured, this political authority became the agency for disbursing funds and for overseeing the construction of the key dams on the Colorado.

By 1940, three dams had been completed, including the Marshall Ford Dam (later renamed Mansfield Dam) that would create Lake Travis, and the Buchanan Dam that produced Lake Buchanan. These new dams now furnished the much-needed electricity and flood control on the river. Behind their construction lay not only the millions of dollars of federal funds but also a host of political contacts and bonds, a number of them initiated by Lyndon Baines Johnson, who succeeded Buchanan in office upon the latter's death. Johnson carefully knit together a network of friends and allies, both in Washington and in central Texas, and eventually helped to create the vast fortunes of private figures, particularly those of his friends, George and Herman Brown, who would go on to become very wealthy contractors, the beneficiaries of a host of federally funded projects, many of them secured through suspicious circumstances, at best.

The dams clearly brought to Austin the capacity to support a much larger population and to be attractive to the new migrants from the northern United States who were seeking refuge from, among other things, bitter winters and economic hardships. In the meantime, the Austin economy had made limited progress, based on a small number of local concerns, a handful of local banks, and a few firms in industrial manufacturing. In fact, the chief enterprises in the city were the state government, which brought visibility and glamour if not wealth to the city, and the University of Texas, which, as often as not, would provide the springboard for new radical ideas that would offend many in the state legislature. Some academic departments became hothouses for the growth of radical ideas, especially the Economics faculty who became well known for their pro-labor, anticapitalist stands. Even in the face of resistance and opposition from state legislators, the university became the heart of ideas that would help to fashion a far more liberal and progressive ideological climate than in most parts of the rest of Texas. It was here, for example, on the campus of the university that many of the anti-growth and pro-environmental ideas would take root—ideas that would later spread to other parts of the state.

By the mid-1940s, the city was poised to take advantage of the growing numbers both of World War II veterans and of other migrants who now sought new opportunities outside the Northeast and Midwest United States. A direction for the destiny of the city had been carefully crafted, one that in the words of one prominent citizen, C. B. Smith, Sr., sought to exclude the old smokestack industries of the North and to secure the new clean industries of the growing technology industry.[11] That the University of Texas was located in the city helped immensely to construct this "high-tech" vision for the engineers and the other scientists at the university who were themselves most receptive to firms and to industries in the growing field of high technology. Such firms came slowly to the city—but they did come. And they settled into the outward regions of Austin. Moreover, with the establishment of Bergstrom Air Force Base nearby the city and with the number of veterans drawn to the region following their Army service, Austin by 1950 had picked up in size considerably, almost tripling over the course of only two decades. It now was on the verge of becoming a great metropolitan area in Texas, one that would not yet rival the great growth cities of Dallas or Houston, but one that, because it housed state government, still carried some substance and some power.

Between the efforts of the University of Texas and the local Chamber of Commerce, along with a number of key business figures, Austin was able to shape and to direct its fortunes during the second half of the twentieth century. The federal government played a prominent role in this shaping, far more so than it had in either Cleveland or Milwaukee, or in countless cities outside the Sunbelt. The federal government had furnished the funds to build the dams; it had also served to inspire the vast expanse of interstate expressways, roads that brought new citizens daily into the state of Texas. Further, of course, it had also decided to locate such major enterprises as the Bergstrom Air Force Base near Austin. But its work went on and on, subsidizing and directing growth in the city. It furnished major grants to university departments to fund their research, and it also provided monies to new firms that specialized in the manufacturing of new technologies—firms such as Texas Instruments, a fledgling enterprise with offices in, among other places, Austin. The handiwork of the federal government was as central to the hopes of the city as that of any set of individuals or figures within the city or the state.

Throughout the 1960s and 1970s, while the decline of Milwaukee had set in and the city's enterprises were seeking to relocate to sites in the South and the Southwest, the fortunes of Austin continued to expand. A number of small firms were begun in the city by faculty who decided their own destinies lay outside the University of Texas, the most prominent of those firms being Tracor, a plant that specialized in the production of electronic equipment. Such firms helped to create a strong industrial base in high technology, one that would share central links to the university and begin to give a definite character to the local economy. At the same time, the city government, itself, began to assume a more definite form. Dominated for years by a few key figures—in particular, Mayor Tom Miller, who personified the city through his expansive ambitions—the government now became transformed into a more substantial and autonomous agency. Businessmen were displaced on its boards and in its local council quarters by younger, more progressive individuals. By the early 1970s, moreover, holding office was no longer the exclusive province of the rich and enterprising local businessmen but became the prize for well-educated and enterprising graduates of the university, men and women who wanted to leave their own, very different mark on the city of Austin. In these years, a struggle emerged within the halls of the local city council between the pro-growth and the environmental forces, a struggle that continues to dominate headlines and to shape local rhetoric today.

At present, Austin stands in great contrast to a city such as Milwaukee or Cleveland. It represents the urban frontier of the United States, both in direct physical terms and in terms of the opportunities it furnishes to new residents. Still a beautiful setting of rolling, wooded hills, interlaced with bodies of water and gently running rivers, the metropolitan region of Austin is a special mixture of laid-back Texan and intense entrepreneurial activity. University of Texas professors, particularly on such prominent faculties as that of Physics, not only shape the directions of Austin but help in the formulation of major American scientific undertakings, including the ill-fated Superconducting Super Collider project. Former university students, such as Michael Dell, run some of the most successful and ambitious computer companies in America. New residents are drawn to the city in the thousands annually, people who seek an escape from the declines of the North and seek to prosper in the great opportunities of Austin and the rest of the Sunbelt.

Moreover, unlike Milwaukee or Cleveland—whose fortunes seemed to level off in the 1930s and 1940s in the midst of such events as the bitter labor disputes and the Great Depression, the fortunes of Austin show no sign of imminent decline. The numbers of people living in the city continue to grow, even in the shadows of the land-bust of the mid-1980s. Once home only to state government and the University of Texas, it now houses the industries of the future—those in computer hardware and software and in the information-processing field, generally. No smokestacks here, nor the tenement-infested lands so dreaded by Austin's visionaries of the 1940s and 1950s; rather, a city that is primarily white and primarily middle- and upper-middle class. Its hills continue to fall victim to new residential developments and to new industrial enterprises of the post-industrial age. To visit and to see Austin is to witness America's future, for better or worse, a future cast in the taut symbols of information and tarnished only by the periodic contests that erupt between those who embrace growth unconditionally and those who wish to preserve the hills and rivers discovered by the city's earliest explorers.

City-Building in Austin and Milwaukee: A Comparative Analysis

If there is something to the notion that cities develop and acquire a life of their own, then presumably there must be certain common features that attend the building of cities and that accordingly structure the lives of city residents and their own fortunes. To understand all of this moves us well beyond asking whether Milwaukee—in terms of the previous comparison with Cleveland—is unique, seeking to discover whether city-building undertaken at an entirely different point in history, and involving an entirely different configuration of social and political circumstances produces features in Austin that parallel those of Milwaukee.

For example, if our choice of Milwaukee has been an apt one, then we should discover that cities like Austin will display the stages and configurations of institutional forces that are similar to those of Milwaukee. We should also find in Austin that an institution such as the municipal government arises over time, and that it takes over as a generative force for the expansion—or the decline—of the city. Furthermore, this institution should look in basic respects similar to the one that we uncovered in Milwaukee.

Austin is a particularly critical example on which to focus to learn both the extent of the generic process of city-building and the creation of urban institutions in America. It perhaps is as different a city as one might imagine from its northern counterparts of Milwaukee and Cleveland. As we have learned, Austin is a city without a strong base in heavy industrial manufacturing. It is a city that has literally exploded, in people and in wealth, only in the past several decades—the post–World War II period. It is a city whose life has been dominated by state government and by the University of Texas. In brief, Austin is a much different city than Milwaukee.

We now turn to learn what parallels exist between Austin and Milwaukee. Moreover, in light of the vast differences between these two cities, if we do discover important parallels we must take these findings as very strong evidence for the general theoretical view that I advanced at the outset of this analysis—one in support of a general model of the institutional imperatives that accompany the building of cities in American society.

Stage and Sequence in Austin, Cleveland, and Milwaukee

We begin our analysis with a very obvious parallel in the case of city-building between Austin and its northern counterparts, Cleveland and, especially, Milwaukee. All three cities show evidence over time of a change in the impetus for growth, from the energies of a group of entrepreneurs to the energies of institutions. In Austin, entrepreneurs—especially figures such as Lyndon Baines Johnson but also local political and economic entrepreneurs—played a major part in cultivating the city's potential for expansion. However, what is especially remarkable—*and of which we must constantly remind ourselves*—is that the growth of this Texas city took place at a much different time in American history than the development either of Cleveland or of Milwaukee.

Yet the entrepreneurial impetus for growth is only one parallel, however provocative. When we consider other possible similarities, especially in the stages through which these cities grew, we discover even more important correspondences—but also several crucial differences. There seem to be three distinct (pre-expansionist, expansionist, and mature) stages in the growth and expansion of Austin (a discussion I will return to momentarily), and in one critical respect these stages parallel those of Milwaukee and of Cleveland. Each stage is notable for the fact that the forces that generate growth and expansion are different and, in particular, that the character and role of local political forces change markedly over time.

But there is something of even greater significance to emerge out of the comparison of Austin and Milwaukee, as well as the parallels to be observed in the stages of their growth and expansion. Milwaukee and Cleveland, as well as a host of other northern industrial cities, suggest by their patterns of growth that many of the circumstances that emerged in the period following each city's industrial boom were the complex product of the growth of their capitalist enterprises. In Austin, by contrast, there was no such boom in the growth of capitalist industry but simply a rapid growth in numbers of people; yet key events such as the emergence of municipal government as an institution followed on the heels of rapid population expansion.

What this comparison between Austin and Milwaukee clearly reveals, then, is that it is not *industrialization* but simply *population growth* that promotes a set of citizen needs that, lacking a substantial commitment from the private sector, must be met by *public institutions*—namely, *municipal government*. In other words, there is a broader, more general phenomenon that is at work in causing the growth of local government—*not industrialization but rapid population growth.* The implications of this discovery, it would appear, are quite profound. Among other things, it tells us that previous histories of American cities that, like the history of Milwaukee, traced the emergence of local government to the simple consequences of the Industrial Revolution were wrong. Likewise, it also informs us that while human ecologists may have been misguided in many of the terms they brought to bear on understanding the city in America, they appear to have gotten one central fact right: *Population growth*, especially rapid population growth, *plays a key role in determining the shape of a city,* particularly its local political institutions.

Let us return now to consider at somewhat greater length the actual shape of the three stages of Austin's development to gain some further insight into the process of city-building in America.

Pre-Expansionist Austin. As in the case both of Milwaukee and of Cleveland, early Austin was a city whose life and whose growth were dominated by a handful of entrepreneurs. Unlike those in Milwaukee, however, the fortunes of these men were not exclusively devoted to land and to real estate. But like Milwaukeeans Solomon Juneau and Byron Kilbourn, and George Walker and Alexander Mitchell, Austin's entrepreneurial figures shouldered much of the responsibility for the city's growth.

Late in the nineteenth century, the key figure in Austin was Alexander Wooldridge. Banker and statesman, as well as a lawyer, Wooldridge played a key part in helping to promote a certain vision for the expansion of Austin. He articulated the view that the city should grow in certain essential ways. In this regard, he played the same role in Austin as the early entrepreneurs had in Milwaukee—he articulated a key set of futures for the city.

However, there were other figures as well. Among them, in the twentieth century, were Walter Long, manager of the Austin Chamber of Commerce from 1915 through 1949; Edgar Perry, one of the city's wealthiest citizens, and Tom Miller, the longtime mayor of Austin and one of its most beloved figures. Theirs was a collaborative venture, designed to promote the interests of the city—and of much of central Texas and the Hill Country, in general—throughout both the state and the nation. Owing to the efforts of these men, along with Lyndon Baines Johnson, the dams finally were constructed on the Colorado River, subsequently facilitating the great growth of the region.

Among other things, the case of Austin also illustrates that the efforts of individuals to promote the fortunes of a city in America *may take far longer to materialize* than the experience of Milwaukee or Cleveland would suggest. Whereas Milwaukee required only three decades to witness a great explosive boom, Austin required nearly a century in order to expand in the same prosperous fashion. Furthermore, during this whole period of time, the life and the limited growth of the city were anchored essentially in the works of but a handful of individuals and their activities. The reason for the delay in the expansion of Austin, it would seem, lay not in the failures of those men who promoted growth from within but lay rather in the *inability of the city to acquire the essential foundations*—for instance, electricity—*that would permit it to expand.*

Expansionist Austin. Beginning in the 1940s, however, Austin began to expand rapidly. The city only grew incrementally during the first couple of decades of the twentieth century, but by the 1930s it began to expand noticeably. Large numbers of new immigrants came to the city, many from the North. There was an initial development of certain key industries in the high-technology and electronic fields that would later play a major role in Austin's future.

What prompted this period of rapid expansion in the numbers of people and of jobs in Austin? At this point in the expansion of Austin, a subtle and powerful interplay began between the institutional imperatives of city-building, those that attend the creation of cities in America, and the configuration of the larger forces—what the historian Fernand Braudel has referred to as the *historical conjuncture*—that shape the details of this process, forces that themselves will change over time. Whereas in Milwaukee the Industrial Revolution gave birth to the great number of jobs and new wealth and provided opportunities for new migrants, the key force in the life of Austin would prove to be that of the federal government. At the end of the nineteenth century, the federal government was but a limited agency for shaping the lives of Americans; yet in the period of the 1930s and 1940s, it had become an essential factor. In many cities of the Sunbelt—in particular, places like Austin—the federal government proved to be the impetus that would provide the great engine for later development. Moreover, in Austin that engine would create such by-products as the dams (and the jobs attending such projects for local residents) and, later, Bergstrom Air Force Base.

Thus, the expansion that began in the 1940s was one fueled fundamentally by the federal government and its largess. Other factors soon would come into play as well. In the period in Austin from about 1950 through 1970, the equivalent of Milwaukee's time of industrial revolution, a number of new industries began to take form that would help to create the basis for the high-technology enterprises that soon would take off. Among the key firms were Tracor, the spin-off of the University of Texas; Radian, a firm that also specialized in electronics goods; and Motorola. Texas Instruments and Houston Instruments also would locate firms in Austin at this time, helping to secure the character of the marketplace that would take over.

In some respects, the remarkable characteristic of the outlines of the marketplace that took shape in Austin was that it had been so carefully constructed by the handiwork of the key entrepreneurs. A high-technology marketplace did not simply occur by happenstance. Rather, some of the second generation of economic entrepreneurs—who played a parallel role to that of Alexander Mitchell in Milwaukee—held a distinct vision for the marketplace. By design, C. B. Smith, Sr., one of the central characters in this drama, would claim the city had avoided the smokestack industries and the teeming tenements of working-class residents in places like Milwaukee and Cleveland. The city was to be fashioned, in other words, to look very differently than its northern counterparts—that is, to be in some respects better than them by avoiding their perceived flaws. Moreover, it was not by chance that the Chamber of Commerce, driven by the energies of people like C. B. Smith, Sr., sought not the steel nor machine industries of the North but rather those firms that placed their bets on technology and the petrochemical industry. The fate of Austin, certainly in this, its expansionist phase, *was not one of chance but one of design.*[12]

Finally, as in Milwaukee at a parallel stage of development, the municipal government of Austin played the role of handmaiden to the developing firms and industries of the marketplace. Although local government had been an active player in the fortunes of Austin previously, it had not been as an institutional force, but rather through the energies of central individuals, especially Mayor Tom Miller and his counterpart, Guiton Morgan, the city manager of Austin.[13] In this expansionist stage, the local government played a backseat role to the work of economic leaders. City government also remained a fairly undeveloped political institution. Indeed, one of the features that would mark the beginning of the city's next stage of growth—its mature industrial stage—was that local government would begin to play a far more active role as an institution in determining the city's fortunes— and it would do so in ways that very much came to resemble those of Milwaukee's municipal government.

Maturing Austin. The contemporary phase of Austin, from about 1970 to the present, is one that is similar to that of the third stage in Milwaukee—a "maturing city." And, as in that phase in Milwaukee, a number of key events have unfolded in Austin, almost as though they were scripted precisely to follow the Milwaukee pattern. The principal and most evident one is that local government has become a major institutional force in the life of the city. In addition, deep conflicts have emerged over the issue of what the city should look like and whom it should benefit in the future. Whereas in Milwaukee such differences focused about the workplace, in Austin, at this different historical conjuncture, those differences are centered on residence and the nature of the lifestyle people display. In Milwaukee, *work* became the basis for political struggle; but in Austin, the basis for political struggle has become the home, land—in short, *residence.*[14]

In this stage of Austin's growth, local government has become a central actor and has begun to exercise its power across the entire metropolitan region. Just as happened in Milwaukee at a parallel point early in the twentieth century, Austin municipal government has emerged as an institution of considerable power to rival that in the marketplace. Further, just as in Milwaukee municipal government engaged in such expansion through vigorous efforts to annex new territories—a sign of its own newly discovered autonomy—so, too, a similar chain of episodes has unfolded in Austin. Local government in Austin has sought in this period of time to expand its power and to increase its revenues, although, unlike Milwaukee, its revenues come principally through its control of the local utilities, not property taxes. Over the period from 1970 through 1990, in fact, the size of local Austin grew substantially, reaching an estimated population of 476,000 by 1992.[15]

This comparison, however, though once again portraying real similarities in the stages of the evolution of cities in America, also points to a key and very critical difference—one of great import to life in Austin and in Milwaukee. Consider this simple fact: The city of Milwaukee in 1965 was a city of roughly 95 square miles, whereas the city of Austin in 1965 was one of 61.3 square miles. Twenty-five years later, the city of Milwaukee still was roughly 95 square miles in area, *but Austin had more than tripled, to* 226 square miles. Therein lies yet another crucial discovery about how difference emerges in city-building in America and about the ways in which city-building at different historical conjunctures entails very different consequences. Milwaukee remains surrounded by a ring of suburbs— the "iron ring"—suburbs that refuse to become part of a larger metropolitan effort to provide a decent quality of life for every citizen, including the poor residing in its central city. But Austin, like virtually every other post-industrial city in the Sunbelt, has no such problems to confront it. Its planners actually have learned from the experience of cities like Milwaukee and Cleveland, and thus have sought to avoid the real difficulties facing those cities by taking in vast amounts of land well in advance of its actual residential and commercial development.[16]

While the municipal government expanded its power by increasing the territory over which it ruled in this, its mature phase, it also grew in other respects into a far more powerful institution as well. As we discovered in Milwaukee, local government at this point in its evolution introduced changes in its own internal operations—changes that stressed a growing emphasis on efficiency and professionalization. The same now took place in Austin, and it happened in several respects.

For example, where once local government had been under the thumb of Austin business interests, and thus virtually inseparable from them, it now introduced a number of changes that would give it far greater autonomy from the local marketplace. For example, in 1972 salaries began to be paid to members of the Austin City Council, thereby enabling people other than businessmen to hold such positions. The effect would be to make local government more autonomous from the business sector than it had been during the reign of Tom Miller and those mayors who followed him immediately in office.

For another thing, there was an effort to rationalize and to systematize the operations of local government, far more so than had ever been accomplished in the city's history. Although the "city manager" form of government had been introduced in 1928 to take politics out of local government, in fact, the changes that occurred in this era truly began to make Austin's municipal government into an autonomous institution, one separate from the interests that run local business and that also, of course, make it one of considerably greater power and authority within the confines of the city. There are two simple and suggestive indices of the growing scope and power of municipal government in this stage. One is that the proportion of people employed by the City of Austin, as a percentage of the total population in the city, doubled between 1950 and 1990. In 1950, one of every one thousand people living in Austin was employed by local government; by 1990, more than two of every one thousand people living in the city were employed by the City of Austin.[17] Similarly, the per-capita cost of local government in Austin skyrocketed during this period, going from a mere $85 in 1950 to almost $2,150 in 1990—a much greater increase than any other cost of living expense for Austin residents.[18]

Furthermore, just as we previously noted in Milwaukee that the police department seemed to furnish an illustration of the internal revamping of municipal government's procedures, so the same is evident in Austin's police department. Whereas there had been only a minimal set of changes in the department's operations from the period from about 1930 through 1970, beginning in 1970 there are a series of efforts to upgrade and to rationalize the department's operations. Some began with the appointment of a new chief of police in 1976. But the major changes were initiated in 1986, following a comprehensive survey of the department's operations. This survey, requested by the new chief of police, was conducted through the auspices of the International Association of Chiefs of Police. The survey recommended many changes in how the police department carried out its operations, ranging from improvements in the training of police officers to improved methods for cost-accounting in the police department. As of early 1993, many of these changes, in fact, had been implemented. Moreover, their net effect was to make more systematic and careful the varied routines employed in the operations of Austin's police force.[19] What was true for the police department of Austin would also prove to be true for its municipal government as a whole.

Austin and Milwaukee: Additional Critical Differences

We have so far focused on the parallels that exist between the experience of city-building in Austin and in Milwaukee. These parallels have alerted us to two things. First, they strongly suggest that there are, indeed, basic underlying institutional imperatives that accompany the growth of cities in America. One such imperative is that cities grow by stages and that the stages themselves resemble one another regardless of the city being built or the historical moment at which its construction occurs. Second, our analysis also reveals important differences in the process of city-building. As we have discovered, for example, the trigger for sustained growth in Milwaukee was the Industrial Revolution, but the trigger for sustained growth in Austin was the federal government. The differences happened because the growth of these two cities occurred at different historical conjunctures in American history.

Now let us turn to explore some further differences between the two cities and to discover their implications. One such difference has to do with the social composition of the two cities. Milwaukee became largely a working-class city by the early years of the twentieth century, based on its roots in heavy manufacturing. This fact had a host of implications for the subsequent development of the city, including the great social hiatus that grew up between the central city and the "iron ring" suburbs surrounding Milwaukee.

Austin, by contrast, is a city whose social composition has been primarily middle class, especially in its period of rapid expansion and development. It is a city that has been built around state government and the University of Texas, as well as the industrial offshoots of these two primary institutions of the city. Accordingly, it also is primarily a white-collar city, with a highly specialized workforce. While there exists both ethnic difference and income inequality within Austin, neither such phenomena is nearly so pronounced nor as marked as in Milwaukee.

These differences in the social composition of the two cities seem to have major consequences for the nature of life as it has unfolded in them. First, as we noted earlier, the political conflicts that emerge in Austin are fundamentally different from those of Milwaukee. Milwaukee was, and is, a manufacturing city. It gave birth to a strong union movement and to an equally strong Social Democratic party, both of which forged important alliances and created substantial ideological divisions within the city over the course of its history. Among other things, it remains true that the strength of unions have, according to many accounts, prompted many industries to move away from the city. The nature of division in Austin, a post-industrial city, is fundamentally different. The divisions that occur are ones over lifestyle and over issues of the environment and how people are to treat it. Even though capitalism is the same in both places, the locus and site of conflict is so very different as to convey the clear sense that these cities, indeed, represent very different worlds.

In addition, because Austin government is run on a nonpartisan basis, created out of the effort to rid city government of politics, it lacks the development of the vigorous political forces, such as unions, that took root in Milwaukee. Thus, Austin's politics is not shaped or informed as much by ideological battles as happened in Milwaukee. The city, in other words, is not only post-industrial in terms of its economic base, but it is almost post-modern in the nature of its politics. The battles that take place are over residence and lifestyle—over symbols—and are centered about the question of how to treat the environment. It is a city more obviously of symbols than of material difference as in Milwaukee.

Correspondingly, it is notable that a sector of the local Austin economy plays a role in the city unlike the role played by its counterpart in Milwaukee at a parallel stage in its development—the real estate community. As in so many Sunbelt cities today, the real estate industry plays a leading role in helping to promote the expansion of the city. The industry's efforts do not lead directly to the creation of jobs, but they do reinforce the tendency of local government to seek to expand outward and to take in new territories. There has developed a very close alliance between the real estate sector of the Austin economy and the fortunes of municipal government—both actors see it in their interests to seek for further, almost endless expansion of the city's boundaries and territories. By contrast, in the industrial cities of Milwaukee and Cleveland, the real estate community did not play such a vigorous role in the primary creation of these two cities, though it does so today in their suburban regions.

This alliance between the real estate sector and local government in Austin, as in other post-industrial cities of the Sunbelt, appears to be so natural and powerful as to have given birth to a theory about its origins and unfolding—the theory of the "growth machine," posited by John Logan and Harvey Molotch. (See Chapter 2, particularly the text associated with Note 26.) However, as the experience of Milwaukee and Cleveland so clearly show, such a growth machine is not based by any means simply on the *natural powers of the real estate community* as the driving force of expansion, but the *engine for growth will vary* with the *particular historical conjuncture* at which a city begins to develop and to expand in America. Industrial capitalism played the role of central engine in Milwaukee, whereas it has not done so in Austin.

None of this is to suggest that capitalism has ceased to play a role as it did in Milwaukee. In Milwaukee, capitalist industry became the culprit and the source of a strong opposition force created by the Social Democrats. Nothing of that sort has taken place in Austin. This largely middle-class city has not suffered the same deep social class divisions; but its divisions, over the environment and over the central fact of growth, are often felt as deeply by its citizens. Yet they are not so prominent and severe as to drive industry away. In fact, although there are many people and neighborhoods opposed to growth in Austin, growth still occurs, and people (and enterprises) do not abandon the city for sites elsewhere.

In addition, because deep class conflict has not developed in Austin as it has in Milwaukee, efforts to create escapes to suburban areas also have not developed. At most, what one finds as a measure of escape in Austin from the force of local government is the effort to create local municipal utility districts (MUDs). Since the city gains the majority of its monies from utilities, the forces of opposition, seeking to resist the encroachment of local government, have fashioned these new districts to escape the city. Presently there are many such MUDs in the Austin metropolitan area—the legal innovation of the state in the early 1980s.

Finally, because Austin is populated largely with middle-class, highly educated citizens—and in spite of Austin's form of nonpartisan politics—there seems to be considerably more active citizen involvement in the governing of Austin than occurred at a similar stage in the development of Milwaukee. People in Austin seem to take political democracy, as a credo and ethos, more seriously, and therefore Austinites seem to become more involved in the activities of local governance. Further, even though growth continues unabated in Austin in the face of local concerns, this greater activity means that more citizens are actively involved in trying to shape their futures and in seeking to make their municipal institutions bend to their collective will. Whether they prove to be more successful in this effort than their Milwaukee counterparts remains to be seen—and perhaps to be vigorously sought.

Summary

I have disclosed a number of important lessons in this comparative chapter on Austin and Milwaukee. First, important parallels exist in the city-building efforts that resulted in Austin and Milwaukee. Both cities show evidence of a change over time—from expansion efforts that were rooted in the energies of individual entrepreneurs to efforts rooted in the moves and manipulations of institutions. Second, both cities reveal a growth and development by stages and, in particular, the emergence of a powerful local government between the date of the city's original founding and the years when it developed into a mature city. Moreover, at each stage of the development of these cities, different actors were involved in promoting the city's fortunes: In the early pre-expansionist stage, the entrepreneurs provided the main energy for expansion; but in the later, mature stage, municipal government took over to play a crucial role.

Because these cities are so very different from one another, such findings as these are strong support for the general perspective I have offered here on the nature of city-building in America. But I have also disclosed critical differences between the two cities—differences that further illuminate the nature of city-building in America. For example, the triggers for rapid growth in Austin and in Milwaukee differed from one another. Rapid growth in Milwaukee followed on the heels of the Industrial Revolution, whereas in Austin growth was promoted by the monies and efforts of the federal government. In addition, the comparison of these two cities has demonstrated that it was not the industrialization of Milwaukee but, instead, simply rapid population growth by itself that created a set of needs of local residents that were met by the growth of local government.

Both these similarities and differences, along with others that I have noted earlier, thus provide a nuanced view of city growth in America. The general view, on the evolution of cities through stages, seems secure based on the comparison here, but the unfolding of growth and development of a particular city will depend on the historical conjuncture at which city-building takes place. In short, the Austin-Milwaukee comparison has enabled us to see a blend both of the general and of the particular and, therefore, to come to an even more profound understanding of the rise and fall of American cities.

11

The Rebirth of Minneapolis–St. Paul: Creating a Post-Industrial City in the Midwest

The Twin Cities of Minneapolis and St. Paul, Minnesota, represent an exception among the great cities of the American Midwest. Although subject to the same loss of population from their central cities to their suburbs as other Midwestern cities, they seem to be much more akin to the boom cities of the Sunbelt. In Minneapolis, for example, tall glass skyscrapers reach upward, giving every appearance of a setting like Dallas or Denver rather than one like St. Louis or Detroit. Electronics industries seem to lie everywhere throughout the city, as do financial firms, both features much more characteristic of newer, post-industrial cities than of older, industrial ones.

All of this represents something of a great puzzle to the student of cities. How have Minneapolis and St. Paul managed to recover so quickly from the legacy of their pasts, while Cleveland and Milwaukee still are mired in the residue of that legacy? Is it merely a matter of smoke and mirrors—of great glass structures lining downtown Minneapolis and of a vital and restored downtown St. Paul—but of the same lingering problems that face other older cities? Why, in particular, do the Twin Cities regularly rank among the very best cities in America, in terms of their overall quality of life, while so many of their counterparts, such as Detroit or St. Louis, rank so much lower than them?[1]

These are the questions I will pursue in this last comparative analysis of my book. In particular, I will illustrate the special features of Minneapolis and St. Paul that make them stand out among many older American cities. In the process of examining whether there is any truth to both appearances and to the images of the popular press, I also will try to determine the conditions that might have fostered the Twin Cities' post-industrial boom. Armed with this kind of knowledge, we should be better able to understand the condition, or set of conditions, that promotes the vitality of older cities and thus be in a position to point the way to changes that might be instituted in cities still suffering from the legacies of their industrial past.

City-Building in the Twin Cities:
A Comparative Analysis

The Parallels

According to the logic of comparative analysis among a small sample of cases, such as we have here, if one is to make the claim that there exist special causes, or conditions, that promote differences among cities, one must first establish that the cities are alike in most fundamental respects. For instance, when I undertook my comparative analysis of Milwaukee, Cleveland, and Austin, I was required to identify key parallels—to show that all three cities were, as cities, similar to one another—in order to even examine the major differences among them in the nature of their present development.

So it is when I analyze and compare the situation of Minneapolis and St. Paul with that of Cleveland and Milwaukee. I must be able to identify the essential similarities in their origins and development as cities to be able to even speak to the nature of the features that distinguish them from one another. What, then, are the essential similarities among these several cities?

First of all, Minneapolis and St. Paul, along with Milwaukee and Cleveland, all were founded at roughly the same historical period, in the early part of the nineteenth century.[2] Although Cleveland did possess something of a head start on the other cities, by the latter decades of the nineteenth century all the cities had become attractive sites for new settlers to the Midwest. By the 1870s, Cleveland was the largest, with a population of 92,829, followed by Milwaukee with 71,440, then Minneapolis with a population of 13,066, and St. Paul with one of 20,030.[3] Secondly, all of the cities followed roughly the same course in their patterns of growth. Each city underwent a rapid expansion in the period of great industrial boom in America, from 1870 through 1900. Just as Milwaukee and Cleveland had literally exploded in this time period, so, too, did Minneapolis and St. Paul. The former city, which for a time had been the lesser of the two, grew to become a city of 300,000 people by 1910, only about 70,000 less than Milwaukee.[4]

At yet a deeper level, the patterns of growth among all cities—here, even including Austin—essentially have been identical. All five cities have followed the same course of development by stages. Thus, for example, just as the municipal governments of Cleveland and Milwaukee became active forces for shaping their cities in the early part of the twentieth century, so the very same thing happened both to Minneapolis and St. Paul.[5] Furthermore, the parallels in the patterns of development continued well beyond this time. Just as Milwaukee and Cleveland would become landlocked by their suburbs, isolating the rich from the poor, so the same thing happened both to Minneapolis and to St. Paul. By the 1950s, both cities had reached the maximum point of their expansion and would grow no larger in terms of land area, though their suburbs would flourish. Finally, just as their Midwestern counterparts would begin to lose population by the 1960s, so the same events happened to the central cities of Minneapolis and St. Paul. Between 1950 and 1990, the central cities lost almost 200,000 people in population—not as great as Cleveland but higher than that of Milwaukee.[6]

In brief, over the course of their respective histories, the patterns of growth as well as of decline in land area and population of the Twin Cities are virtually identical to those of Cleveland and of Milwaukee. And yet, the Twin Cities appear to be vastly different. But are they truly so?

The Differences

Differences seem apparent from the very moment one sets foot in the downtown areas of these respective cities. Minneapolis and St. Paul provide livable downtowns. The Nicollet Mall area of downtown Minneapolis, for example, is a place where people can be observed walking freely, day and night. It provides a weekly farmers market in the spring and summer, an attraction for hundreds, if not thousands, of shoppers. The Minneapolis Symphony holds regular indoor and outdoor concerts for local residents during the summers—concerts that draw in a host of people. Although both Cleveland and Milwaukee have made efforts to bring people back into their downtowns, such efforts truly pale by comparison with those of Minneapolis and St. Paul. The Grand Avenue Mall, constructed in the late 1970s in downtown Milwaukee, removes people from the streets and places them in a crowded indoor area, lined mainly with small shops and youngsters in their teens. Further, while there are regular outdoor performances of concerts in downtown Milwaukee, they fail to attract the same numbers or enthusiasm of the regular pedestrian traffic as in downtown Minneapolis. Cleveland is much the same, with an array of imposing buildings, and the majestic Great Mall downtown, but furnishing nothing of the livable and comfortable amenities of either downtown Minneapolis or St. Paul. A Sunday in downtown Minneapolis during the warmer months is friendly, lively, and sociable; in Milwaukee, by contrast, it feels as though one is walking in a ghost town.

The differences stretch far below the surfaces. Downtown construction and reconstruction have been a major part of the Twin Cities, especially since the 1960s.[7] Unlike Milwaukee, which essentially destroyed its downtown by creating expressways and parking lots, along with allowing older buildings to slowly deteriorate, Minneapolis and St. Paul remade their central cities by eliminating much of the older, industrial construction. Although there are many residents of the Twin Cities who rue the loss of a number of key historic older buildings, a few buildings remain to this day, and efforts pervade the cities to reconstruct the downtown, both in terms of apartment buildings and new industrial enterprises.[8] Some of this same effort is taking place in Cleveland and Milwaukee, but on a far smaller scale and without the simultaneous encouragement of furnishing a livable and sociable central city.

Yet it is not simply within the industry and economy that one finds central differences between the Twin Cities, and their Midwestern counterparts, so alike in so many other ways. Both Cleveland and Milwaukee witnessed the social fragmentation and political division between their central cities and suburbs early in the twentieth century. Both cities tried to overcome these divisions through efforts at municipal restructuring—as in Milwaukee, for example, through an effort to create some kind of metropolitan governance structure (see Chapter 7)—but to no avail.

Minneapolis and St. Paul, however, managed to create just such a framework for governance in 1967; in this regard, they stand out among not only Midwestern cities but also among most American cities. Growing out of a period of lengthy discussion about metropolitanwide problems, a group of local citizens and legislators managed to create the Metropolitan Council in 1967, a body that is appointed by the governor of Minnesota and that serves to deal with issues of metropolitan importance.[9] Although in recent years the Metropolitan Council has not worked as well as many people would prefer, it clearly provides a basic framework for governance through which people can try to address key metropolitan issues, and is thus unlike anything that now exists in Cleveland or Milwaukee.[10]

These differences between the Twin Cities and their Midwestern counterparts, coupled with striking similarities to a city like Austin, provide us then with the rudiments of a puzzle to solve. To recapitulate: We know of the essential parallels in the course of development of all the Midwestern cities, but we must wonder why the central areas of Minneapolis and St. Paul have become so prosperous and so livable and why the region has been able to fashion a form, however effective, for metropolitan governance. *How and why, in other words, have the Twin Cities managed not to become like Cleveland and Milwaukee?*

In Search of an Explanation

The logic of the comparative analysis I use here is rather simple. If key differences in the current circumstances of the several cities are observed, we must then proceed to look for the key differences in the cities' origins—in their historical development—to identify possible sources for the differences. Having found such differences, we shall begin our search by dispensing with three popular explanations: (1) the special marketplace niche of the Twin Cities; (2) the legacy of political progressivism in the Twin Cities; and (3) the dominance of Chicago over its urban environs, especially Milwaukee.

The Twin Cities as the Market for the Upper Midwest. One of the more popular explanations for the comparative success of the Twin Cities, particularly for that of Minneapolis, in forging a livable and prosperous future for themselves has been the prominent place these cities have occupied as the major market for the Upper Midwest.[11] To be sure, this feature of the region helped to explain much of the boom and growth, especially until about the 1930s. Minneapolis possessed a hinterland that stretched as far west as Montana and as far south as South Dakota. Goods flowed back and forth between the hinterlands and Minneapolis, producing, among other things, the concentration of grains and, later, the flour industry in the Twin Cities. Firms such as Pillsbury arose here largely because of the ease with which grains could be produced and marketed in the area, along with special inventions that came about at Minneapolis plants to mill the hard spring wheat. Moreover, the Twin Cities also became a regional financial center, and Minneapolis now is the site of the Ninth Federal Reserve District.

Accordingly, some analysts therefore argue it is the special marketplace niche that the Twin Cities have occupied that has led them to be more prosperous today. But such an explanation is not very compelling. Cleveland, for example, is also the site of a Federal Reserve District, but it does not enjoy the prosperous and livable conditions of Minneapolis. Moreover, there now exist cities in the Northwest that rival the Twin Cities, among them Seattle, for example, thus further undermining the special market explanation. In addition, the marketplace, itself, has become transformed, and grain and flour no longer represent the driving vehicles of the Twin Cities' economy. In short, the special marketplace explanation simply does not work very well as an explanation in today's world to account for the special differences in life in Minneapolis and St. Paul.

The Twin Cities as the Site of Political Progressivism. There is an even more popular and widespread explanation for the success of the Twin Cities—particularly for the features of livability, a sense of community, and for the specific creation of the Metropolitan Council. Many residents have convinced themselves that the national origins of the Twin Cities' residents, together with the ideological program carved out in this Upper Midwest region, lend themselves to such novel products as the Metropolitan Council, along with such important political parties as the Democratic-Farmer-Labor (DFL) party, a party that, among other things, gave the country the strong liberal politicians Hubert H. Humphrey and Walter F. Mondale.[12]

There is much to recommend this particular explanation. Minnesota, in general, and the Twin Cities, in particular, have witnessed a number of important political innovations that simply are to be found nowhere else in America. The state, for example, regularly provides more benefits to its residents, in the way of healthcare and other services, than virtually any other state in the country. Local municipal governments also have been able to provide for the well-being of their residents in a way that is very substantial. Efforts to speak out against racial segregation also happened much earlier in the Twin Cities than elsewhere in the Midwest. In 1948, Humphrey, for example, became the first white politician to speak out forcefully against racial segregation in America.

Consequently, some analysts argue that the Twin Cities almost inevitably became the site of an inventive metropolitanwide form of governance, because in so many ways politics in the region are so very progressive. Yet, again, this argument seems to lose force if we compare the histories and outcomes in Milwaukee with those in the Twin Cities. Milwaukee is not nearly so livable a city as Minneapolis and St. Paul, and Milwaukee also was unable to put into effect some form of consolidation between its central city and its suburbs. But it was at one time the home of very progressive political ideas. As I have discussed at length earlier in this book (Chapters 3 and 4), the Social Democrats took hold in the city and made a number of efforts to provide for reform. For at least thirty years, the Social Democrats represented a very strong force in the city; indeed, Frank Zeidler was the only Socialist mayor in America by the mid-twentieth century.

In other words, the Social Democrats in Milwaukee represented as strong a force for political progressivism as the DFL party, and other elements, did in Minneapolis and St. Paul. And yet Milwaukee today is not nearly so attractive and livable a city. Thus, we must conclude that the explanation for the comparative success of the Twin Cities lies not with its political traditions, but, indeed, in other quarters.

The Dominance of Chicago. There is yet one more argument designed especially to account for the failure of Milwaukee to continue to be a growing and booming urban site as compared to Minneapolis–St. Paul. The explanation rests on the dominance achieved by Chicago as a major metropolis. The argument here is that Chicago has become so large that it simply dwarfs the city of Milwaukee as well as Milwaukee's greater environs, condemning Wisconsin's longtime rival city to be but a satellite of the larger Chicago metropolitan vicinity.

Once more this argument, as the previous two, seems to make some sense on a superficial level. Milwaukee lies only 80 miles to the north of Chicago, and many Chicagoans treat Milwaukee as though it were simply a suburb—a place to visit briefly at Summerfest or to pass through on the way to the recreational areas of northern Wisconsin. But this argument fails to account for the decline of the central city of Cleveland, which has undergone a loss of almost 400,000 residents in the past 40 years. Cleveland, of course, is seven hours by car from Chicago and thus is far out of Chicago's reach of dominance. Moreover, the argument also seems weak when we consider that in the state of Texas, cities such as Austin lie within the reach of major urban centers such as San Antonio—80 miles away—or Dallas–Fort Worth—200 miles to the north—and yet these outlying cities boom in all sorts of ways. In brief, just as the arguments about the marketplace and about political progressivism fail when we examine them critically, the argument for Chicago's dominance cannot account for the failure of Milwaukee to be a booming and thriving metropolis today.

The Real Explanation: A Causal Cluster

We have thus discovered that three popular explanations fail to account either for the current success of the Twin Cities or, obversely, for the failure of Milwaukee and of Cleveland to become viable and vital cities in a post-industrial age. What, then, can possibly account for the prosperity and livability of Minneapolis and St. Paul?

Here I want to invoke the notion of *causal clusters.* What I mean to assert is that there exists a set of forces that account for the Twin Cities' prosperity and success in establishing a metropolitan framework for governance and that these conditions are not entirely independent of one another but instead exist as a *concatenation* of causes, each only effective if it acts as a part of a cluster of causes. In other words, these forces, or conditions, each are *historically and analytically necessary to the comparative success of the Twin Cities*; and *only conjointly do they also represent the sufficient condition to have promoted that success.*

Four historical circumstances are important to account for the current viability of Minneapolis and St. Paul. The first is one that probably will come as something of a surprise. Just as industrialization clearly reshaped the social and economic landscape of Milwaukee and of Cleveland, thus producing a residue of great benefits at one time, it is the very *absence of the same degree of industrialization* that has produced the good fortune of the Twin Cities.[13] In fact, both Minneapolis and St. Paul, contrary to much conventional wisdom, have never experienced the depth and extent of industrialization as have Milwaukee and Cleveland. While there is a popular belief that all four cities experienced rapid growth because of their industrial boom periods, both the degree and kind of industrial growth in the Twin Cities were far more limited. Never the site of plants that produced heavy machinery, they also simply never witnessed the growth of a large working class in the same manner as Milwaukee or Cleveland.

Consider the percentages of people in various key occupational groupings as arrayed in Table 11.1. Observe the sharp difference between the percentages of Twin City residents in the basic blue-collar labor force of mechanics and machinists, and those in the parallel categories in Cleveland and Milwaukee. The differences hold up across two time periods, 1910 and 1930. (Other data not shown here reveal the same kind of differences both in 1890 and 1950.) In 1930, for instance, just at the peak of vitality and the onset of the Great Depression both for Cleveland and Milwaukee, the differences among the four cities are very marked: Minneapolis and St. Paul each possess three of every ten members of the labor force in blue-collar jobs, whereas almost half of the entire labor force both in Cleveland and in Milwaukee hold such jobs.

In other words, unlike both Cleveland and Milwaukee, Minneapolis and St. Paul never had to overcome the legacy of industrialization in the same manner. The labor force in the Twin Cities clearly was more diverse. There were substantially more people in white-collar jobs in the Twin Cities, thus providing the ini-

TABLE 11.1   Distribution of Labor Force by Occupations, 1910 and 1930
(in percentages; 1930 in bold)

Occupations	Cleveland		Milwaukee		Minneapolis		St. Paul		Austin
	1910	*1930*	*1910*	*1930*	*1910*	*1930*	*1910*	*1930*	*1930*
Agriculture, Forestry, & Mining	—	**1**	—	**1**	1	**1**	1	—	**2**
Clerical	9	**12**	9	**13**	10	**16**	12	**17**	**10**
Domestic & Personal Service	11	**12**	10	**9**	14	**13**	14	**13**	**23**
Manufacturing & Mechanical	51	**44**	52	**46**	37	**30**	34	**30**	**22**
Professional (including Public Service)	6	**8**	6	**9**	8	**11**	8	**11**	**17**
Transportation & Communication	9	**10**	8	**8**	12	**10**	13	**11**	**7**
Trade	13	**14**	14	**15**	18	**20**	18	**18**	**18**
Total	99	**101**	99	**101**	100	**101**	100	**100**	**99**

SOURCE: U.S. Bureau of the Census, *United States Census of the Population* (Washington, D.C., 1910), Volume 4, Table 3, and 1930, Volume 4, Tables 9 and 10.

tial foundations for an economy that would be able to adapt to a post-industrial world. In fact, it is interesting to note in Table 11.1 that the distribution of occupations in the Twin Cities was *much more akin to that of Austin than it was like either that of Cleveland or Milwaukee.*

Accordingly, the first key circumstance for the ability of the Twin Cities to arise in a post-industrial age was the absence of a substantial legacy from industrialization. This meant, among other things, that residues from the Twin City past—in terms of the nature of the labor force, the actual forms of industries, and even the age distribution of workers—would not be so difficult to overcome as those circumstances in Cleveland and Milwaukee.

The next condition that is so critical to the contemporary vitality of Minneapolis and St. Paul is one that is linked directly to the relative absence of industrialization. In terms of racial and ethnic diversity, Minneapolis and St. Paul, as the rest of Minnesota communities, simply are less diverse than either Cleveland or Milwaukee.[14] For example, in 1970, 38 percent of Cleveland's central city residents were black compared to 15 percent in Milwaukee and only 4 percent in the Twin Cities. Even today, only 8 percent of the metropolitan population of Minneapolis and St. Paul are nonwhite residents.[15] The absence of heavy industries in the region of Minneapolis and St. Paul unquestionably played a part in *not acting as an inducement* for many black migrants to enter the city at the same time as they entered in large numbers of cities such as Detroit and Chicago, about the time of World Wars I and II.[16]

This difference is a significant one, but, perhaps, not for the reasons one might immediately suppose. The Twin Cities' area has been notable for its relative degree of social harmony and consensus, a fact commonly claimed by a variety of observers.[17] One clear explanation for such consensus is the absence of racial and ethnic diversity. This social homogeneity to the region meant, then, that when the time came to discuss creating a metropolitan form of governance in the late 1960s, the divisiveness that was present in other metropolitan regions, such as Cleveland, owing to its diversity, did not present an obstacle in Minneapolis and in St. Paul.[18] Accordingly, it became more likely to reach agreements across cities and suburbs because the differences among them were not nearly so marked and sharp as in other metropolitan regions.

But if the absence of industrialization, and the concomitant absence of racial and ethnic diversity, helped to lay the foundations for such important innovations as the Metropolitan Council, they could not by themselves account for the actual vitality and prosperity present in the Twin Cities today. Two other factors, *along with the absence of industrialization and the absence of diversity,* seem to account for the unique situation of Minneapolis and St. Paul.

One of these conditions is the long-term commitment of wealthy and prosperous families to the Twin Cities' region. This has been singled out by a number of observers as a key fact.[19] But it only represents a key fact if it acts *in concert with the other conditions.* We have already observed that the presence of social alliances among the leading business families in Milwaukee failed to prevent its decline. Now we see that the commitment among leading business families, especially over a period of several generations, can act as a key for promoting a livable and successful urban environment.

Though the reconstruction of downtown Minneapolis, for example, depended on a coalition of both public and private forces, observers remember that it was the public pronouncements of people like David Dayton of Dayton-Hudson enterprises, a firm that runs and owns many American department stores, that were so crucial to reconstructing the downtown area.[20] Other accounts suggest that a number of prominent families have retained this kind of commitment to Minneapolis and St. Paul, many of them remaining as residents of the area today. This sort of loyalty to the region seems to have been essential both in promoting and in retaining key enterprises, such as Cargill, Target, and the Dayton-Hudson headquarters, as well as in fostering the view that the downtown must be a livable site—one where people can freely engage in social intercourse with one another. Lacking these same commitments, in addition to the great social and economic gaps that exist between inner-city residents and those of the suburbs, Cleveland and Milwaukee—and other cities such as Detroit and St. Louis—simply have failed to fashion the same degree of economic vitality and livability as Minneapolis and St. Paul.

There is yet one more piece of the puzzle to add here, namely, the kind of training and expert knowledge so necessary to create a workforce that can operate successfully in a post-industrial world and economy. In this respect, the Twin Cities are in many ways more similar to Austin than they are either to Milwaukee or Cleveland. For the Twin Cities are home to a substantial university—the University of Minnesota—a school that has had a strong faculty in engineering and that has produced important technological innovations in the areas of computers and other technical fields. These products, many of them produced either by the faculty at the university or by people employed in local manufacturing companies spun off from the university, such as Minnesota Mining and Manufacturing (3M) Corporation, have meant that the Twin Cities could more easily support post-industrial enterprises than either Cleveland or Milwaukee. Consider, for example, that today Minneapolis and St. Paul rank far above both Cleveland and Milwaukee in terms of the median education of their residents. According to a recent report of the Metropolitan Council, of the 25 largest metropolitan areas in the United States, Minneapolis–St. Paul rank highest in terms of the proportion of residents who have a high-school degree, whereas Milwaukee ranks 11th and Cleveland ranks 15th.[21] Further, although Milwaukee has been home to two good schools, Marquette University and the University of Wisconsin at Milwaukee, neither school has produced nor supported the kinds of research that can easily furnish successful endeavors in the local economy. Likewise, although Cleveland has become the home of both Cleveland State University and Case Western Reserve, both schools simply do not possess the same kinds of research productivity and enterprise to be found at the University of Minnesota.

Summary

I began this chapter with a puzzle and concluded it with some key observations about the conditions that have promoted the economic success and political inventiveness in the Twin Cities. Although Minneapolis and St. Paul are in some respects very much parallel to Cleveland and Milwaukee—and to a host of other industrial cities in America—in certain essential respects they also are very different. And it is these differences in the histories of the Twin Cities that seem to account for their greater viability today.

In particular, the Twin Cities of Minnesota simply never experienced the depth of industrialization that other Midwestern cities did. Thus, by a twist of fate, Minneapolis and St. Paul were better prepared than their counterparts—just as cities like Austin have been—to take advantage of life in a post-industrial age. Moreover, the relative absence of industrialization, I suggest, also meant that the lure of blue-collar industrial jobs for minority groups, especially African Americans, has not existed in Minneapolis and St. Paul to the same degree as it has in Cleveland and Milwaukee. Accordingly, the metropolitan area of the Twin Cities simply is less diverse in racial and ethnic terms than its Midwestern counterparts. Further, it therefore was easier to create the political structures that could deal with metropolitan problems in the Twin Cities than it has been to do so in cities such as Milwaukee, where both ethnic diversity and economic inequalities divide the central city from its suburbs.

Finally, I maintain that the long-term commitment of wealthy families and prosperous corporations to the Twin City area, coupled with the research and innovations available from the University of Minnesota, have furnished the building blocks on which to create the strong foundations for a post-industrial urban economy. The former condition helped to remake the downtown areas both of Minneapolis and St. Paul long before such reconstruction happened in other downtown areas—a reconstruction also made possible, of course, by the absence of divisiveness between the residents of the central city and its suburbs. The latter condition has provided a continuous flow of ideas and personnel to the construction of industries central to a post-industrial age, particularly those in electronics and other areas of high technology. In this regard, then, the Twin Cities are more akin to Austin, home of the University of Texas, than they are either to Cleveland or to Milwaukee.

My argument in this chapter about the success of the Twin Cities in the contemporary era rests on the notion that the conditions, or causes, of such success cannot easily be isolated from one another, but act in combination. The nature of this particular logic of causality, a *concatenation of circumstances,* also helps to explain why the commitment of wealthy and prosperous families has failed to revive the fortunes of downtown Milwaukee in the same degree that it has benefited the Twin Cities. Specifically, though some of the leading families, such as the Uihleins and, today, the Bradleys, did retain some commitment to the enterprises of downtown Milwaukee, there were other handicaps that the city could not so easily overcome. For example, Milwaukee faced a legacy of much deeper industrialization, hence, a much larger blue-collar workforce, and therefore it was less able to make the transition to a new age and to a new economy.

But is the set of circumstances that have made the Twin Cities so prosperous and livable today entirely unique? Can any, or all, of them be replicated in any fashion to revive the fortunes of other cities? Must Cleveland and Milwaukee remain on the outside looking in, or are there ways in which they and their residents can secure more vital and prosperous lives in the future? I turn now to consider these issues, among others, in the last chapter.

PART FOUR

Conclusion

12
Building Cities
in America

I began this analysis with a series of themes and guiding ideas adopted mainly from writings in the new urban sociology. Such writings are diverse, ranging from the neo-Marxist analyses of Joe Feagin and Mark Gottdiener to those of John Logan and Harvey Molotch. A number of common themes were to be discovered among the works of these scholars, such as the notions that the lives of cities are animated by fundamental conflict and that cities make an effort to balance demands for growth against demands for equity among their residents. These ideas proved very helpful to the historical analysis in this book and I am confident that they have helped my readers to gain special insight into the manner by which cities in America are built over time.

I also added two special themes, moving beyond the general claims of the new urban sociology. I argued that the nature of the variation among cities develops for two major reasons. One is the historical conjuncture at which cities emerge, and the other is the series of stages through which cities develop, giving evidence, in effect, of a life cycle. I further argued that history is very important to understanding the manner by which cities in America have developed. In particular, I disclosed that certain elements become inscribed into the very structure of cities, the main one in America having been the territorial boundaries that separate cities and suburbs and that have accounted for so much of the conflict in metropolitan areas.

Perhaps the major empirical discovery of this research is that cities in America do, indeed, evolve over time and that the configuration of forces that accounts for their growth—as well as their decline—varies from one stage to another. Using this principal discovery, let us review the specific details of my research.

Using Milwaukee, Wisconsin, an older industrial center, as the main case study, we observed that its history could be elaborated into a set of five stages. There was the pre-industrial period, marked by the rule of economic entrepreneurs who dominated much of the life of the city. Both full-scale political and economic in-

stitutions were absent. Next there was the industrial period, in which major transformations took place in the entire character of the city. Again entrepreneurs
dominated the city, and their efforts, through their enterprises, served to expand
the city. Eventually these efforts gave birth to a marketplace and to an array of
firms—in other words, to the institution of capitalism in the city. Again, political
institutions remained relatively weak but gained in form and influence over the
course of this period. By the end of it, municipal government, which had been
run primarily by volunteer efforts, had begun to develop in substantial respects—
from increasing professionalization of its departments to a control over substantial assets in the city.

The third period, that of the mature industrial city, represented the high point
for the development and activity of local government. Municipal government
now became the active agent in seeking to promote the growth of the city, and it
did so primarily through efforts to annex new lands to the city. Moreover, it was
in this period that the barriers grew up between the city and its suburbs, as a
number of suburbs refused to be annexed into the city, setting the stage for a long
and unending period of conflict between city and suburb. Capitalist industrial
enterprises continued to remain strong and to employ large numbers of people.
Moreover, we found in Milwaukee the emergence of a strong upper class, an alliance, in particular, among German families that knit both family and industry
closely together.

The last two periods represent stages when the city, itself, begins to decline.
There are both extra-local and local forces that precipitate the decline. The first
stage, which began during the course of the Great Depression, represented, in effect, the beginnings of the end for Milwaukee. Labor strikes divided the city
deeply, setting employer and worker against one another. Individual enterprises
began to depart the city, seeking to secure higher profits in places where there
were neither labor unions nor high local taxes. Moreover, municipal government
became reshaped in important respects. Certain needs that it previously had met
in the city, such as healthcare and other such benefits, now were shifted to both
county and federal governments. The net effect was to leave local government as
primarily responsible for securing order in the city, rather than also providing for
the welfare of local residents.

By 1950, and the inception of the substantial decline of Milwaukee, the city began to decay both in visible material ways and in terms of its own institutions.
Downtown properties in the city became old and worn-out. As properties declined, so, too, did the revenues that municipal government could secure, thereby
setting into motion a long period of dwindling resources. More and more local
enterprises also began to leave the city, seeking to secure profits more easily elsewhere. The departure of the local industries, to new sites in the South and West or
even in foreign countries, was part of the general restructuring of the American
economy that began in the 1950s and 1960s.

In addition to these changes, more and more wealthy residents sought refuge in nearby suburbs, thus further undermining the ability of local government to fund its own operations. Historically contiguous with this was the rapid influx of large numbers of minority residents, many of whom were poor. Lacking jobs, which had now left the city with the departing industries, such residents became an increasing burden on local government. Local government continued to be faced with a demand for more benefits but ever dwindling revenues with which to supply those needs.

So reads the story of Milwaukee's growth and decline. But is it simply a historical narrative, simply a telling of a story that is so much like the story of other major industrial cities in America? Here the analysis shifted from historical narrative to consider whether there were, indeed, deeper institutional imperatives at work. Specifically, we turned from considering the stages of Milwaukee's growth and decline to learning whether similar stages existed in other cities.

We first turned to consider the story of Cleveland. Cleveland seemed, at first glance, to be very similar to Milwaukee. Upon a searching examination of its own history, we made the significant discovery that there existed key parallels in Cleveland's own development. Cleveland's history, like Milwaukee's, could be seen as a series of stages in the development of the city—stages that, for all intents and purposes, paralleled the growth of institutions and their special configurations. Thus, for example, we found that Cleveland, like Milwaukee, experienced a stage of a mature industrial city. During this period, which in Cleveland, like Milwaukee, ran from 1900 to 1930, municipal government became a key actor in the life of the city. As in Milwaukee, for example, it sought to annex new lands; and, as in Milwaukee, it was successful only to a limited extent, giving birth, among other things, to divisions with its suburbs that would remain in place for decades afterward. We concluded our examination of Cleveland by drawing the inference that the general patterns we found in Milwaukee were duplicated in Cleveland and that, in general, there was important evidence for thinking of the development of cities in terms of the stages we had posited with respect to Milwaukee earlier.

Next, we considered that if our perspective on the evolution of cities by stages in America were correct, then we should find that cities that grew and expanded at an entirely different point in history should show certain parallels to the patterns of growth in Milwaukee and in Cleveland. Here we examined our argument by considering the history of Austin, Texas. Austin is representative of countless cities in the American Sunbelt that have grown in the aftermath of World War II. Significantly, in considering the story of Austin we found important parallels to the cases of both Milwaukee and Cleveland.

These parallels helped to show both what is general in the development of cities by stages in America and what is unique to Milwaukee and Cleveland, as industrial cities on the one hand, and to Austin, as a post-industrial city on the other. With regard to our general notions of stages of development of American cities, we found that Austin experienced the same first three stages of growth as Cleveland and Milwaukee. In particular, Austin's first stage of growth was dominated by entrepreneurs; its second stage was a period of rapid growth, fueled by an array of different enterprises; and its third stage was one in which local government became a key actor in the city's development, both in terms of its own internal operations and in terms of its effort to annex new lands. We thus found additional evidence for our claim that cities in America do develop in terms of stages that are characterized by certain general institutional features. Moreover and of key importance, we found that these stages develop regardless of when cities actually grow in America. Thus, this comparison gave strong evidence for our view that cities evolve in America.

However, the Austin comparison did something more for our analysis and claims. It provided some insight into the unique differences in the way that cities develop in American society by furnishing the story of a city that grew in an entirely different set of historical circumstances than Cleveland and Milwaukee. In this regard, the Austin comparison with Milwaukee and Cleveland revealed the following central differences. First, it showed that, in general, there can be different triggers for the expansion and development of American cities. In Milwaukee and Cleveland, the triggers were industrial expansion and growth. By contrast, the key trigger in Austin, as in so many Sunbelt cities that grew in the wake of World War II, was the infusion of funds from the federal government.

Second, it revealed the vast differences that exist between older industrial cities and newer post-industrial ones, the latter of whose economies rest on high-tech and service enterprises. The newer cities, in contrast to the older ones, are primarily middle-class cities. The style of politics is also radically different from the older ones, especially at a parallel stage in their development. Thus, whereas the workplace provided the locus for conflict in Milwaukee, residence and the environment provide the locus for conflict in Austin.

Third, the Austin comparison further revealed that, in effect, new cities can learn from the experience of older industrial cities. In particular, the local government of Austin managed to annex hundreds of square miles of territory adjacent to it. Its purpose in doing so was to secure greater revenues from utilities it provided to its adjacent suburbs, but also, and equally important, to avoid the same kinds of deep conflicts between city and suburb that had emerged in cities like Milwaukee and Cleveland. This discovery provided, of course, even further nuances to our view of the succession of stages by which cities in America develop, suggesting that though there is a series of such stages, later cities can improve on themselves by avoiding the mistakes of older cities.

Finally, we turned from this extended comparative analysis of Austin, Milwaukee, and Cleveland to consider the case of Minneapolis–St. Paul. In doing so, we sought to address the issue of how and why older industrial cities, such as the Twin Cities, can overcome the experience of industrial decline to become, in effect, a post-industrial city. Our comparative analysis here revealed a very central truth: namely, that Minneapolis–St. Paul never experienced the same degree of industrialization as Milwaukee and Cleveland. This difference underscored the central significance of industrialization as a phenomenon that greatly shaped and affected the futures of both Cleveland and Milwaukee. Furthermore, its very absence had a profound influence on the Twin Cities by, among other things, failing to promote as much racial and ethnic in-migration and diversity as industrialization had in older cities like Cleveland and Milwaukee. For these reasons, we argued, the Twin Cities were able to create a novel form of metropolitan governance, the Metropolitan Council. Both Milwaukee and Cleveland, beset by considerable diversity and divisiveness, between ethnic groups as well as between city and suburb, have failed to generate such a broad structure.

Our analysis of the Twin Cities further revealed that the commitment and alliance among key upper-class families, together with the presence of a major research university, helped the Twin Cities to make the transition from an older city to a newer, revitalized one in a post-industrial age. (In Milwaukee, by contrast, there seemed to be a notable absence of enlightened and aggressive leadership, particularly on issues of inequality within the city.) A number of local families, such as the Daytons, were central in the decisions to undertake a vast renewal of both downtown Minneapolis and St. Paul, as well as in the decisions to invest in new and substantial capitalist enterprises in the downtown areas. Moreover, the University of Minnesota, through its School of Engineering, among others, has helped to spawn a number of key local enterprises, among them, the 3M Corporation, which now provide the bulwark of a post-industrial economy that thrives on high-technology enterprises. In many respects, we further concluded, the Twin Cities are more akin to a Sunbelt city such as Austin than to older industrial cities such as Cleveland and Milwaukee and therefore are able to take advantage of the opportunities to reinvent themselves for a post-industrial age.

Theoretical Implications

There are a number of theoretical implications that grow out of this study. Let me begin with its ramifications for current views and theories about cities.

In most respects, this study affirms the main ideas and themes from the most recent theoretical work on American cities. By and large, the guiding ideas from this body of theoretical work provided important forms of insight into the way that American cities develop. Among other things, we learned that municipal bodies, as sovereign corporations, can exercise a considerable amount of power in determining how and when cities will grow. At some point, such bodies, in fact, become more or less autonomous and, as we learned in Milwaukee especially, they can seek to challenge certain demands even of major capitalist enterprises in the city.

But we also discovered the important way in which history and the stage of urban development shape the city. While the new urban sociology offers many important insights into how cities develop, it is of more limited help in understanding the transformation that occurs in American cities over time. For example, the growth-machine argument of Logan and Molotch, while most compelling, is limited to a rather narrow view of the history of American cities. The growth-machine argument makes it appear as though the real estate community has universally and always been the driving force for the expansion of American cities, as well as that some kind of coalition, a growth coalition, has existed to supplement this force. However, as we have obverved, the forces that actually drive the expansion and growth of American cities vary substantially from one period to another.

Thus, we have made it a special point to demonstrate that between the period of early industrialization in Cleveland and Milwaukee, and that of the mature industrial city, there was a major shift in the impetus for the expansion of the city. In the early industrialization period, economic entrepreneurs and the emerging industrial capitalist firms drove city growth by providing large numbers of jobs. In the mature industrial period, as the economic expansion itself declined, local government assumed the role for the expansion of the city, having itself become transformed into a major institutional force. Its central act in this period was to seek to annex adjacent territories, an act that had only limited success both for Cleveland and for Milwaukee and that resulted in historic barriers between the central city and the suburbs.

Although I took exception to the limitations of the arguments of human ecology, in some respects the discoveries in my work provide support for specific elements of the paradigm. A major discovery is that it is rapid population growth that drives the initial development of municipal government in the American city, not industrialization as many claim—although industrialization does exist as a trigger for rapid population growth. Thus, as the human ecologists are wont to argue, population variables do matter, even to the emergence of social and political institutions. Specifically, we found that local government assumed ever greater power and authority and became increasingly more efficient as an institution, following the rapid growth of local population and the emergence of a wide variety of immediate new needs of residents.

Beyond these conclusions, our research here, in conjunction with the insights of political economists such as R. D. Norton and Ann Markusen, may furnish the beginnings for a more powerful view of the city-building process in America. In particular, we suggest that the notion of the life cycle and development of cities in America over the course of several stages has received considerable empirical verification in our historical and comparative studies. There is a course of stages, each of which differs from both those that precede it and those that follow it, that we have found to characterize the period especially of the expansion and growth of cities. These stages are marked by a unique and distinctive set of forces that promote the growth of the city, as well as by a special configuration of those forces.

In addition, we have found that the transition from stage to stage, and, in particular, the transition from the pre-expansionist city to the expansionist city, are prompted by rapid population growth. Regardless of the trigger for such growth—whether it be the Industrial Revolution or the expansion of federal largess—the effect is to rapidly increase numbers of people in a given local area and thereby to create a host of new needs and demands upon the city. In addition, we have found that the transition from the expansionist to the mature city is to be marked especially by the increasing and central role of local government in fostering the growth of the city. This pattern of the emergence of local government as a central force happened, as we have shown, in Cleveland, Milwaukee, and Austin, cities that developed under entirely different sets of historical circumstances.

Finally, we have made discoveries that enable us to talk distinctively about American cities both in institutional and in historical terms. By having compared the development of Austin with that of Milwaukee and Cleveland, we have revealed the general institutional features that underlie the growth and development of American cities, as well as the unique historical circumstances that give special contents to each city. Here we have shown, for example, that while the development of Austin by stages shares a number of parallels in common with the growth of Milwaukee and Cleveland, Austin is also distinctive from the other two cities—as they are from Austin. Perhaps the most compelling distinction is simply the impact that industrialization had over the entire landscape of Cleveland and Milwaukee, from helping to create the barriers between city and suburb, to helping to give birth to the very nature of classes and class conflict in the two cities. Industrialization, in effect, has left a historical legacy that is hard to escape in Cleveland and Milwaukee. Both Austin and Minneapolis–St. Paul were far better positioned to take advantage of the opportunities for expansion in the current age of post-industrialism *simply because they never experienced industrialization to the same degree or extent as both Cleveland and Milwaukee.*

That we are able here to provide the beginnings of a framework to distinguish between the institutional imperatives for city growth in Milwaukee and the effects of historical conjuncture is perhaps the most central theoretical contribution of this work. Among other things, it helps to disentangle what is often confounded in simple historical narratives of the growth and decline of American cities. Historians have typically told these stories as though it were all narrative and no underlying structure. What we suggest here is that each and every American city is constituted both by the intersection of institutional development and stage, and by the historical conjuncture in which it arises. Thus, differences arise among cities because of the variability both of structural development and of specific historical circumstances. Failure to acknowledge the contribution of both sets of circumstances results not only in bad analysis but also in a limited ability to conceive of ways to refashion and to rebuild American cities, especially those like Cleveland and Milwaukee, which have been in decline.

It is to this last, most pressing of immediate matters, that we now turn.

Rebuilding Cities in America

In the events that give birth to cities in America, certain fundamental tensions arise among participants. The major one appears to be a continuing struggle between the people who endorse the effort to promote new growth at all costs and those who affirm the effort to equitably distribute the rewards from growth. As we have found at several points in the foregoing historical studies, though the forces on behalf of equality sometimes have effectively mobilized themselves, their impact on the shape of local institutions has been minimal. At best, they have produced reforms in the structure of municipal institutions, but they have made only small gains in dealing with fundamental inequalities between social classes or between races.

How might greater equality be achieved, particularly through innovations in public policies that govern cities? To make any difference at all, two central obstacles must be overcome. The first is the sharp, almost irreparable, racial and social polarization. Both in Milwaukee and in Cleveland, we find, for instance, two separate and distinct communities. One consists primarily of black and brown residents, contains the largest proportion of impoverished families, and resides primarily in the inner-city sections of the metropolitan area. The other consists primarily of white residents, resides in the suburban areas, and is generally economically well-off. Milwaukee has assumed this form over the past three decades, while in Cleveland, and in a number of other older industrial cities, the polarization of races and of classes has existed for a far longer time.

The other, but corresponding, problem confronting these cities is the great divide that lies between the suburbs and the central city. We have seen, especially in the case of Milwaukee, that this great divide opened up almost a century ago, and efforts to reduce it or simply to transcend it have failed. This same gap is also to be found in a host of other primarily northern industrial centers, such as Detroit, St. Louis, and Cleveland, among others. Perhaps the separation would not pose so many problems if there existed other governmental structures that could help to redistribute resources throughout the metropolitan area, serving to reduce the considerable inequalities that exist. But in the two cities we have examined, no such structures are to be found.

These two major facts about the older metropolitan areas of America thus confront us with the need to tailor our specific policy recommendations to address them. Much thought already has been given to these issues and how to overcome them. Analysts such as William Julius Wilson argue that the way to overcome the great differences between the people of color who reside in the inner cities and the whites who tend to cluster in the suburbs is to develop new businesses (and thus, jobs) in the inner cities. Clearly, both as Wilson's evidence has shown and as our own historical evidence has shown in Milwaukee, jobs are desperately needed to rejuvenate the lives of those who live in the inner cities. In fact, in Wisconsin, the controversial governor, Tommy Thompson, has just begun a novel effort designed to take people off the welfare rolls and to provide them with jobs within a period of two years. The burden of this effort is to substantially reduce the welfare rolls of the State of Wisconsin while at the same time reinvigorating the lives of those people who reside in the inner cities of metropolitan areas like Milwaukee.

But these problems are so vast, and they have existed for so long, that no single solution is likely to make them disappear. Moreover, the jobs that Thompson promises are not likely to show up overnight, and though they will help solve many difficulties, there are critical issues facing families and children in the inner city that also require solutions. Therefore, let us now consider several possible options for policies that might be taken to reduce the inequalities that exist.

Option 1: Metropolitan Government

In the past, the purpose of metropolitan government structures has been to provide an efficient and effective vehicle for furnishing services to people who reside in different municipalities in metropolitan areas. In the Twin Cities, for example, metropolitan government has helped in the distribution of water to and the development of transportation corridors among the various municipalities—public needs that can be easily supervised within a governance structure. As contemplated years ago in Milwaukee, the metropolitan government seemed to furnish a very helpful mechanism for meeting the common needs of metropolitan residents and doing so without necessarily jeopardizing other services that would be provided within particular localities.

Yet the effort in the 1950s and 1960s to create such metropolitan governance structures failed completely in Milwaukee and in Cleveland, as well as in many other older industrial sites. It failed precisely for the reasons we have identified in tracing the history of different municipalities—namely, that territorial jurisdiction proved so important to the residents and officials of different municipalities that officials were reluctant to relinquish any authority. Is there any reason to believe now that such structures could come into existence in places where they failed in the past or to believe that they would work to reduce inequalities?

One strong reason for seeking to implement some form of metropolitan structure is that the inequalities between the cities and the suburbs are, if anything, far greater today than they were three decades ago. Moreover, every resident suffers so long as the inequalities exist. As David Rusk, author of the notable work, *Cities Without Suburbs,* has said, when foreign investors think of Detroit, they think not of the suburbs but of the decline and the misery that lies among people of color living in the central city of Detroit.[1] Image is a large problem for everyone. But, more than that, by allowing residents of the inner cities to continue to have less— of housing, schooling, and jobs—the metropolitan area as a whole simply is losing a great sector of the population that could contribute to its vitality now and in the future. This is especially true for the children of the inner city.

Nonetheless, the creation of such a structure will face very difficult odds. As our comparative analysis sought to show, the Twin Cities were able to create such a structure two decades ago when inequalities were not nearly so marked as they are now. In addition, the Twin Cities retained a commitment both of social and of political leadership to help guide the passage of the Metropolitan Council. Cities like Milwaukee, however, have shown themselves to lack bold and imaginative leadership, and the challenges that need to be faced today are far greater than those of thirty years ago.

Officials of suburban municipalities are not likely to readily concede their authority and power, nor are city officials. There is no reason to believe that the "iron ring" of suburbs in Milwaukee has rusted, nor that parallel differences in cities like Cleveland have disappeared. But we live in different times today. Industrial jobs have fled abroad. Growing numbers of white-collar workers, especially at the middle-management level, are being lost on a daily basis as well. Various reports suggest that these losses are not temporary but that they represent major transformations of the occupational structure of America. The plight of the cities, in other words, is not simply the plight of the people of color in the central cities, but it also has become the plight of white suburban dwellers as well.

Clearly the multiple political structures that line metropolises such as Milwaukee serve only to confuse and to confound real problems. Some argue that independent municipalities make for a healthy political environment in which individuals can exercise their choice of residence by going to that area where they can optimize their living conditions.[2] But with the residents both of the central city and of the suburbs beginning to suffer in terms of lost jobs and lower incomes, it only makes sense to try to effect some kind of change that would have an influence on all residents of the metropolis. Metropolitan governments, such as the Metropolitan Council of the Twin Cities, do provide a vehicle that can keep municipal authority intact, while at the same time furnishing a means for meeting common public needs, such as water and sewage treatment. In addition, as recent efforts in Minnesota have shown, metropolitan governments also can provide vehicles through which special needs, such as subsidized housing for low-income families, might be provided in certain areas. But there exist other options, too.

Option 2: Annexation, or Consolidation

As our history of Milwaukee also demonstrates, cities have tried in the past to annex adjacent areas—or to consolidate them with the city. Frank Zeidler in Milwaukee was especially effective in the 1950s in almost doubling the size of Milwaukee through annexation. The advantage of annexation is that it eliminates the duplication of municipal authority throughout the metropolis, and it brings new industry, with its jobs and tax revenues, directly into the city. David Rusk argues that annexation and consolidation truly represent the only way for metropolitan areas today to move, and he demonstrates convincingly, in the case of cities like Indianapolis, Indiana, how consolidation proved a boon to the residents of the entire new metropolitan region.[3]

To effect such annexation, however, especially given the entrenched political interests that exist in municipalities, will prove exceedingly difficult. If suburban authorities in cities like Milwaukee are unwilling to relinquish authority to metropolitan governments, which would retain certain functions for the suburbs, imagine how they would feel if they were to disappear under some acts of annexation? And yet annexation has much to recommend it. It concentrates political authority in the hands of relatively few structures, permits decisions to be made about the future of an entire region without having to take into account the problems created by multiple taxing authorities, and allows political officials to concentrate their efforts to improve the metropolitan area through such strategies as providing certain inducements to new business.

Most of all, I believe, the advantage of annexation or consolidation is that it rids a metropolitan area of the inequalities that exist when suburbs and city lie side by side. Such inequalities are currently built into the metropolis in the form of property taxes, which furnish much of the public revenue for schools. Suburban and inner-city schools differ mainly today precisely because the suburbs have had an abundance of public revenues, secured through the property tax, to target to education, while inner-city schools, suffering an ever diminishing amount of revenues, have been left to languish. State aid, as found in states like Wisconsin, has helped to remedy the situation. But so long as property tax continues to be tagged to municipality, the inequities are likely to continue. Consolidation, or annexation, would effectively eliminate such policies.

Various cities have begun a serious effort to consider annexation, or consolidation. Memphis, Tennessee, for example, has undertaken such an effort in the hope to avoid the kinds of problems that are produced with countless municipalities littering metropolitan areas.[4] But in light of the time, and the many authorities that in the past have approved municipal autonomy in places like Wisconsin—including, we shall repeat, the affirmation by the state supreme court—the effort to annex adjacent suburbs is likely to require considerable political muscle. In the end, however, it might be well worth it.

Option 3: State Policies

A third major option is to pursue policies principally at the state level. Governor Thompson of Wisconsin, for example, has been very aggressive in coming up with new initiatives designed to remedy problems in cities like Milwaukee. His policy designed to take people off the welfare rolls is only one such example. Yet Thompson has angered a number of people because his underlying position condemns the impoverished citizens of Milwaukee rather than appropriately targeting the sorry state of Milwaukee and Wisconsin institutions.

But such policies require considerable imagination and need to take into account the host of problems that exist in metropolitan areas like Milwaukee and Cleveland. One of the most serious, I believe, is the vast disparity in the funding that has existed for schools in the suburbs and those in the cities. Schools represent the very heart of our future. To the extent that we fail to provide adequate funding for schools, we effectively shortchange our children and how they will be able to lead their lives. Though we may understand the roots of the social, political, and economic polarization that exist in many cities, such as Milwaukee and Cleveland, we should not permit them to furnish an excuse for callously abandoning our future and that of our children.

There are likely to be a variety of efforts that can happen at the state level. Dawn Clark Netsch, Democratic candidate for governor of Illinois in 1994, has provided a very imaginative plan that would increase the state income tax, reduce the local property tax, and provide public revenues *exclusively targeted* for public education. Although her plan has drawn much criticism, she has been willing to confront head-on a major problem that exists not only in Illinois, but in a host of other states, including those of Wisconsin and Ohio. Such a tax would provide considerable revenues that could be distributed throughout the many school districts of the state, and it would do so in such a way as to avoid the great disparities created by tagging school funding to local property taxes. The State of Michigan also has recently passed a measure that will effectively do the same thing. Other states, such as Texas, though inclined to enact such laws, have proven politically unable to come up with appropriate legislation.

There are both advantages and disadvantages of any initiatives taken at the state level. The main advantage is that such policies would create the largest bank of public revenues and thus would provide a flow of funds that could be distributed throughout the various legislative areas of a state. In addition, state initiatives also enable local municipalities to remain intact and to take independent initiatives that they believe are in their own best interests. But, unless there are certain limits placed on the powers of local municipalities, many of the problems of the past, such as competing authorities and petty squabbling, are likely to remain.

Newer Post-Industrial Cities

It is not only among the older industrial cities that problems are to be found. Even among the rapidly growing, post-industrial cities, such as Austin, there are important issues that remain to be resolved. Here let me briefly conclude my analysis by discussing two of them.

Problem 1: Balancing Growth and Equity

The kinds of problems faced today by post-industrial cities in the South and West are the sort of problems faced decades ago by cities such as Milwaukee and Cleveland. Growth of the population, essentially, has gotten out of hand. Instead of decline, especially at the inner core of the city, these metropolitan regions face the problem of how to limit growth, and, more especially, of how to balance explosive growth with the issue of equality among the population.

What has happened in places like Austin is that some groups have profited more from the growth, particularly of the addition of new land developments, than other people. The big winners here are the developers and, of course, city governments, inasmuch as they manage to bring in new revenues and new lands over which they can exercise their control. But there are big losers in this process as well. In particular, many neighborhood groups, which have formed to limit growth and development, have proven unable to prevent the real estate community from coming into their areas, rezoning them, and then constructing vast new housing developments.

In addition to these problems, there are the issues of how to handle the explosive growth. Rapid new populations create massive new traffic jams, prove difficult for the transportation systems to solve, and overextend utilities, such as sewer lines and the like. Moreover, often the jobs that are promised by virtue of the new growth of industry are not available to everyone equally. In cities like Austin, for example, the kinds of jobs created by the new high-technology industry mainly bring in white-collar work and do not provide ready employment for people of color, especially those with more limited training and education.

Obviously, the issues here seem less pressing, simply because there is a continuous supply of new resources. But issues of equity remain and are likely to be most effectively solved by initiatives taken by state officials rather than by local officials.

Problem 2: Anticipating Decline

Perhaps one of the most important discoveries to emerge from this research is that cities do, indeed, seem to go through cycles of growth and of decline. Thus, although many of the newer cities, in Texas, Florida, and Utah, among other states, today seem to face rosy futures, their decline awaits them just around the corner. Moreover, though this decline may be tied very much to the fates and fortunes of industry, it really has ramifications that flow throughout the community.

It is imperative, therefore, that such growing cities anticipate declines today and prepare for them. Ann Markusen, in her remarkable book on profit cycles, argues that such cities need to stay one step ahead of decline by constantly recruiting enterprises in new and growing industries.[5] But clearly they must do other things as well. The most essential act is to plan for the inevitable local decline and to anticipate substantial job losses, particularly among the older population.

The experience of many such local governments has been that, however hard "planning departments" work, they rarely, if ever, seem able to effectively forecast or to shape the future. But if they plan far enough ahead, recognizing that the problems faced by the inner cities of older northern industrial sites are apt to become their problems someday, they can act accordingly. Among other things, they need to expand and to conserve public revenues as effectively as possible to be able to ward off the likely drain on public resources that will occur when a larger proportion of their residents face unemployment. This calls for making local municipal governments even more effective instruments for local action than they are at present. While the most successful among these governments, such as that in Austin, already have taken important steps to annex adjacent territories, there are other important acts for them to take.

Such acts would include steps to increase local investment in education and schooling, particularly for the people of color, so as to avoid the vast disparities that have emerged in places like Milwaukee and Cleveland. The experience of these latter two cities should indicate that if a large section of the local population is left out of major decisions, its handicaps will become handicaps for the entire community simply because it creates such a drain and demand on local revenues. At the same time, other efforts must be taken to ensure that the investment in local services is such that they can continue to meet the needs of the local population. Among other things, such initiatives might consider ways to create suitable partnerships with private firms and corporations. By heeding the lessons of Milwaukee, the architects of city-building in America may reinvent the discipline and rejuvenate our aging cities.

Notes

Chapter 2

1. Some of the ideas I discuss here were previously examined in two other articles I wrote about cities: Anthony M. Orum, "City Politics and City Growth," in Richard G. Braungart (ed.), *Research in Political Sociology*, Volume 3 (Greenwich, CT: JAI Press, 1987), pp. 223–244; and Anthony M. Orum, "Apprehending the City: The View from Above, Below and Behind," *Urban Affairs Quarterly*, Volume 26, Number 4 (June 1991), pp. 589–609.

2. My italics. Mark Gottdiener, *The New Urban Sociology* (New York: McGraw Hill, 1994), p. 4. Also see Mark Gottdiener and A. Lagopoulos, *The City and the Sign: Introduction to Urban Semiotics* (New York: Columbia University Press, 1986).

3. John R. Logan and Harvey L. Molotch, *Urban Fortunes: The Political Economy of Place* (Berkeley: University of California Press, 1987), p. 17. At present, this award-winning work is perhaps the best comprehensive work on the nature and dynamics of the American city.

4. For an interesting work on the Chicago school and its influence, see Martin Bulmer, *The Chicago School of Sociology: Institutionalization, Diversity and the Rise of Sociological Research* (Chicago: University of Chicago Press, 1984).

5. Robert E. Park, "Human Ecology," *American Journal of Sociology* 42 (July 1936), pp. 1–15; and Louis Wirth, "Human Ecology," *American Journal of Sociology* 50 (May 1945), pp. 483–488.

6. Park, "Human Ecology," p. 1–15.

7. Park wrote: "The fact seems to be then, that human society, as distinguished from plant and animal society, is organized on two levels, the biotic and the cultural. There is a symbiotic society based in competition and a cultural society based on communication and consensus" (ibid., p. 13).

8. Frederic Thrasher, *The Gang* (Chicago: University of Chicago Press, 1927); Clifford S. Shaw, *The Jackroller* (Chicago: University of Chicago Press, 1930); Louis Wirth, *The Ghetto* (Chicago: University of Chicago Press, 1928); Nels Anderson, *The Hobo* (Chicago: University of Chicago Press, 1923); and Walter P. Reckless, "The Distribution of Commercialized Vice in the City: A Sociological Analysis," *Publications of the American Sociological Society* 20 (1926), pp. 164–176.

9. Gottdiener, *The New Urban Sociology*, p.114.

10. Ernest W. Burgess, "The Growth of the City: An Introduction to a Research Project," in Robert E. Park, Ernest W. Burgess, and R. D. McKenzie (eds.), *The City* (Chicago: University of Chicago Press, 1925), pp. 47–62.

11. Ibid., p. 61.

12. Ibid., p. 50.

13. Louis Wirth, "Urbanism as a Way of Life," *American Journal of Sociology* 44 (January 1938), pp. 1–24.

14. For an excellent treatment of this article, plus many other facets of social theory about the city, see Peter Saunders, *Social Theory and the Urban Question* (New York: Holmes & Meier Publishers, 1981), chapter 3. Gottdiener *(The New Urban Sociology,* chapter 6) also contains a very thoughtful discussion of this work along with the other writings of the Chicago school.

15. Wirth, "Urbanism," p. 22.

16. See the various articles contained in George A. Theodorson (ed.), *Studies in Human Ecology* (Evanston: Row, Peterson and Company, 1961), especially parts 2 and 3.

17. Amos Hawley, *Human Ecology* (New York: Ronald Press, 1950).

18. Walter Firey, "Sentiment and Symbolism as Ecological Variables," *American Sociological Review* 10 (April 1945), pp. 140–148.

19. See, for example, Louis Althusser and Etienne Balibar, *Reading Capital* (London: Verso, 1979), translated from the French by Ben Brewster.

20. Manuel Castells, *The Urban Question: A Marxist Approach* (Cambridge, Mass.: MIT Press, 1977); originally published as *La Question Urbaine* (Paris: François Maspero, 1972), especially chapter 8. Another excellent treatment of some of the same themes that appeared in Castells's work is that of Michael P. Smith, *The City and Social Theory* (New York: St. Martin's Press, 1979), especially chapter 6. Also, a very incisive discussion of Castells's work is included in Saunders, *Social Theory and the Urban Question,* especially chapters 5 and 6.

21. Castells, *The Urban Question,* chapter 9 and afterword, 1975.

22. David Harvey, *Social Justice and the City* (Baltimore: Johns Hopkins University Press, 1973). The introductory chapter is most fascinating in the manner in which it portrays Harvey's intellectual odyssey, an adventure that took him from an initial obligation to a liberal democratic stance to absolute conviction in the radical ideas of Marx.

23. Ibid., chapter 5. For the original discussion on *exchange value* and *use value* in Marx, see Karl Marx, *Capital,* Volume 1 (Moscow: Foreign Language Publishing House, 1961), chapters 1 (Commodities) and 2 (Exchange).

24. Ibid., p. 159.

25. See, for example, David Harvey, *Consciousness and the Urban Experience: Studies in the History and Theory of Capitalist Urbanization* (Baltimore: Johns Hopkins University Press, 1985).

26. In this regard, Molotch's claims not only challenged the arguments of the human ecologists, but they also challenged the reigning paradigm about American politics at the time, that of pluralism found in the writings of Robert Dahl. Dahl had insisted that local politics was an arena in which various interests could be mobilized and in which numbers of actors could freely exercise their influence over political outcomes. See Robert Dahl, *Who Governs?* (New Haven: Yale University Press, 1961); Harvey Molotch, "The City as a Growth Machine," Volume 82 (May 1976), pp. 309–332.

27. Ibid., p. 314.

28. For further elaboration on some of these themes, see my article on "City Growth and City Politics."

29. Logan and Molotch, *Urban Fortunes.*

30. Ibid., chapter 2 et infra.

31. Mark Gottdiener, *The New Urban Sociology;* Mark Gottdiener and Joe R. Feagin, "The Paradigm Shift in Urban Sociology," *Urban Affairs Quarterly,* Volume 24, Number 2

(December 1988), pp. 163–187; and David A. Smith and Michael T. Timberlake, "The New Urban Sociology," in J. John Palen, *The Urban World* (New York: McGraw Hill, 1992, 4th edition), pp. 339–356.

32. Susan Fainstein, "Local Mobilization and Economic Discontent," in Michael Peter Smith and Joe R. Feagin (eds.), *The Capitalist City: Global Restructuring and Community Politics* (Oxford and New York: Basil Blackwell, 1987), p. 335.

33. Logan and Molotch, *Urban Fortunes,* chapter 3.

34. Gottdiener, *The New Urban Sociology,* chapter 1; and Mark Gottdiener, *The Social Production of Urban Space* (Austin: The University of Texas Press, 1985).

35. Harvey, *Consciousness and the Urban Experience,* chapter 2.

36. Joe R. Feagin, *Free Enterprise City: Houston in Political and Economic Perspective* (New Brunswick, N.J.: Rutgers University Press, 1988), pp. 28–30 and chapter 7. Also see Joe R. Feagin and Robert Parker, *Building American Cities: The Urban Real Estate Game,* 2nd ed. (Englewood Cliffs, N.J.: Prentice-Hall, 1990).

37. Harvey, *Social Justice and the City;* and Burgess, "The Growth of the City."

38. Molotch, "The City as a Growth Machine," p. 310.

39. See, for example, Feagin, *Free Enterprise City.*

40. One of the most helpful works that I have read on the issue of Marxist writings on the city is by Ira Katznelson, *Marxism and the City* (Oxford: Clarendon Press, 1992). This surely represents one of the most thoughtful and intelligent renderings of the city among all recent writings.

41. Raymond Pahl, *Whose City?* 2nd ed. (Harmondsworth, Middlesex, England: Penguin Books, 1975); and R. E. Pahl, "Managers, Technical Experts and the State: Forms of Mediation, Manipulation and Dominance in Urban and Regional Development," in Michael Harloe (ed.), *Captive Cities* (London: John Wiley & Sons, 1977), pp. 49–60.

42. Desmond King, "The State, Capital and Urban Change in Britain," in Smith and Feagin (eds.), *The Capitalist City,* pp. 215–236; also, for relevant work on the United States, see Ted Robert Gurr and Desmond King, *The State and the City* (London: Macmillan, 1987).

43. Feagin, *Free Enterprise City,* chapter 6.

44. There are some urbanists who are particularly appreciative of the role of timing and how it figures into the city-building process. John Mollenkopf, a political scientist, is instructive on how both federal and local governments became key actors in shaping American cities during and after the New Deal. See his *The Contested City* (Princeton: Princeton University Press, 1983). Yet there are others who seem to think that the nature of city-building is virtually untouched by historical variation and change. See, for example, Paul E. Peterson, *City Limits* (Chicago: University of Chicago Press, 1981).

45. Saskia Sassen, *Cities in a World Economy* (Thousand Oaks, Calif.: Pine Forge Press, 1994); also see Saskia Sassen, *The Global City: New York, London, Tokyo* (Princeton: Princeton University Press, 1991), as well as Smith and Feagin (eds.), *The Capitalist City.*

46. Richard Wade, *The Urban Frontier: The Rise of Western Cities,* 1790–1830 (Cambridge, Mass.: Harvard University Press, 1959). Also see Charles N. Glaab, "Visions of Metropolis: William Gilpin and Theories of City Growth in the American West," *Wisconsin Magazine of History* 45 (1961), pp. 21–31.

47. William Cronon, *Nature's Metropolis: Chicago and the Great West* (New York: W. W. Norton, 1991). This work truly is one of the modern historical masterpieces on the American city.

48. Castells, *The Urban Question.*

49. Castells, *The City and the Grassroots* (Berkeley: University of California Press, 1983). I found the discussion in Katznelson on these matters especially helpful and illuminating; see Katznelson, *Marxism and the City,* especially chapter 3. Moreover, as Gottdiener and Feagin observe, "the new critical sociologists ... (take) ... agency seriously by highlighting how powerful actors operate in the urban development process in the manner that does not simply follow some structural imperative or system logic" ("The Paradigm Shift in Urban Sociology," p. 310).

50. See, for example, Logan and Molotch, *Urban Fortunes,* pp. 29–31.

51. Susan Fainstein and Norman Fainstein, *Urban Political Movements* (Englewood Cliffs, N.J.: Prentice-Hall, 1974). Also see Castells, *The City and the Grassroots,* for a number of vivid illustrations, as well as Matthew Crenson, *Neighborhood Politics* (Cambridge, Mass.: Harvard University Press, 1983), for more specific detail on how such groups are organized and how they operate in one urban setting.

52. Logan and Molotch, *Urban Fortunes,* chapter 3.

53. Clarence N. Stone, *Regime Politics: Governing Atlanta, 1946–1988* (Lawrence: University of Kansas Press, 1989).

54. Orum, "Apprehending the City."

55. Eric Monkkonen, *America Becomes Urban: The Development of U.S. Cities and Towns, 1780–1980* (Berkeley and Los Angeles: University of California Press, 1988), p. 236.

56. Feagin, in fact, is particularly alert to these possibilities, which accounts for his emphasis on the second circuit of capitalism in urban growth as opposed to emphasizing the primary circuit, that of industrial capitalism. Personal communication, February 1994.

57. Mollenkopf, *The Contested City.*

58. Anthony M. Orum, *Power, Money and the People: The Making of Modern Austin* (Austin: Texas Monthly Press, 1987), pp. 308–309.

59. Castells, *The City and the Grassroots.*

60. Also see Orum, "City Politics and City Growth."

61. Feagin, *Free Enterprise City,* chapter 8.

62. Gregory D. Squires, Larry Bennett, Kathleen McCourt, and Philip Nyden, *Chicago: Race, Class and the Response to Urban Decline* (Philadelphia: Temple University Press, 1987), especially chapter 6; Joe T. Darden, Richard Child Hill, June Thomas, and Richard Thomas, *Detroit: Race and Uneven Development* (Philadelphia: Temple University Press, 1987); and Carolyn Adams, David Bartelt, David Elesh, Ira Goldstein, Nancy Kleniewski, and William Yancey, *Philadelphia: Neighborhoods, Division, and Conflict in a Postindustrial City* (Philadelphia: Temple University Press, 1991), especially chapter 4.

63. Todd Swanstrom, *The Crisis of Growth Politics: Cleveland, Kucinich, and the Challenge of Urban Populism* (Philadelphia: Temple University Press, 1985), p. 117. Also see Clarence Stone, *Regime Politics,* chapter 10.

64. Ira Katznelson, *City Trenches* (New York: Pantheon, 1981).

65. Barry Bluestone and Bennett Harrison, *The Deindustrialization of America: Plant Closings, Community Abandonment and the Dismantling of Basic Industries* (New York: Basic Books, 1982).

66. See the relevant discussion in W. Parker Frisbie and John Kasarda, "Spatial Processes," in Neil J. Smelser (ed.), *Handbook of Sociology* (Newbury Park, Calif.: Sage Publishers, 1988), pp. 629–666.

67. Logan and Molotch, *Urban Fortunes,* pp. 52–57. It is notable that these analysts, while in many respects absolutely original and thoroughgoing in their pathbreaking work, only devote a matter of about five pages to the history of growth politics in America.

68. R. D. Norton, *City Life-Cycles and American Urban Policy* (New York: Academic Press, 1979).

69. Ann Roell Markusen, *Profit Cycles, Oligopoly, and Regional Development* (Cambridge, Mass.: MIT Press, 1985), especially chapter 3.

70. Ibid., p. 291.

71. Kenneth T. Jackson, *Crabgrass Frontier: The Suburbanization of the United States* (New York: Oxford University Press, 1985). Also see the excellent essay on suburbs in America by Michael Ebner in Howard Gillette, Jr., and Zane L. Miller (eds.), *American Urbanism: A Historiographical Review* (New York: Greenwood Press, 1987), chapter 10.

72. Jon C. Teaford, *The Unheralded Triumph: City Government in America, 1870–1900* (Baltimore: Johns Hopkins University Press, 1984).

Chapter 3

1. James S. Buck, "Reminiscences: 1875," excerpted in Frank Flower, *History of Milwaukee, Wisconsin, from Pre-Historic Times to the Present Date* (Chicago: Western Historical Company, 1881), p. 105.

2. One older history suggests some question about Josette's origins but then goes on to claim she was mainly Menomonee. See John G. Gregory, *History of Milwaukee, Wisconsin,* Volume 1 (Chicago/Milwaukee: S. J. Clarke Publishing, 1931), p. 130.

3. For an excellent piece on Martin and Juneau and their relationship, see Barbara Whalen, "The Lawyer and the Fur Trader: Morgan Martin and Solomon Juneau," *Milwaukee History: The Magazine of the Milwaukee County Historical Society,* Volume 11, Number 1 (Spring–Summer 1988), pp. 17–32.

4. Solomon Juneau to Morgan Martin, December 1, 1833, written by Albert Fowler. Solomon Juneau Papers, Milwaukee County Historical Society.

5. Albert Fowler to Morgan Martin, December 13, 1834. Solomon Juneau Papers, Milwaukee County Historical Society.

6. James S. Buck, *Pioneer History of Milwaukee from the First American Settlement in 1833, to 1841, with a Topographical Description, as It Appeared in a State of Nature* (Milwaukee: Swain & Tate Printers, 1890), pp. 284–285.

7. Byron Kilbourn to Micajah Williams, February 27, 1837. Reprinted in John G. Gregory, *History of Milwaukee, Wisconsin,* Volume 1 (Chicago/Milwaukee: S. J. Clarke Publishing, 1931), pp. 126–28.

8. Alexander F. Pratt, "Reminiscence," in Frank Flower, *History of Milwaukee, Wisconsin,* p. 167.

9. Silas Chapman, "Pioneer Land Speculation in Milwaukee." Read before the Old Settlers' Club, December 5, 1893; in *Early Milwaukee: Papers from the Archives of the Old Settlers' Club of Milwaukee County* (Milwaukee: The Old Settler's Club, 1916), pp. 25–27.

10. Flower, *History of Milwaukee,* p. 166 et passim.

11. Russell Austin, "Solomon Juneau," August 9, 1949. Unidentified newspaper article. Solomon Juneau Papers, Milwaukee County Historical Society.

12. Indenture contract between Solomon Juneau and Josette Juneau, and Morgan Martin, December 1, 1835; and letter from Solomon Juneau to Morgan Martin, March 31, 1836. Solomon Juneau Papers, Milwaukee County Historical Society.

13. Letter from Daniel Wells, Jr., to Jacob H. Kimball, Green Bay, Wisconsin, August 30, 1835. Daniel Wells, Jr., Papers, Milwaukee County Historical Society.

14. Buck, *Pioneer History of Milwaukee*, pp. 76–78; letter from Daniel Wells, Jr., to Jacob Kimball, Green Bay, August 30, 1835. Daniel Wells, Jr., Papers, Milwaukee County Historical Society.

15. Wells's papers at the Milwaukee County Historical Society consist of a large number of notes and certificates of property, indicating a vast range of holdings. What is perhaps further notable, as well as a sharp indication of the man's personality, is that his own personal letters, even those drafted approximately during this period, rarely give any sign of feelings or emotion. Most of his letters instead are very straightforward, and some, to his brother, suggest that he was a man whom today we would call "all business."

16. Stanley Mallach, "Alexander Mitchell: Business Stories from Wisconsin's Past," in *Investor: Wisconsin's Business Magazine*, Volume 6, Number 6 (August 1975), pp. 27–29; and Alice E. Smith, "Banking Without Banks: George Smith and the Wisconsin Marine and Fire Insurance Company," *Wisconsin Magazine of History*, Volume 48, Number 4 (Summer 1965), pp. 268–281.

17. Buck, *Pioneer History of Milwaukee*, pp. 256–293; and Smith, "Banking Without Banks."

18. Matt Clohisy, "History of the Wells Family in Wisconsin, 1835–1919" (unpublished manuscript, circa 1934). Daniel Wells, Jr., Papers, Milwaukee County Historical Society, chapter 3, p. 1.

19. Daniel R. Madden, "City-State Relations in Wisconsin, 1835–1901: The Origins of the Milwaukee Home Rule Movement" (Ph.D. thesis, University of Wisconsin–Madison, Department of History, 1972), p. 14.

20. Letter from Daniel Wells, Jr., to Jacob Kimball, Green Bay, August 30, 1835. Daniel Wells, Jr., Papers, Milwaukee County Historical Society.

21. Richard Wade, *The Urban Frontier: The Rise of Western Cities, 1790–1830* (Cambridge, Mass.: Harvard University Press, 1959).

22. Edward D. Holton, "Commercial History of Milwaukee," November 22, 1858. Speech delivered at the Chamber of Commerce of Milwaukee. Reprinted in *Collections of the State Historical Society of Wisconsin*, Volume 4 (Madison State Historical Society of Wisconsin, 1906), pp. 253–284.

23. Eric Reinelt, "Early Grain Trading in Milwaukee," *Milwaukee History: The Magazine of the Milwaukee County Historical Society*, Volume 9, Number 1 (Spring 1986), p. 26.

24. Reinelt, "Early Grain Trading in Milwaukee," pp. 24–32.

25. On lake tonnage of various ports between 1860 and 1870, see *Thirteenth Annual Statement of the Trade and Commerce of Milwaukee, for the Year Ending December 31, 1870*, compiled by William J. Langson, secretary (Milwaukee: Evening Wisconsin Printing House, 1871), p. 64.

26. Margaret Walsh, *The Manufacturing Frontier: Pioneer Industry in Antebellum Wisconsin, 1830–1860* (Madison: State Historical Society of Wisconsin, 1972), chapter 7.

27. *Compendium of the Seventh United States Census* (Washington, D.C.: Bureau of the Census, 1850), p. 337; and *Eighth Census of the United States* (Washington, D.C.: Bureau of the Census, 1860), "Manufactures, Milwaukee County," pp. 648–649.

28. *Eighth Census of the United States*, pp. 648–649.

29. *Thirty-Fourth Annual Report of the Trade and Commerce of Milwaukee, Year Ending December 31, 1891* (Milwaukee: Milwaukee Chamber of Commerce, 1892), pp. 33, 73, 92, 94, and 97.

30. Ibid.

31. *Thirteenth Annual Statement of the Trade and Commerce of Milwaukee, for the Year Ending December 31, 1870*, pp. 15–16.

32. Walsh, *The Manufacturing Frontier*, chapter 7; and Robert C. Nesbit, *Wisconsin: A History* (Madison: University of Wisconsin Press, 1973), part 4.

33. Charles A. Beard, *An Economic Interpretation of the Constitution of the United States* (New York: Free Press, 1965). Originally published 1935.

34. Laurence Larson, "A Financial and Administrative History of Milwaukee," *Bulletin of the University of Wisconsin* (Madison), Number 242 (June 1908), p. 15.

35. Buck, *Pioneer History of Milwaukee*, p. 41.

36. Excerpt from "McLeod's History of Wiskonsan, 1842–43," in Flower, *History of Milwaukee, Wisconsin*, p. 190.

37. Flower, *History of Milwaukee, Wisconsin*, p. 169.

38. Madden, *City-State Relations in Wisconsin*, p. 24.

39. Buck, *Pioneer History of Milwaukee*, p. 289.

40. For an excellent work on the whole subject of city-state relations involving Milwaukee and Wisconsin, see Madden, *City-State Relations in Wisconsin*.

41. See, for example, Madden, *City-State Relations in Wisconsin*, pp. 47–64; and Nesbit, *Wisconsin: A History*, pp. 201–202.

42. Clohisy, *History of the Wells Family*, chapter 4, pp. 11–12.

43. See, for example, Bayrd Still, *Milwaukee: The History of a City* (Madison: State Historical Society of Wisconsin, 1948).

44. "Rules and Regulations," Milwaukee County, March 13, 1837, photocopy.

45. Buck, *Pioneer History of Milwaukee*, p. 282.

46. On the importance of this general theme, see Still, *Milwaukee: The History of a City*, especially chapter 10. Still writes of this phenomenon in Milwaukee as follows: "Throughout the fifties the city's leading businessmen continued to participate in the fire-fighting function and the volunteer fire companies to be supported by civic subscriptions as well as public funds. The roster of a sack company, organized in September 1851, constituted a list of the city's most 'solid citizens.' ... The members of the company, each vested with the powers of a special constable, were to act as special police at all fires, carrying white canvas sacks and staves and taking charge of exposed property. In 1853, a Chicagoan contrasted the fire departments of the cities in the East with that of Milwaukee where 'the best citizens and most respectable business men are members.'" (p. 234)

47. Flower, *History of Milwaukee, Wisconsin*, pp. 346–347.

48. Sam Bass Warner, Jr., *The Private City: Philadelphia in Three Periods of Its Growth* (Philadelphia: University of Pennsylvania Press, 1968).

49. Holton, "Commercial History of Wisconsin," p. 272.

50. Ibid.

51. Flower, *History of Milwaukee, Wisconsin*, p. 504.

52. I have reconstructed the episode of the Bridge War from several historical documents, none of which seem to precisely agree with one another. Thus, I have had to piece together a story, making the best possible sense out of disagreements over some of the ac-

tual facts. These documents include John G. Gregory, *History of Milwaukee, Wisconsin,* Volume 1, chapter 9; Flower, *History of Milwaukee, Wisconsin,* chapter 16; and the address of Holton on the "Commercial History of Milwaukee."

53. Robert R. Dykstra, *The Cattle Towns* (New York: Atheneum, 1970).

54. See an excellent discussion of this topic in Carl Abbott, "Frontiers and Sections: Cities and Regions in American Growth," in Howard Gillette, Jr., and Zane L. Miller (eds.), *American Urbanism: A Historiographical Review* (New York: Greenwood Press, 1987), chapter 13.

55. John G. Gregory writes the following of Kilbourn: "Having in mind at the beginning the idea of improving communication between Lake Michigan and [the] Mississippi [River], it was natural that Mr. Kilbourn's main concern should be the acquisition of land on the west side of the river, commanding the spot for the opening of the projected canal. Compelled eventually to abandon the canal project, he found consolation in the fact that incidentally it had supplied a water-power stimulating the establishment of manufactures in Milwaukee. For the improvement of transportation, railroads would be superior to canals, and now he concentrated his energies upon railroads. ... Byron Kilbourn's indomitable energy in the promotion of early railroad-building is remembered as an outstanding factor in the making of Milwaukee." Gregory, *History of Milwaukee, Wisconsin,* Volume 1, p. 140.

56. Herbert William Rice, "Early History of the Chicago, Milwaukee and St. Paul Railway Company" (Ph.D. thesis, University of Iowa, Department of History, 1938), especially pp. 15–19.

57. James Seville, "Milwaukee's First Railway," in *Early Milwaukee: Papers from the Archives of the Old Settlers' Club of Milwaukee County* (Milwaukee: The Old Settlers' Club, 1916), pp. 88–100.

58. Seville, "Milwaukee's First Railway," p. 95.

59. On the history of railroads in and about Milwaukee, see Rice, "Early History of the Chicago, Milwaukee and St. Paul Railway Company," and Gregory, *History of Milwaukee, Wisconsin,* Volume 1, chapter 16.

60. Rice, "Early History of the Chicago, Milwaukee and St. Paul Railway Company," and Gregory, *History of Milwaukee, Wisconsin,* Volume 1, chapter 2.

61. Rice, "Early History of the Chicago, Milwaukee and St. Paul Railway Company"; Gregory, *History of Milwaukee, Wisconsin,* Volume 1, chapter 5; and Nesbit, *Wisconsin: A History,* pp. 200–206.

62. Rice, "Early History of the Chicago, Milwaukee and St. Paul Railway Company," and Gregory, *History of Milwaukee, Wisconsin,* Volume 1, chapter 2.

63. Nesbit, *Wisconsin: A History,* p. 314.

64. Ibid., chapter 21, and Mallach, "Alexander Mitchell."

65. Mallach, "Alexander Mitchell," pp. 33–34.

66. There are differences in the reports on these numbers. Mallach writes that Mitchell held control to more than 2,400 miles, of which 1,000 were in Wisconsin; Nesbit cites a different set of figures. See Mallach, "Alexander Mitchell," and Nesbit, *Wisconsin: A History,* chapter 21.

67. As quoted in Rice, "Early History of the Chicago, Milwaukee and St. Paul Railway Company," p. 190.

Chapter 4

1. William George Bruce (ed.), *History of Milwaukee City and County* (Chicago/Milwaukee: S. J. Clarke Publishing, 1922), Volume 1, p. 237.

2. W. J. Anderson and Julius Bleyer (eds.), *Milwaukee's Great Industries* (Milwaukee: Association for the Advancement of Milwaukee, 1892), p. 102.

3. This layered social morphology to the city is evident to many urban scholars and has given rise to a special metaphor—that of the city as a "palimpsest."

4. *Sixteenth Annual Report of the Trade and Commerce of Milwaukee, for the Year Ending December 31, 1873* (Milwaukee: Milwaukee Chamber of Commerce, 1874), p. 87

5. *Twenty-Third Annual Report of the Trade and Commerce of Milwaukee, for the Year Ending December 31, 1880* (Milwaukee: Milwaukee Chamber of Commerce, 1881), p. 105.

6. *United States Census of Manufactures* (Washington, D.C.: Bureau of the Census, 1880), Table 6.

7. Anderson and Bleyer, *Milwaukee's Great Industries*, p. 87.

8. *United States Census of the Population, Compendium* (Washington, D.C.: Bureau of the Census, 1870), Tables 19 and 20. For the full and rich story of the creation of the early German community in Milwaukee, see Kathleen Neils Conzen, *Immigrant Milwaukee, 1836–1860: Accommodation and Community in a Frontier City* (Cambridge, Mass.: Harvard University Press, 1976).

9. Anderson and Bleyer, *Milwaukee's Great Industries*, p. 163; Frank Flower, *History of Milwaukee, Wisconsin, from Pre-Historic Times to the Present Date* (Chicago: Western Historical Company, 1881), p. 1468.

10. Bruce, *History of Milwaukee City and County,* Volume III, pp. 52–53, 435–436j, 694–698, and 706; also Anderson and Bleyer, *Milwaukee's Great Industries,* p. 163.

11. Anderson and Bleyer, *Milwaukee's Great Industries,* p. 162; and James S. Buck, *Milwaukee Under the Charter* (Milwaukee: Swain & Tate Printers, 1886), Volume 4, pp. 345–348.

12. Bruce, *History of Milwaukee City and County,* Volume II, pp. 391–392; Buck, *Milwaukee Under the Charter,* Volume 3, pp. 450–453; Herbert W. Rice, "Pioneer in Leather," *Historical Messenger of the Milwaukee County Historical Society,* Volume II, Number 1 (March 1955), pp. 9–10.

13. Margaret Walsh, "Industrial Opportunity on the Urban Frontier: 'Rags to Riches' and Milwaukee Clothing Manufacturers, 1840–1880," *Wisconsin Magazine of History,* Volume 57, Number 3 (Spring 1974), pp. 175–194.

14. Ibid.

15. Bernhard C. Korn, "The First Steel Mill," *Historical Messenger of the Milwaukee County Historical Society,* Volume 9, Number 1 (June 1953), pp. 12–15; Anderson and Bleyer, *Milwaukee's Great Industries,* p. 80.

16. An excellent history of the Allis-Chalmers/Reliance Iron Works is found in Walter F. Peterson, *An Industrial Heritage: Allis-Chalmers Corporation* (Milwaukee: Milwaukee County Historical Society, 1976).

17. Ibid.; also see the Allis-Chalmers Papers, Milwaukee County Historical Society (hereafter referred to as MCHS).

18. Edwin Reynolds File, Allis-Chalmers Papers, MCHS.

19. Ibid.; also Peterson, *An Industrial Heritage,* chapter 3.

20. William Dixon Gray File, Allis-Chalmers Papers, MCHS, and Peterson, *An Industrial Heritage*, pp. 28–39.

21. Gray File, Allis-Chalmers Papers, MCHS.

22. George Madison Hinckley File, Allis-Chalmers Papers, MCHS.

23. Walsh, "Industrial Opportunity on the Urban Frontier."

24. For an excellent general discussion of these matters in Milwaukee, see Gerd Korman, *Industrialization, Immigrants and Americanizers* (Madison: State Historical Society of Wisconsin, 1967), Part I.

25. See also Roger D. Simon, "The City-Building Process: Housing and Services in New Milwaukee Neighborhoods, 1880–1910," *Transactions of the American Philosophical Society*, Volume 68, Part 5 (1978). This is an especially useful and informative article. Among other things, it provides data that support the argument here. In Table 2 of his article, Simon shows that in 1910 Milwaukee ranked second among the largest American cities in the proportion of men employed in manufacturing. Also see Roger D. Simon, "Foundations for Industrialization: 1835–1880," *Milwaukee History*, Volume 1, Numbers 1 and 2 (Spring and Summer 1978), pp. 38–56.

26. Bruce, *History of Milwaukee City and County*, Volume 1, p. 357.

27. Ibid.

28. U.S. Bureau of the Census, *United States Census of the Population*, 1890, "Manufacturing Industries" (Washington, D.C., 1890), Part 2, Table 3. These data pertain to wages of male officers, firm members and clerks, and male operatives. United States Census of the Population, *Statistics of Manufacturers, 1900* (Washington, D.C., 1901), Table 8. These data pertain to salaries of officials, clerks, etc., and male wage-earners.

29. Korman, *Industrialization, Immigrants and Americanizers*, chapter 5, contains an excellent discussion of this issue and includes a wide array of evidence.

30. Ibid., chapter 3.

31. Judith Walzer Leavitt, *The Healthiest City: Milwaukee and the Politics of Health Reform* (Princeton: Princeton University Press, 1982), chapter 2, especially pp. 54–55.

32. Peterson, *An Industrial Heritage*, pp. 8, 14, and 48.

33. *The P&H Chronicle*, 1920, pp. 9–10; Henry Harnischfeger Papers, Milwaukee County Historical Society.

34. *Forty Years of Progress*, 1884–1924, p. 7; Henry Harnischfeger Papers, Milwaukee County Historical Society.

35. Ibid.

36. Anderson and Bleyer, *Milwaukee's Great Industries*, "Our Iron and Steel Industries"; *Thirty-Third Annual Report of the Trade and Commerce of Milwaukee*, 1891, (Milwaukee: Milwaukee Chamber of Commerce, 1892), pp. 56–57; and Peterson, *An Industrial Heritage*.

37. Simon, "The City-Building Process." Simon's study provides detailed and informative research on several sample wards in Milwaukee, including Ward 14 that represents an illustrative example of a southside, primarily Polish, working-class ward.

38. Bruce, *History of Milwaukee City and County*, Volume 3, pp. 875–877; Peterson, *An Industrial Heritage*, p. 107.

39. Simon, "The City-Building Process," pp. 44ff.

40. The story was much the same in Cleveland, Cincinnati, St. Louis, and Detroit, among others. On Cleveland, see, for example, David D. Van Tassel and John J. Grabowski (eds.), *The Encyclopedia of Cleveland History* (Bloomington: Indiana University Press,

1987), and Todd Swanstrom, *The Crisis of Growth Politics: Cleveland, Kucinich, and the Challenge of Urban Populism* (Philadelphia: Temple University Press, 1985).

41. Bayrd Still, *Milwaukee: The History of a City* (Madison: State Historical Society of Wisconsin, 1948), p. 288. For a fuller story of the Knights of Labor as well as the labor movement more generally in Milwaukee, see Thomas W. Gavett, *Development of the Labor Movement in Milwaukee* (Madison: University of Wisconsin Press, 1965), especially pp. 48–50. Gavett estimates that there were only 12,000 members of the Knights of Labor by 1886.

42. Gavett, *Development of the Labor Movement*, chapter V. For an additional description of the strikes, see Howard Louis Conard (ed.), *History of Milwaukee from Its First Settlement to the Year 1895* (Chicago: American Biographical Publishing, 1895), Volume 1, pp. 64–66.

43. Gavett, *Development of the Labor Movement*, p. 60.

44. Ibid., p. 64.

45. U.S. Bureau of the Census, *United States Census of the Population, 1900*, Compendium (Washington, D.C., 1901).

46. *Milwaukee Sentinel*, June 26, 1865, as quoted in Still, *Milwaukee*, p. 242, fn. 26.

47. As quoted in Leavitt, *The Healthiest City*, p. 58, fn. 48; also in Conard, *History of Milwaukee*, p. 253.

48. Leavitt, *The Healthiest City*, pp. 61–63; also Conard, *History of Milwaukee*, p. 253.

49. The best account of this particular history is Bruce Jordan, "Origins of the Milwaukee Water Works," *Milwaukee History*, Volume 9, Number 1 (Spring 1986), pp. 2–16.

50. James Johnson, quoted in *Annual Report of the Milwaukee Board of Health, 1871*, p. 39.

51. Jordan, "Origins of the Milwaukee Water Works."

52. Ibid.; also Conard, *History of Milwaukee*, chapter 42.

53. Peterson, *An Industrial Heritage*, pp. 10–14.

54. Jordan, "Origins of the Milwaukee Water Works," p. 16.

55. City of Milwaukee Reports, 1890.

56. For the more general treatments of these developments in this era, see Eric Monkkonen, *America Becomes Urban: The Development of U.S. Cities and Towns, 1780–1980* (Berkeley and Los Angeles: University of California Press, 1988); and Jon C. Teaford, *The Unheralded Triumph: City Government in America, 1870–1900* (Baltimore: Johns Hopkins University Press, 1984). Monkkonen is particularly emphatic about how, from this period onward, the nature of municipal government changes from a passive to an active service institution—see especially chapter 9 of his book. This change is by no means trivial; the effect is to insert local government, as an institution, more powerfully into the affairs of the city—from the doings of the lowliest ironmonger to those of the wealthiest manufacturer. Further, it would be precisely because of this change in the character of local government that added divisions would emerge to make consensus in Milwaukee even more fragile.

57. *Annual Report of the Milwaukee Board of Health, 1880*.

58. Leavitt, *The Healthiest City*, p. 24.

59. In their chapter covering the Milwaukee Health Department, Walter Kempster and Solon Marks devote unusual attention to this problem. See Conard, *History of Milwaukee*, chapter 36. Years later, however, Leavitt's meticulous statistical evidence came to the same conclusion. See Leavitt, *The Healthiest City*, pp. 32ff.

60. Leavitt, *The Healthiest City*, pp. 63–65.

61. *Annual Report of the Milwaukee Board of Health, 1875*.

62. The *Annual Report of the Milwaukee Board of Health, 1871,* contains an extensive description of the various public and private facilities then available in Milwaukee for healthcare.

63. Leavitt, *The Healthiest City,* pp. 69–70.

64. *Annual Report of the Milwaukee Board of Health, 1871; Report of the Health Commissioner, December 31, 1900.*

65. Leavitt, *The Healthiest City,* p. 41.

66. City of Milwaukee Reports, 1890.

67. City of Milwaukee Reports, *Tenth Annual Report of the Park Commissioners, 1901.*

68. Ibid. Also see Harry H. Anderson, "Recreation, Entertainment and Open Space: Park Traditions of Milwaukee County," pp. 255–323, in Ralph M. Aderman, (ed.), *Trading Post to Metropolis: Milwaukee County's First 150 Years* (Milwaukee: Milwaukee County Historical Society, 1987).

69. See, e.g., *Annual Report of the Commissioner of Health, 1891,* pp. 27–34.

70. For an excellent general treatment on transportation in Milwaukee, see Clay McShane, *Technology and Reform: Street Railways and the Growth of Milwaukee, 1887–1900* (Madison: State Historical Society of Wisconsin, 1974).

71. *Annual Report of the Milwaukee Fire Department, 1881,* p. 68.

72. Milwaukee Writers Project, *History of Milwaukee County* (Milwaukee Public Library, 1947), p. 661.

73. *Annual Report of the Milwaukee Fire Department, 1881,* p. 7.

74. *Annual Report of the Milwaukee Fire Department, 1882,* p. 9.

75. *Annual Report of the Milwaukee Fire Department, 1883,* p. 1.

76. City of Milwaukee Reports, *Controller's Report, 1880,* p. 19.

77. City of Milwaukee Reports, *Annual Report of the Chief of Police, 1885,* p. 19; *Annual Report of the Chief of Police, 1887,* p. 1.

78. *Annual Report of the Chief of Police, 1901,* pp. 1–10.

79. *Annual Report of the Chief of Police, 1891,* p. 9.

80. *Annual Report of the Chief of Police, 1901;* see, e.g., p. 27.

81. See, for example, *Annual Report of the Board of School Commissioners, 1869–70.*

82. *Annual Report of the Milwaukee School Board* (Milwaukee, 1870, 1880, and 1900).

83. *Annual Report of the Milwaukee School Board, 1880.*

84. For one description of the school at the end of the nineteenth century, there is a section in Anderson and Bleyer's *Milwaukee's Great Industries,* pp. 41–42. Prominent German families such as the Uihleins and Vogels made it a point to send their children to the German-English Academy.

85. *Annual Report of the Milwaukee School Board, 1900.*

86. For the arguments on behalf of these programs, the remarks of Superintendent William Anderson in 1891 are instructive. See his report in *Annual Report of the Milwaukee School Board, August 31, 1891.*

87. "President's Address," *Annual Report of the Milwaukee School Board, 1895,* p. 31.

88. *Annual Report of the Superintendent of Schools, August 31, 1871,* p. 4.

89. *Superintendent's Report, August 31, 1873,* p. 145.

90. By-laws of the Milwaukee School Board, 1871.

91. Rules and Regulations of Milwaukee Public Schools, 1874–75.

92. On this period, see Still, *Milwaukee,* pp. 369–78; also the excellent treatments in McShane, *Technology and Reform,* chapter 7; and the excellent analysis in David P. Thelen,

The New Citizenship: Origins of Progressivism in Wisconsin, 1885–1900 (Columbia: University of Missouri Press, 1972), especially chapter 12.

93. Thelen, *The New Citizenship.*

94. City of Milwaukee Reports, 1869–70.

95. City Clerk of Milwaukee, *Milwaukee Assessments and Taxes, 1901–1930.*

Chapter 5

1. U.S. Bureau of the Census, *U.S. Census of Manufactures, 1910* (Washington, D.C., 1910), Table 1, "Summary for 75 Leading Cities in Manufacturing Industries, as Measured by Value of Products." p. 84.

2. See, for example, Walter F. Peterson, *An Industrial Heritage: Allis-Chalmers Corporation* (Milwaukee: Milwaukee County Historical Society, 1976), especially chapters 5–7.

3. There are dozens of important works by historians, sociologists, and political scientists on the American city. To get a sense both of the variety of these works and of the limited attention given to municipal government—not the political machine but the government—see Howard Gillette, Jr., and Zane L. Miller (eds.), *American Urbanism: A Historiographical Review* (New York: Greenwood Press, 1987), especially chapter 5 by Jon Teaford.

4. See, for instance, my discussion of the history of the old view in Anthony M. Orum, *Introduction to Political Sociology* (Englewood Cliffs, N.J.: Prentice-Hall, 1989), 3rd edition, pp. 216–218.

5. There are different approaches to the nature of federalism. Morton Grodzins, for example, has suggested that federalism describes the shared responsibility among federal, state, and local governments, and has sought to capture this cooperation in terms of a metaphor of a marble cake. In the most recent extended discussion of federalism, particularly in terms of the authority of local governments, Paul Peterson has argued that local governments are limited as to the type of policies they can pursue. He has argued specifically that local governments can only pursue matters of development, whereas issues of the redistribution of resources must be pursued at the federal level. He then goes on to elaborate this distinction at some length. (See Paul E. Peterson, *City Limits* (Chicago: University of Chicago Press, 1981), especially chapters 1 and 4.) The problem both with Grodzins and Peterson, however, is that both assume that the federal allocation of power and responsibility is fixed over time. In fact, as we learn in the case of Milwaukee, it is not fixed at all, but changes to meet changed circumstances. While there may be some appeal in the simplicity of Peterson's approach, it also is a distortion of historical fact.

6. The best general treatment of this matter is to be found in Jon C. Teaford, *The Unheralded Triumph: City Government in America, 1870–1900* (Baltimore: Johns Hopkins University Press, 1984), especially chapters 4 and 5.

7. U.S. Bureau of the Census, *United States Census of the Population*, Volume 9, *Manufactures* (Washington, D.C., 1910), Table 1, "The State of Wisconsin."

8. Records of these detailed annexations, which trace the growth of the city from January 1900 onward, may be found in the Annexation microfilm file of the Legislative Reference Bureau, Milwaukee City Hall. In the first decade, for example, the city grew by just about 10 percent, and in the next two decades it expanded considerably more.

9. For this particular history, see Ralph M. Aderman (ed.), *Trading Post to Metropolis: Milwaukee County's First 150 Years* (Milwaukee: Milwaukee County Historical Society, 1987).

10. See, especially, Frederick I. Olson, "City Expansion and Suburban Spread," in Aderman, *Trading Post to Metropolis*; and the magnum opus, of more than 700 pages, by Charles Davis Goff, *The Politics of Governmental Integration in Metropolitan Milwaukee* (Ph.D. diss., Northwestern University, Department of Government, 1952), especially chapter 5.

11. An excellent history of this railway is to be found in Clay McShane, *Technology and Reform: Street Railways and the Growth of Milwaukee, 1887–1900* (Madison: State Historical Society of Wisconsin, 1974).

12. Ibid., chapter 6.

13. See, for example, Teaford, *The Unheralded Triumph*, pp. 105–122, and Charles R. Adrian, *A History of American City Government: The Emergence of the Metropolis, 1920–1945* (New York: University Press of America, 1987), pp. 59–61.

14. See, for example, Frederick I. Olson, *The Milwaukee Socialists, 1987–1941*, Ph.D. diss., Harvard University, Department of History, 1952).

15. One of the first public pronouncements on behalf of the consolidation of city and county governments that I discovered was made by William George Bruce, a Republican and city tax commissioner at the time. To quote: "Mr. Bruce spoke in advocacy of the consolidation of the city and county governments, giving a detailed account of the manner in which many large manufacturing concerns escape their just share of taxation by moving their plants into suburban districts, like West Allis, North Milwaukee, South Milwaukee, Cudahy, Wauwatosa and other outside localities. ... Rural assessors, he said, are always lenient in assessments, and by moving into the suburbs, many large manufacturing concerns receive the benefit of this leniency (*Evening Wisconsin,* May 29, 1906)." The effort to annex, or consolidate, governments continued throughout this period, as a review of actual annexations will demonstrate. The inception and the continuity of this effort must be acknowledged clearly to recognize that annexation and consolidation were not a creation of the Social Democrats, as some might argue, but were, in fact, a product of the emerging and growing needs of city government, itself.

16. Annual Report of the City Comptroller of Milwaukee, 1910; and City of Milwaukee Financial Survey, Comptroller's Department, 1894–1931.

17. For example, between 1910 and 1920 the tax revenues required for purposes of the city government's operations increased fourfold, from just about $4 million to almost $16 million. City of Milwaukee Annual Reports, 1910 and 1920.

18. A considerable protest developed over this issue in the 1920s. See, for example, issues of the *Milwaukee Sentinel* from July 2 through July 5, 1923.

19. "West Allis Is Industrial City," *Milwaukee Journal,* May 28, 1922.

20. "Fear High Tax in Annexation," *Milwaukee Journal,* November 29, 1920.

21. *Milwaukee Journal,* April 28, 1922.

22. See, for example, the report on the Whitefish Bay meetings, R. E. Stoelting, Commission of Public Works, "City Congested, Musty Annex Territory," *Milwaukee Journal,* February 9, 1928.

23. See, for instance, "Borough Plan of Rule Urged," *Milwaukee Journal,* March 29, 1928.

24. Also see the review of these debates in *The Wisconsin News,* March 1928 (Milwaukee Legislative Reference Bureau, Annexation File, card 6, line 4, fiche 5).

25. "Annexation Bill Meets Objection," *Milwaukee Sentinel,* April 20, 1917.

26. See Goff, *The Politics of Governmental Integration in Metropolitan Milwaukee* for further details, as well as the work by Gordon Ross Stephens, *Metropolitan Reorganization: A Comparison of Six Cases* (Ph.D. diss., University of Wisconsin, Department of Political Science, 1961). Stephens goes into considerable detail on the case of St. Louis. It is notable that the Milwaukee newspapers, all of which were sympathetic to the city's efforts in this period, also periodically ran annexation stories, both successful and otherwise, on other cities such as St. Louis and Cleveland. See *Milwaukee Journal,* June 22, 1928, on St. Louis and also the *Journal,* circa March 1929, for lengthy articles on Cleveland.

27. David Rusk, *Cities Without Suburbs* (Baltimore: Johns Hopkins University Press, 1993).

28. Kenneth T. Jackson, *Crabgrass Frontier: The Suburbanization of the United States* (New York: Oxford University Press, 1985).

29. There was a general move afoot in this era to make governments more efficient and more akin to capitalist enterprises. Milwaukee was not immune to this movement, as attested to by the activity of groups like the Municipal Reform League. But their effect would be ultimately to make city governments *more* effective as sovereign powers, not less so, and thereby to help exacerbate the conflicts between the territorial pursuits of city government and the separate purposes of local corporations. For some general readings that take the more conventional point of view that the source of change in government actually came from outside, rather than from within, see David P. Thelen, *The New Citizenship: Origins of Progressivism in Wisconsin, 1885–1900* (Columbia: University of Missouri Press, 1972), especially chapter 12; and Martin J. Schiesl, *The Politics of Efficiency: Municipal Administration and Reform in America, 1800–1920* (Berkeley: University of California Press, 1977), especially chapter 6.

30. For details, see reports of the Police Department, City of Milwaukee, 1921–1923.

31. *Annual Report,* Milwaukee Police Department (1923), p. 7.

32. Some of the overall increase, of course, could be attributed to the enforcement of the Prohibition laws, which went into effect in 1917. But, in the five years prior to Laubenheimer's regime, relatively few people had been arrested under these laws. Once he came to office and the new systems were introduced, enforcement and arrests went up accordingly.

33. "Superintendent's Report," in the *Annual Report of the Milwaukee School Board, June 30, 1912,* p. 71.

34. Edward J. Muzik, "Victor Berger's Early Career," *Historical Messenger of the Milwaukee County Historical Society,* Volume 17, Number 1 (March 1961), pp. 15–20.

35. *Milwaukee Sentinel,* July 8, 1897; as reported in Joseph Anthony Gasperetti, *The 1910 Social-Democratic Mayoral Campaign in Milwaukee* (master of arts thesis, University of Wisconsin–Milwaukee, Department of Communication, June 1970), pp. 16–17.

36. U.S. Bureau of the Census, (Washington D.C., 1910), Volume 9, *Population/Occupation Statistics,* Table 3, pp. 166–179; and *United States Census of the Population, 1920,* "Population/Occupational Statistics," Table 2, pp. 1140–1144.

37. For a review of the policies of the Social Democrats, see any of the following: John G. Beratti, *Socialist Rule in Milwaukee, 1910–1912* (master of arts thesis, Marquette University, Department of History, 1968); Sally M. Miller, "Casting a Wide Net: The Milwaukee Movement to 1920," in Donald T. Critchlow (ed.), *Socialism in the Heartland: The Midwestern Experience, 1900–1925* (Notre Dame, Ind.: Notre Dame Press, 1986), pp. 18–45; and Sally M.

Miller, "Milwaukee: Of Ethnicity and Labor," in Bruce M. Stave (ed.), *Socialism and the Cities* (Port Washington, N.Y.: Kennikat Press, 1975), pp. 41–71.

38. Gasperetti, *The 1910 Social-Democratic Mayoral Campaign,* pp. 38–42; Miller, "Milwaukee: Of Ethnicity and Labor," p. 47.

39. Miller, "Casting a Wide Net," p. 29.

40. Miller, "Milwaukee: Of Ethnicity and Labor," p. 47.

41. See also Beratti, *Socialist Rule in Milwaukee,* pp. 34–36, and Gasperetti, *The 1910 Social-Democratic Mayoral Campaign.*

42. The actual facts of corruption, especially in Milwaukee, are hard to pin down. One fact to keep in mind is that claims of corruption were as much a part of the political strategy of the Social Democrats, to oust Rose, as anything else. Even more significantly, at this time in the city's evolution, corruption would be difficult to distinguish from the emerging practices of politics, as a profession. Capitalist enterprises still sought to retain some control over municipal government—control that was as often exercised through the exchange of money for political favors as anything else.

43. *Milwaukee Journal,* April 6, 1910, p. 6; as cited in Beratti, *Socialist Rule in Milwaukee,* p. 28.

44. Miller, "Milwaukee: Of Ethnicity and Labor," p. 50.

45. The *St. Louis Herald,* for example, in its issue of April 16, 1911, claimed that Milwaukee suffered under the Socialists and that the "Socialists in Milwaukee have been a mere horde of office-seekers and officeholders."

46. See, for example, Bruce M. Stave, "Socialism and the Cities: An Introduction," in Stave (ed.), *Socialism and the Cities,* pp. 3–12.

47. As Sally Miller notes, for instance, "The Socialists streamlined city government." She also rightly acknowledges the important contribution of the Bureau of Economy and Efficiency—created by Seidel and headed by John R. Commons, famed University of Wisconsin economist—that, among other things, introduced new cost accounting and centralized purchasing procedures to the operations of Milwaukee city government. Miller, "Milwaukee: Of Ethnicity and Labor," p. 51. On this matter of the accomplishments of the Socialists, also see Douglas E. Booth, "Municipal Socialism and City Government Reform: The Milwaukee Experience, 1910–1940," *Journal of Urban History,* Volume 12, Number 1 (November 1985), pp. 51–74.

48. I want to acknowledge the thematic inspiration of Robert Michels's wonderful work, *The Iron Law of Oligarchy Political Parties: A Sociological Study of the Oligarchical Tendencies of Modern Democracy,* translated by Eden and Cedar Paul (New York: Free Press, 1958). Originally published in 1911. But, I also want to point out a very important and fundamental difference between my argument and his. Michels was interested in demonstrating that inevitably a kind of bureaucratic momentum would develop as political parties evolved, and that, ironically enough, this momentum happened even in Socialist parties that sought to improve conditions for the working class. His point was that once organization takes root, it is driven forward by an inexorable logic all its own. My point is that this inexorable logic took root in Milwaukee's municipal government and was so overpowering in its overall features as to limit what any social alliance, including that of the Social Democrats, could effect in office.

49. For the most part, the evidence for this section comes from the extensive files in the Milwaukee County Historical Society. Of particular value were the several boxes of materi-

als in the Otto Falk files, the materials on the Pfister family, and the materials in the Uihlein files.

50. Third Annual Banquet, Milwaukee Metal Trades and Founders Association, January 30, 1908.

51. "Strikes at Social Democrats in Talks at M & M Meeting," *Milwaukee Sentinel,* February 7, 1911.

52. Pfister, who remained a bachelor throughout his life, owned a special resort called Lake Five, which was about 25 miles from Milwaukee. Pictures in the Falk file show him and his cohorts, such as Otto Falk, Sr., Gustave Pabst, Jr., and Fred Vogel, Jr., periodically enjoying themselves in recreational and other pursuits.

53. The details on the Uihlein brothers come from Frank Flower, *History of Milwaukee, Wisconsin, from Pre-Historic Times to the Present Date* (Chicago: The Western Historical Company, 1881); William George Bruce (ed.), *History of Milwaukee City and County* (Chicago/Milwaukee: S. J. Clarke Publishing, 1922), Volume 3; and Jerome A. Watrous (ed.), *Memoirs of Milwaukee County* (Madison: Western Historical Association, 1909), Volume 3.

54. See the obituary for Vogel in the Falk papers, Milwaukee County Historical Society.

55. See, for example, the article on Falk in *Forbes Magazine,* February 15, 1926.

56. In the obituary for Charles Pfister, who died in 1927, the *Milwaukee Journal* wrote that he "was identified with a strong financial group in Milwaukee, including the Vogel, Falk, Uihlein, Pabst, and Nunnemacher families." *Milwaukee Journal,* November 12, 1927.

57. Among sociologists, there are two different points of view of the forces that generate the expansion of a place. One, which some might call the elite view, insists that alliances are central in the expansion of places. Among others who take this point of view is G. William Domhoff. The other point of view, the institutional view, insists that institutions are central to the life and expansion of a place. My own point of view on this subject is that institutions became the central dynamic of urban life in the late nineteenth and early twentieth centuries, and that alliances played a far more circumscribed—one might say, short-term—role.

58. Walter F. Peterson, *An Industrial Heritage: Allis-Chalmers Corporation* (Milwaukee: Milwaukee County Historical Society, 1976), pp. 102–108.

59. "First Milwaukee Bank Organized in 1836 Never Opened Its Doors; 1839 Saw Birth of Oldest Institution," *Milwaukee Sentinel,* June 1, 1921.

60. *An American Dream: A Commemorative History of Cutler-Hammer, Inc., 1892–1978* (Milwaukee: Cutler-Hammer, 1979), pp. 9–24.

61. *Business Milwaukee: A Trade Review, 1919* (Commercial Service Department, First Wisconsin National Bank, 1919); and *Industrial Milwaukee: A Trade Review* (First Wisconsin National Bank, 1929).

62. *Official Directory of Companies of Milwaukee, Wisconsin,* compiled by R. H. Odell (Milwaukee: Odell & Owen, 1904).

63. Charles Ernest Schefft, *The Tanning Industry in Wisconsin: A History of Its Frontier Origins and Its Development* (master of arts thesis, University of Wisconsin at Madison, Department of History, 1938).

64. Patrick Cudahy, *Patrick Cudahy: His Life* (Milwaukee: Burdick & Allen, 1912).

65. *Milwaukee Sentinel,* May 17, 1924, p. 1.

66. Peterson, *An Industrial Heritage;* and Harold F. Williamson and Kenneth H. Myers, III, *Designed for Digging: The First 75 Years of Bucyrus-Erie* (Evanston, Ill.: Northwestern University Press, 1955).

67. U.S. Bureau of the Census, *Twelfth Census of the United States, 1900,* "Comparative Summary for Principal Cities Shown Separately, 1880, 1890, and 1900," Table 74 (Washington, D.C., 1901); and *Fifteenth Census of the United States, Manufacturers, 1929,* Volume III, *Report by States* (Washington, D.C., 1930), p. 562.

68. *Industrial Milwaukee: A Trade Review* (1929).

69. This problem only became evident some years later, in hindsight, as city officials sought to assess the reasons for disproportionate tragedies visited upon Milwaukee business by the depression of the 1930s. See Robert L. Filtzer and William L. Slayton, *Manufacturing in Milwaukee and 22 Metropolitan Cities, 1919–1929–1939* (Milwaukee: Board of Public Land Commissioners, March 20, 1944).

70. See the various articles on taxes and the potential loss of industry to Milwaukee and Wisconsin in the following issues of the *Milwaukee Sentinel* during the 1920s: March 7, 1923; September 21, 1923; May 23, 1923; and May 19, 1925.

71. Ira Katznelson, *City Trenches* (New York: Pantheon, 1981).

Chapter 6

1. See the very nice analysis presented in Robert Filtzer and William L. Slayton, *Manufacturing in Milwaukee and 22 Metropolitan Cities, 1919–1929–1939* (Milwaukee: Board of Public Land Commissioners, March 20, 1944). This sophisticated use of statistical regression techniques shows that the concentration of heavy industry in Milwaukee, and the character of the workforce thereby created, led to a far sharper impact of the Depression on the local economy than in many other cities.

2. Walter F. Peterson, *An Industrial Heritage: Allis-Chalmers Corporation* (Milwaukee: Milwaukee County Historical Society, 1976), p. 313.

3. Stephen Meyer, *"Stalin over Wisconsin": The Making and Unmaking of Militant Unionism, 1900–1950* (New Brunswick, N.J.: Rutgers University Press, 1992), p. 39.

4. *Milwaukee Sentinel,* January 1, 1931.

5. Meyer, *"Stalin over Wisconsin,"* p. 39. Also see the following for additional information on the figures and the trends in employment in Milwaukee in this period: Thomas W. Gavett, *Development of the Labor Movement in Milwaukee* (Madison: University of Wisconsin Press, 1965), p. 152; and the *Milwaukee Sentinel,* September 1936, Business Page, which displays a graph of employment trends in Milwaukee based upon information from the "Milwaukee office of the state employment service." Data from the United States Census taken in 1930 and 1940 reveal a drop in employed workers in Milwaukee from 94,873 to 61,672, the first decade to report a decline in employment in the city's history. (*Fifteenth Census of the United States, Manufacturers: 1929,* Volume 3, *Reports by States, 1933,* p. 562; and *Sixteenth Census of the United States, Manufacturers,* Volume 3. *Reports for States and Outlying Areas, 1942,* Table 2, p. 1098.)

6. *Milwaukee Sentinel,* November 17, 1936, p. 1.

7. Gayle Koprowski-Kraut, "The Depression's Effects on a Milwaukee Family," *Milwaukee History* (Autumn 1980), Volume 3, Number 3, pp. 84–92; at pp. 85–86.

8. Ibid., p. 87.

9. Doug McAdam, *Political Process and the Development of Black Insurgency, 1930–1970* (Chicago: University of Chicago Press, 1982).

10. Since the late 1970s, the study of collective action by sociologists has been dominated by a perspective—resource mobilization—that insists, among other things, that it is mag-

nitude of organization rather than the depth of grievance that serves to mobilize people to undertake collective action. See, for example, Charles Tilly, *From Mobilization to Revolution* (Cambridge, Mass.: Addison-Wesley Press, 1978).

11. Federated Trades Council of Milwaukee, as reported in Frank Sinclair, *Milwaukee Journal*, October 20, 1935. For comparable figures on union membership, also see Gavett, *Development of the Labor Movement in Milwaukee*, p. 166.

12. Gavett, *Development of the Labor Movement in Milwaukee*, chapter 13.

13. Meyer, *"Stalin over Wisconsin,"* passim.

14. *Milwaukee Journal*, December 13, 1931.

15. Gavett, *Development of the Labor Movement in Milwaukee*, p. 178.

16. For other reports on their activities in the city, see, for example, reports in the *Milwaukee Sentinel* of March 1 and 5, 1936, as well as May 4, 1936. Also see Meyer, *"Stalin over Wisconsin,"* and Gavett, *Development of the Labor Movement in Milwaukee.*

17. An article written by Frank Sinclair and published in the *Milwaukee Journal* on October 20, 1935, provided a somewhat different accounting of the numbers. Sinclair reported that between January 1, 1934, and October 1935, there had been a total of 138 strikes, involving 30,000 workers. His numbers, he wrote, were provided by the Milwaukee Federated Trades Council (FTC).

18. Sinclair, *Milwaukee Journal*, October 20, 1935.

19. "Phoenix Strike Ended, Peace Terms Signed," "Hosiery Labor Troubles Over," *Milwaukee Journal*, October 24 and 25, respectively, 1931.

20. "Milk Is Spilled on East Side; More Clashes Mark Strike," *Milwaukee Journal*, June 20, 1935.

21. This strike took place from June 25 through June 29, 1934, and resulted in the arrest of hundreds of people. Eventually, TMER&L and its president, S. B. Way, relented and granted recognition to the local union as a legitimate bargaining agent for workers. All three major Milwaukee newspapers at the time—the *Milwaukee Leader*, the *Milwaukee Journal*, and the *Milwaukee Sentinel*—include detailed coverage of the strike.

22. "Fond du Lac Riot in Two Sections," *Milwaukee Journal*, June 28, 1934.

23. Ibid.

24. "The Crisis Passes," *Milwaukee Sentinel*, June 30, 1934.

25. The *Milwaukee Sentinel* reported in its issue of April 10, 1931, that Milwaukee was ranked second in the nation in health by the U.S. Chamber of Commerce.

26. *Milwaukee Sentinel*, August 2, 1931.

27. *Milwaukee Sentinel*, January 10, 1932.

28. *Buffalo News*, as quoted in the *Milwaukee Sentinel*, January 10, 1932.

29. *Milwaukee Sentinel*, November 12, 1932. The Annual Report of the Milwaukee Common Council in 1940 noted that the tax delinquency in 1933 was $17.5 million or roughly 83 percent of the entire tax levy for the year. For further evidence on the problems that this created for city government, see also the *Milwaukee Sentinel*, November 12, 1932, and February 26, 1933.

30. "Relief Report Is Sent to U.S.," *Milwaukee Journal*, February 26, 1933.

31. There are a host of writings that discuss both the motives and the detailed history of the New Deal programs, as well as how they asserted the power of the federal government over cities in new and fundamentally changed respects. The best of these treatments is to be found in John Mollenkopf, *The Contested City* (Princeton: Princeton University Press, 1983), especially chapter 2. Mollenkopf's thesis is that "political entrepreneurs" in the fed-

eral government developed specific urban policies that would secure votes for themselves and ensure the federal government's power over the cities. He observes, for example, that the "programs developed by the New Deal strongly reflected the need to mobilize the urban electorate, the need to command congressional majorities, and the need to align competing interests in urban politics. … Through … legislative titles (such as the Public Works Administration and the Works Progress Administration) the federal government began all the basic activities which have come to be called 'national urban policy.'" Pp. 64–65.

32. *Milwaukee Journal*, June 12, 1934.

33. "County Relief Cost 110 Million Dollars in the Last Nine Years," *Milwaukee Journal*, June 19, 1938.

34. Reports of the Works Progress Administration, Milwaukee, 1935–1943.

35. "County Funds Were Expended," *Milwaukee Journal*, April 16, 1922.

36. Obituary of Benjamin Glassberg, superintendent of the Department of Outdoor Relief, Milwaukee County, in the *Milwaukee Journal*, November 17, 1953.

37. "More Relief Is Prospect Here for Fall, Winter," *Milwaukee Journal*, July 31, 1932.

38. "Relief Report Is Sent to U.S.," *Milwaukee Journal*, February 26, 1933.

39. "More Relief Is Prospect Here for Fall, Winter."

40. *Annual Report of the Milwaukee Common Council, 1930.*

41. *Annual Report of the Milwaukee Common Council, 1940.*

42. *Annual Report of the Milwaukee Common Council, 1950.*

43. Filtzer and Slayton, *Manufacturing in Milwaukee and 22 Metropolitan Cities,* p. 3.

44. Remarks by Otto Falk to the Third Annual Banquet of the Milwaukee Metal Trades and Founders Association, January 30, 1908.

45. "Mayor Uses Hot Words in Reply to S. B. Way," *Milwaukee Sentinel*, June 28, 1934.

46. A certain amount of caution must be exercised in digesting the reports of industrial losses in both the *Journal* and the *Sentinel*. Both papers, but especially the latter, were notorious outlets of conservative opinions. The *Sentinel*, for example, was highly critical of the New Deal. In a banner editorial in the midst of the Depression, the *Sentinel* (July 28, 1936), for example, opined that "day after day the New Deal is making unemployment a more permanent condition. If the problem is never solved, most of the blame will rest on the shoulders of President Roosevelt and his aides. … Business, hurt in the past by New Deal interference, has lost its confidence in the government." Accordingly, when both papers reported on the departures of plants from Milwaukee, they also were trying to drum up support for their own point of view—namely, to endorse efforts to protect industries in the city, both from the workers and from the New Deal. Nevertheless, the facts as they report them seem to concur with other evidence on the loss of jobs and industries to the city, and the general perception that both the city and the state were becoming increasingly unfriendly to business.

47. *Milwaukee Sentinel*, September 11, 1932.

48. "Shoe Factory Pay Roll Lost to Milwaukee," *Milwaukee Sentinel*, November 16, 1934.

49. "13,850 Jobs, Toll of Trend," *Milwaukee Journal*, March 10, 1938.

50. Articles, under the byline Arch Ely, ran in the *Milwaukee Sentinel* from November 15 through 18, 1935, and they suggested the magnitude of loss of industry from the city. The article of November 15, 1935, reported that six of the city's shoe companies had already departed, taking a payroll estimated at $4 million annually.

51. *Milwaukee Sentinel*, September 11, 1932. Several years later, the publisher of the *Sentinel,* Paul Block, became so concerned about the loss of industry in Milwaukee and so out-

raged by the apparent inability both of Mayor Hoan and other officials to recruit new industry, that he addressed a lengthy letter to the mayor in which he urged the mayor to take steps to attract new industry. It said, in part, that "'industry, which is fearful and apprehensive due to the antics of the Washington New Dealers, feels doubly fearful about Wisconsin. Businessmen say that many of Wisconsin's state laws and some of Milwaukee's local laws are so harmful to industry that, if there is to be any removal of plants, they prefer most other states to Wisconsin and most other cities to Milwaukee.'" Upon receipt of a letter from Mayor Hoan that claimed the loss of industry to be an illusion, Block submitted to the *Sentinel* a lengthy reply in which, among other things, he listed a number of plants that had expanded outside Milwaukee. They included the Heil Company of Milwaukee, Holeproof Hosiery, and the Palmolive Company (*Milwaukee Sentinel*, May 9, 1936). The deeply imbedded conflicts between the *Sentinel,* and the many industrialists it represented, and the regime of Mayor Hoan are very evident in the exceedingly hostile tone of Block's editorial.

52. See the excellent treatment of this economic issue, as well as many other related issues, in William F. Thompson, *The History of Wisconsin,* Volume 6, *Continuity and Change: 1940–1965* (Madison: State Historical Society of Wisconsin, 1988), chapter 5. This is a magnificent history of the state over the course of this period, and Thompson's work contains a number of important observations on the nature of the economic decline in Milwaukee. Thompson argues that, in fact, the city and state did not exact higher taxes than a number of other nearby states—but that a perception developed that Wisconsin and Milwaukee were unfriendly to business. This perception then became so real as to lead many businesses to leave and others to refrain from opening plants in the state.

53. "Bucyrus-Erie Earnings Boomed over Last Year," *Milwaukee Journal,* March 4, 1940.

54. Peterson, *An Industrial Heritage,* pp. 312–313.

55. "Harnischfeger Earnings Rise," *Milwaukee Journal,* February 23, 1941; and "Defense Orders Boost Heil Co. Profits," *Milwaukee Journal,* April 7, 1941.

56. "Defense Orders Boost Heil Co. Profits."

57. "Harnischfeger Plant Is Awarded the Navy E," "Falk Receives 'E' Pennant for War Work," "Nordberg Given Navy High Award," *Milwaukee Sentinel,* May 7, 10, and 16, respectively, 1942.

58. "First State Firm Unfurls Joint E," "Another Plant Flies Joint E," *Milwaukee Sentinel,* August 11 and 18, respectively, 1942; "Kearney-Treaker Production Award Plans Announced," "Harvester Co. Given 'E' Flag," September 3 and 15, respectively, 1942.

59. "Plants Drain Lists of WPA," *Milwaukee Journal,* May 18, 1941.

60. Thompson, *History of Wisconsin,* Volume 6, pp. 93–94.

61. Ibid.

62. "Plants Drain Lists of WPA."

63. U.S. Bureau of Labor Statistics, "Strikes of Milwaukee Labor Organizations, 1929–1945," as reported in the files of the Legislative Reference Bureau, Milwaukee, "Labor Strikes."

64. Peterson, *An Industrial Heritage,* pp. 316–317.

65. For a superb history of the unions at Allis-Chalmers and the larger questions invoked by their efforts, see Meyer, *"Stalin over Wisconsin."* I am very grateful to Professor Meyer for enabling me to see his manuscript before its actual publication. Another, very different view of the history of unions at Allis-Chalmers is available in a paper, "Résumé of Pertinent Phases of Collective Bargaining History at West Allis Works," which is in the Allis-

Chalmers files held by the Milwaukee County Historical Society. This paper presents a radically different view of this story.

66. Meyer, *"Stalin over Wisconsin,"* chapter 3; and Gavett, *Development of the Labor Movement in Milwaukee,* chapters 13 through 15.

67. Subsequent claims that Christoffel was a member of the Communist party highlighted his effectiveness and suggested that his skills had proven attractive to party leaders by the mid-1930s when the American Communist party developed its popular-front strategy and worked to infiltrate existing unions with their own members. Meyer, *"Stalin over Wisconsin,"* chapter 1.

68. Ibid., pp. 111–112.

69. Ibid., pp. 88–90.

70. Besides Meyer, *"Stalin over Wisconsin,"* and Gavett, *Development of the Labor Movement in Milwaukee,* also see the accounts in Julian L. Stockley, "'Red Purge': The 1946–47 Strike at Allis-Chalmers," in *Transactions of the Wisconsin Academy of Science, Arts and Letters,* Volume 76, 1988, pp. 17–31.

71. The pieces in the *Sentinel* ran from late September through November 1946.

72. The company apparently had been convinced for years that Communist influence dominated the actions of Local 248 and animated the decisions of Christoffel, in particular. The company review of this history claimed, for example, that while "the Company was fully aware of Communist machinations in Local 248 affairs, the employees and the general public were ignorant of the basic cause for disturbed relations at West Allis Works. For years the Company had carried on a silent, desperate behind-the-scenes fight to discharge management responsibilities and protect employes [sic] and the public against a powerful and deeply entrenched conspiracy operating behind the front of a legitimate labor organization fortified in its status as exclusive bargaining representative by the majesty of the law of the United States of America." "Résumé of Pertinent Phases," p. 18.

73. "Blames Communists for 1941 A-C Strike," *Milwaukee Journal,* February 16, 1947.

Chapter 7

1. U.S. Bureau of the Census, *United States Census of the Population, Compendium,* (Washington D.C., 1960); and *United States Census of the Population, Compendium* (Washington, D.C., 1990).

2. For precise details on the years and amounts of annexations, see Arnold Paul Fleischmann, "The Politics of Annexation and Urban Development: A Clash of Two Paradigms" (unpublished diss., University of Texas at Austin, Department of Government), pp. 79–81.

3. On Chicago, see Gregory D. Squires, Larry Bennett, Kathleen McCourt, and Philip Nyden, *Chicago: Race, Class and the Response to Urban Decline* (Philadelphia: Temple University Press, 1987), especially pp. 25–37; on Detroit, see Joe T. Darden, Richard Child Hill, June Thomas, and Richard Thomas, *Detroit: Race and Uneven Development* (Philadelphia: Temple University Press, 1987), especially pp. 18–26; and on Philadelphia, see Carolyn Adams, David Bartelt, David Elesh, Ira Goldstein, Nancy Kleniewski, and William Yancey, *Philadelphia: Neighborhoods, Division, and Conflict in a Postindustrial City* (Philadelphia: Temple University Press, 1991), chapter 2.

4. Barry Bluestone and Bennett Harrison, *The Deindustrialization of America: Plant Closings, Community Abandonment and the Dismantling of Basic Industries* (New York: Basic Books, 1982).

5. Kirkpatrick Sale, *Power Shift: The Rise of the Southern Rim and Its Challenge to the Eastern Establishment* (New York: Random House, 1975); and Carl Abbott, *The New Urban America: Growth and Politics in Sunbelt Cities* (Chapel Hill: University of North Carolina Press, 1987), especially chapter 1.

6. See, for example, the essays in David Perry and Alfred Watkins (eds.), *The Rise of the Sunbelt Cities* (Beverly Hills, Calif.: Sage Publications, 1977), especially the lead essay by Perry and Watkins, "Regional Change and the Impact of Uneven Urban Development."

7. Mayor's Study Commission on Social Problems in the Inner Core Areas of the City, "Final Report to the Honorable Frank P. Zeidler, Mayor, City of Milwaukee, April 15, 1960."

8. Milwaukee Municipal Reference Library, *City Planning and Taxation*, 1943 (now found in Milwaukee Legislative Reference Bureau, Milwaukee, Wisconsin).

9. "Report from Thomas A. Byrne, Tax Commissioner, City of Milwaukee, to Honorable John L. Bohn, Acting Mayor, Milwaukee, Wisconsin, January 21, 1943," p. 4.

10. Redevelopment Coordinating Committee, City of Milwaukee, "Blight Elimination and Urban Redevelopment in Milwaukee," June 1948, Milwaukee, Wisconsin.

11. William J. Manly, "The Blight Within Us," *Milwaukee Journal*, May 1954.

12. For other reports substantiating the matter of decline at this time, see Board of Public Land Commissioners, City of Milwaukee, "Blight Elimination," Number 1, January 1950; and George C. Saffran, "Blight Elimination and Prevention," Budget Supervisor, City of Milwaukee, July 1954.

13. See, for example, the reports in the *Milwaukee Journal*, May 12, 1946, and January 7, 1947.

14. See, for example, the *Milwaukee Journal*, January 7, 1947, and *Milwaukee Sentinel*, January 9, 1947.

15. The columns by William Norris appear to begin in July 1950 and continue periodically over the next several years; see, for instance, his series of opinions in the *Sentinel* of July 1950. Also, it was Arthur Werba who apparently believed that the lack of support eventually from the *Journal* led to the difficulties experienced by the city in gaining new land acquisitions. This absence of support, according to Werba, stood in contrast to the *Journal*'s great enthusiasm for annexations in the 1920s ("Let Milwaukee Grow," editorial, *Milwaukee Sentinel*, May 11, 1952).

16. "Werba Urges Annexing of Seventy-five Square Miles," *Milwaukee Sentinel*, June 5, 1952.

17. See, for instance, "Decide Annexation Issue, Zeidler Asks Legislators," *Milwaukee Journal*, April 7, 1949.

18. The key figure in the fight between the city and its surrounding territories seems to have been Leland McParland, a Democratic assemblyman from Cudahy, who acted to represent the collective interests of the suburbs in the Wisconsin State Legislature.

19. See the reports on the state supreme court decision in the *Milwaukee Journal*, April 3, 1951, and April 4, 1951, as well as the William Norris column entitled "Annexation Ruling Fosters Bewilderment" in the *Milwaukee Sentinel* of April 11, 1951. Also for a good discussion of the court's role, in general, in Milwaukee's efforts at annexation, see Fleischmann, *The Politics of Annexation*, chapter 4.

20. "Zeidler Points to City Growth," *Milwaukee Sentinel*, February 28, 1956.

21. See the reference in the *Milwaukee Journal,* June 13, 1954.

22. William A. Norris, "We're Committing Suicide with Our Annexation Policy," *Milwaukee Sentinel,* September 5, 1952.

23. Ibid; William A. Norris, "Can Milwaukee Afford to Subsidize Annexation?" *Milwaukee Sentinel,* August 1, 1952.

24. For details, see Fleischmann, *The Politics of Annexation,* pp. 140–145.

25. The last major annexation to the city, of portions of Brown Deer, also was the most debated in court. It took eight full years to resolve the dispute, but it finally led to the annexation of 16 square miles of Brown Deer, on the northeast side of the city. See Joseph R. Aicher, Jr., "The Brown Deer Annexation: A Case Study in the City of Milwaukee's Consolidation Activity" (unpublished master's thesis, Marquette University, Milwaukee, Wisconsin, 1968).

26. *Milwaukee Sentinel,* May 5, 1966.

27. City of Milwaukee, Office of the Tax Commissioner, *Assessments and Taxes* (1980), p. 4.

28. For an interesting analysis of the Milwaukee school system, see the article by Marc Levine and John Zipp, "A City at Risk: The Changing Social and Economic Context of Public Schooling in Milwaukee," in John L. Rury and Frank A. Cassell (eds.), *Seeds of Crisis: Public Schooling in Milwaukee Since 1920* (Madison: University of Wisconsin Press, 1993), pp. 42–72.

29. Reports of the Milwaukee School Board, 1949–50 and 1969–70.

30. Report of the Milwaukee School Board, 1989–90.

31. Reports of the Milwaukee School Board, 1949–50 and 1989–90.

32. The appropriate consumer price index for this period was taken from the *Economic Report of the President, 1992* (Washington, D.C., 1992), Table B–56, "Consumer Price Index, Major Expenditure Classes, 1950–1991."

33. Reports of the Milwaukee School Board, 1959–60, 1969–70, and 1979–80.

34. The state and national figures for 1980 are reported in the *Milwaukee Journal,* November 3, 1983, p. 16.

35. Office of the Tax Commissioner, City of Milwaukee, *Assessments and Taxes* (1980), pp. 6–9A; also *City of Milwaukee Annual Report* (1980). There are somewhat differing figures given for the city property in these reports. Those data used here for the calculations are the following figures: City property, 1980 = $1,028,982,000, and the total of private property (land, improvements, and personal property) = $7,680,433,829. The ratio of one to the other, then, is 0.13, or 13 percent.

36. The percentages of the federal government's contribution to city government operations went from 0.4 percent in 1957, to 3.2 percent in 1967, and 12.0 percent in 1977; by 1987, it had dropped down to 4.2 percent. These data come from the following sources (all from the U.S. Bureau of the Census): *1957 Census of Governments,* Volume 3, *Finances of Municipalities and Township Governments,* Table 24; *Financial Statistics for Individual Municipalities,* Part A, "Municipalities Having 5,000 or More Inhabitants"; *1967 Census of Governments,* Volume 4, *Governmental Finances,* Table 22, "Finances of Individual Municipalities and Townships with 1960 Population of 10,000 or More"; *1977 Census of Governments,* Volume 4, *Governmental Finances,* Table 22, "Finances of Municipal and Township Governments with 1975 Population of 10,000 or More"; and *1987 Census of Governments,* Volume 4, *Governmental Finances,* Table 18, "Finances of Individual Municipal Governments with a Population of 10,000 or More."

37. U.S. Bureau of the Census, *1977 Census of Governments.*

38. Annual Report of the Milwaukee School Board, 1959–60.

39. Annual Report of the Milwaukee School Board, 1989–90.

40. The best analysis of this general phenomenon is to be found in John H. Mollenkopf, *The Contested City* (Princeton: Princeton University Press, 1983).

41. For an excellent review of a number of different urban-renewal projects, through 1976, see Roger L. Franks, "The History of Urban Renewal in Milwaukee" (master's thesis, University of Wisconsin–Milwaukee, Urban Affairs, August 1976).

42. Patricia A. House, "Relocation of Families Displaced by Expressway Development: Milwaukee Case Study," *Land Economics,* Volume 46 (1970), pp. 75–78.

43. See, for example, Franks, "The History of Urban Renewal," and Marilyn R. Johannsen, "The Potential for Displacement in the Riverwest Community of Milwaukee: An Exploratory Study"(master's thesis, University of Wisconsin–Milwaukee, Urban Affairs, December 1982).

44. Judith A. Simonsen, "The Third Ward: Symbol of Ethnic Identity," *Milwaukee History: The Magazine of the Milwaukee County Historical Society,* Volume 10, Number 2 (Summer 1987), pp. 61–76.

45. I am extremely grateful to Paul Geib of the University of Wisconsin–Milwaukee for sharing this information with me.

46. Franks, "The History of Urban Renewal."

47. One of the continuing concerns of the efforts to create "master plans" for the city in the post-war period was to create better parking in the downtown area. Blight, and urban, renewal thus became seen as a means for achieving exactly that end. See, for example, the report of the Board of Public Land Commissioners, City of Milwaukee, "Downtown Milwaukee: 1975," May 1, 1957 (with an attached letter from the Board's executive secretary, Elmer Krieger; copy at the Legislative Reference Bureau, Milwaukee, Wisconsin).

48. Ann Roell Markusen, *Profit Cycles, Oligopoly, and Regional Development* (Cambridge, Mass.: MIT Press, 1985).

49. "Strike Effects Grow Wider," *Milwaukee Journal,* March 6, 1952.

50. On the whole array of these strikes, see the *Milwaukee Journal,* April 27, 1952, as well as the series of articles that appears throughout April and May 1952.

51. "Strike Swells Jobless Total," *Milwaukee Sentinel,* July 16, 1952; "Idle Workers Total 23,000," *Milwaukee Journal,* August 1, 1952.

52. "Workers Vote for a Walkout 6,652 to 18," *Milwaukee Journal,* May 14, 1953.

53. "Beer Strike Ends; Pay Hike Looms," *Milwaukee Journal,* July 29, 1953.

54. *Milwaukee Sentinel,* July 29, 1953. "Now It Can Be Told," full-page ad,

55. This particular observation was made to me in conversation with Walter Kasten, a member of an old and distinguished Milwaukee family, at the occasion of a lecture I gave in May 1992 at the Newberry Library.

56. See the lengthy report on Hohl's research, "MU Expert Says City Has Not Attracted Growth Firms While Older Companies Have Lost Ground," *Milwaukee Journal,* March 10, 1963.

57. "Buying Industry," *Milwaukee Sentinel,* August 25, 1962.

58. See, for example, the remarks of the president of the Marquette Cement Company, who in early 1963 reported that his firm was considering moving its operations from Milwaukee because the "real estate and personal property taxes in Milwaukee are excessive" ("Firm Stirs Tax Issue," *Milwaukee Sentinel,* January 4, 1963).

59. "New Plant in Bowling Green, KY, One C-H Unit to Move," *Milwaukee Journal,* March 12, 1964.

60. "Schlitz Plans to Construct Texas Plant," *Milwaukee Journal,* March 28, 1964; "Milsteel Firm Will Move from City to Cedarburg," *Milwaukee Sentinel,* March 27, 1964; and "Harnischfeger Picks Indiana," *Milwaukee Sentinel,* March 31, 1964.

61. Ray Kenney, "Trostel Ends 111 Years of Tanning," *Milwaukee Sentinel,* June 3, 1969.

62. "IH to Move: Milwaukee to Lose 700 Jobs," *Milwaukee Journal,* August 20, 1971.

63. "Four Efforts Push for Growth," *Milwaukee Journal,* December 6, 1963.

64. Descriptions of the land-bank program are to be found in Department of City Development, City of Milwaukee, "The Land Bank," March 1972; and City of Milwaukee, Industrial Land Bank, Selected Statutes, Exhibits and Resolutions, 1982.

65. For an example of Maier's vision for restoring and improving Milwaukee, see his "Economic Development Program," delivered to the Milwaukee Common Council on August 29, 1968. The report also included the creation of a special Economic Development Committee of the Common Council.

66. James Parks, "Cities Fight But Industries Move," *Milwaukee Journal,* May 3, 1977. This is an excellent and extremely informative article. The figures on percentages of people employed in manufacturing for 1950 and 1990 come, respectively, from the following sources: U.S. Bureau of the Census, *Census of the Population, 1950,* Volume 2, *Characteristics of the Population,* part 49, "Wisconsin," Table 35, "Economic Characteristics of the Population by Sex, for Standard Metropolitan Areas, Urbanized Areas, and Urban Places"; U.S. Bureau of the Census, *Census of the Population, 1990, Social and Economic Characteristics, Wisconsin,* section 2, Table 182, "Geographic Mobility, Community, and Industry of Employed Persons by Race and Hispanic Origin."

67. "Milwaukee: Suspicions of City, Suburbs Hurt Them Both," *Milwaukee Journal,* December 5, 1963.

68. Parks, "Cities Fight," May 3, 1977.

69. U.S. Congress, Joint Economic Committee, *The Economic Future of Metropolitan Milwaukee: Hearings Before the Joint Economic Committee,* 97th Cong., 1st Sess., October 8 and 9, 1981 (U.S. Government Printing Office, Washington, D.C., 1981).

70. Joint Economic Committee, *The Economic Future of Metropolitan Milwaukee,* p. 57.

71. Jean Peterman interview of Frank Zeidler, April 4, 1991.

72. For the best general discussion about these problems in Wisconsin and whether there was any truth to the claims made by departing industrialists, see the excellent chapter by William F. Thompson, "Industry," in his *The History of Wisconsin,* Volume 6: *Continuity and Change: 1940–1965* (Madison: State Historical Society of Wisconsin, 1988), pp. 160–225.

73. See one of the central works that articulates this theme—Sam Bass Warner, Jr., *Streetcar Suburbs: The Process of Growth in Boston* (Cambridge, Mass.: MIT and Harvard University Press, 1962).

74. Clay McShane, *Technology and Reform: Street Railways and the Growth of Milwaukee, 1887–1900* (Madison: State Historical Society of Wisconsin, 1974), pp. 87–94.

75. Board of Public Land Commissioners, "Downtown Milwaukee: 1975."

76. See, for example, Board of Public Land Commissioners, City of Milwaukee, *History of Planning Activity in Milwaukee, 1892–1952* (March 1952), especially pp. 10–16; and the discussion of a proposed central city (central area) plan of the 1948 Corporation, in the *Milwaukee Sentinel,* October 19, 1947.

77. For a record of the debate in Milwaukee over the issue of the expressways at this time, see the following issues of the *Milwaukee Sentinel*: June 5, 1947 (Second News Section); August 17, 1947, p. 2; Sunday, October 19, 1947 (Section C); October 21, 1947, p. 2; October 22, 1947, p. 1; October 25, 1947 (Second Section); October 26, 1947, Section A, p. 10. Finally after several years of debate, the city council voted in November 1950 to commence the expressway system in Milwaukee (*Sentinel*, November 25, 1950).

78. See, for example, the articles in the *Milwaukee Sentinel* of December 11, 13, and 17, 1947.

79. For an excellent synopsis of this matter as well as the more general treatment about city-suburban conflict at this time, see Henry J. Schmandt with William H. Standing, *The Milwaukee Metropolitan Study Commission* (Bloomington: Indiana University Press, 1965), especially pp. 60–61.

80. *Milwaukee Sentinel*, December 19, 1953. The committee actually was later expanded to be a group consisting of 21 members representing different key segments of the metropolitan area.

81. The availability of millions of dollars in monies for expressways was made clear to Milwaukeeans in heated debates on the issue in late 1947. See, for example, issues of the *Milwaukee Sentinel*, December 13 and 17, 1947.

82. *Milwaukee Sentinel*, March 18, 1952, p. 2.

83. U.S. Bureau of the Census, *General Population Characteristics, 1950*, Volume 1, Tables 26 and 27 (Washington, D.C.); the actual number of nonwhites recorded was 21,772.

84. U.S. Bureau of the Census, 1970.

85. An exemplary history of the black population in Milwaukee is to be found in Joe William Trotter, Jr., *Black Milwaukee: The Making of an Industrial Proletariat, 1915–1945* (Urbana and Chicago: University of Illinois Press, 1985).

86. *City Planning and Taxation* (see Note 8).

87. Citizens Governmental Research Bureau, "Milwaukee's Negro Community" (Milwaukee, Wisconsin, March 1, 1946), p. 25.

88. Ibid., pp. 17–18.

89. Zeidler is truly an extraordinary figure. His great knowledge about the nature of local government is to be found, for example, in a lengthy document now available at the Milwaukee Public Library, *Municipal Government and Its Improvement*. The work, in mimeograph form, was produced in 1960, the year he left office.

90. Mayor's Study Commission on Social Problems in the Inner Core Areas of the City, "Final Report to the Honorable Frank P. Zeidler, Mayor, City of Milwaukee, April 15, 1960."

91. Ibid., p. 5.

92. Ibid., p. 8.

93. Ibid., p. 9.

94. Ibid., Annex G, March 1960, p. 17. This bias against the residents of the Inner Core continued years later in the inability of the residents to secure adequate home insurance for their housing. See the excellent and incisive piece by Gregory Squires and William Velez, "Insurance Redlining and the Transformation of an Urban Metropolis," *Urban Affairs Quarterly*, Volume 23, Number 1 (September 1987), pp. 63–83.

95. Mayor's Study Commission, "Inner Core Study," Main Report, p. 11.

96. Frank A. Aukofer, *City with a Chance* (Milwaukee: Bruce Publishing, 1968), chapter 6.

97. Ibid., p. 136.

98. The dimensions are depicted graphically in the *Milwaukee Urban Atlas* (City of Milwaukee, Department of City Development, 1990; based on the 1990 U.S. Census), Map 3, p. 9.

99. For further detail on the black population at this time, see the excellent study by R. L. McNeely and M. R. Kinlar, *Milwaukee Today: A Racial Gap Study* (Milwaukee: Milwaukee Urban League, Research Publication, 1987).

100. Ibid., Table 2, "City of Milwaukee Population by Race: 1940–1985."

101. For the most general and compelling treatment of this entire issue, see William Julius Wilson, *The Truly Disadvantaged: The Inner City, the Underclass and Public Policy* (Chicago: University of Chicago Press, 1987).

102. Clarence N. Stone, *Regime Politics: Governing Atlanta, 1946–1988* (Lawrence: University of Kansas Press, 1989).

103. But, in his interview with Jean Peterman, Zeidler expressed the opinion that, regardless of the strength of his convictions, he was disappointed that in his tenure in office he had failed to "educate the Milwaukee public about the profound racial changes taking place" (April 4, 1991).

104. Thompson, *The History of Wisconsin*, Volume 6, *Continuity and Change, 1940–1965* p. 370. Thompson provides a detailed and illuminating characterization of Milwaukee leadership during this period and also offers important insights into the ideas of Frank Zeidler.

105. I am particularly grateful to Jack Norman, business reporter for the *Milwaukee Journal,* for furnishing me with some important insight and knowledge about the GMC in the course of an interview on October 26, 1992. Also see the articles by Jack Norman and Marilynn Marchione, "The Gatekeepers," which ran in the *Journal* between January 6 and January 9, 1991. Also see the following materials for information on the GMC over the course of its history: Jack Norman, "Congenial Milwaukee: A Segregated City," in Gregory D. Squires (ed.), *Unequal Partnerships: The Political Economy of Urban Redevelopment in Postwar America* (New Brunswick N.J., and London: Rutgers University Press, 1989), pp. 178–201; the reports by Ron Elving and Joel McNally on "Who Runs Milwaukee?" in the *Milwaukee Journal* in late May 1980, which go into detail on the GMC; and, finally, the general discussion of the GMC in Schmandt, with Standing, *The Milwaukee Metropolitan Study Commission* (1965), especially pp. 33–47. Also, I am extremely grateful here, as many places elsewhere, for the materials that Margo Anderson of the University of Wisconsin–Milwaukee provided me.

106. The 1948 Corporation did a number of important things in the course of its work to help celebrate the centennial of the city. One was to help foster specific plans for remaking downtown Milwaukee and for ridding the city of some of its "blight." William Norris, for example, provides a full discussion of the plans put together by Maynard W. Meyer, a leading city planner and architect in Milwaukee in the late 1940s, at the behest of the 1948 Corporation. See William Norris, "1948 Plan Seeks to Free City's Central Area Traffic Arteries of Congestion," *Milwaukee Sentinel,* October 19, 1947. Miraculously, almost, the model plans provided by Meyer anticipated much of what would be constructed in the downtown area, including the new East-West Expressway to be elevated across the downtown area. Meyer, incidentally, was the architect who eventually designed the Lincoln War Memorial Museum.

107. Schmandt, with Standing, *The Milwaukee Metropolitan Study Commission,* pp. 60–61.

108. Norman and Marchione, "The Gatekeepers."

109. For a company history of Northwestern Mutual Life, see John Gurda, *The Quiet Company: A Modern History of Northwestern Mutual Life* (Milwaukee: Northwestern Mutual Life Insurance Company, 1983); and for a more scholarly, if not also more tedious, history, see Harold F. Williamson and Orange A. Smalley, *Mutual Life: A Century of Trusteeship* (Evanston, Ill.: Northwestern University Press, 1957).

110. Fitzgerald's importance and his views are evident in a conference convened in Milwaukee in 1960 to discuss general problems of growth in and about the city. See the report, "Central City Growth Conference" (Milwaukee, May 10, 1960). The conference was convened in conjunction with work being undertaken by the Milwaukee Metropolitan Study Commission. Here, by the way, Fitzgerald is identified with the Milwaukee Development Group, an offshoot of the GMC.

111. The articles by Elving and McNally on "Who Runs Milwaukee?" speak directly to this issue of residence and participation, and cite the Uihlein family as the primary example of a set of wealthy citizens whose interests eventually became divorced from the city, itself.

112. See, for example, Marchione and Norman, "The Gatekeepers."

113. See, for example, the excellent paper, Jeannine E. Klein, "The Grand Avenue from Concept to Concrete," prepared for a class taught by Margo (Conk) Anderson, University of Wisconsin–Milwaukee, May 18, 1983.

114. Commission on the Year 2000, "Milwaukee Goals/Action 2000: Assess 88," July 25, 1988, p. xi.

115. One of the best general treatments of the role of neighborhood in modern city and, more generally, American political life is that of Matthew A. Crenson, *Neighborhood Politics* (Cambridge, Mass.: Harvard University Press, 1983).

116. Legislative Reference Bureau, City of Milwaukee, Public Welfare Microfiche Documents, Card Number 6, Line Number 1, Fiche Number 6 (there is no other identifying material contained therein).

117. Miriam G. Palay, "Citizen Participation: Issues and Groups" (Milwaukee: Milwaukee Urban Observatory, University of Wisconsin–Milwaukee, Spring 1969), p. 9.

118. See, for example, David John Olson, "Racial Violence and City Politics: The Political Response to Civil Disorders in Three American Cities" (doctoral diss., University of Wisconsin–Madison, Department of Political Science, 1971), pp. 167–218.

119. Palay, "Citizen Participation," p. 12.

120. "Milwaukee Goals/Action 2000: Assess 88," p. vi.

121. The discussion here and in the following paragraphs draws heavily on Schmandt, with Standing, *The Milwaukee Metropolitan Study Commission.* Schmandt was the principal academic adviser to the Milwaukee Study Commission.

122. Metropolitan Study Commission, *Report of Executive Committee Concerning the Determination of the Type of Government Best Suited to Discharge Metropolitan Functions* (Milwaukee, December 29, 1958), p. 1.

123. Ibid.

Part Three Introduction

1. For two recent books on these matters, see Joe R. Feagin, Anthony M. Orum, and Gideon Sjoberg (eds.), *A Case for the Case Study* (Chapel Hill: University of North Carolina

Press, 1991), and Charles Ragin and Howard Becker (eds.), *What Is a Case?* (New York: Cambridge University Press, 1992).

Chapter 9

1. This narrative account is based upon two major sources, both of which provide excellent recent histories of the city of Cleveland. They are: David D. Van Tassel and John J. Grabowski (eds.), *The Encyclopedia of Cleveland History* (Bloomington: Indiana University Press, 1987), especially pp. xvii–iv; and Carol Poh Miller and Robert Wheeler, *Cleveland: A Concise History, 1776–1990* (Bloomington: Indiana University Press, 1990). The latter book is drawn largely from the narrative account in the former one. The other major work to figure in the historical description in this chapter is by Todd Swanstrom, *The Crisis of Growth Politics: Cleveland, Kucinich, and the Challenge of Urban Populism* (Philadelphia: Temple University Press, 1985). Swanstrom's work is truly one of the best analytic works on the issues facing declining industrial centers.

2. "Consistently throughout its first decade, the Connecticut Land Company demonstrated that its primary goal was not settlement but quick sale for profit." Miller and Wheeler, *Cleveland*, p. 10.

3. Ibid., p. 46

4. Ibid., p. 24.

5. Van Tassel and Grabowski, *Encyclopedia of Cleveland History*, p. xxii.

6. Miller and Wheeler, *Cleveland*, p. 70.

7. Ibid., p. 51.

8. Ibid., chapter 6.

9. Harold C. Livesay, "From Steeples to Smokestacks: The Birth of Modern Corporations in Cleveland," pp. 54–70 in Thomas F. Campbell and Edward M. Miggins (eds.), *The Birth of Modern Cleveland* (Cleveland: Western Reserve Historical Society, 1988); and Darwin H. Stapleton, "The City Industrious: How Technology Transformed Cleveland," pp. 71–95 in Campbell and Miggins, *The Birth of Modern Cleveland*.

10. U.S. Bureau of the Census, *Thirteenth Census of the United States, 1910*, Volume 1, *Population*, Table 59.

11. *Annual Report of the Cleveland Chamber of Commerce* (April 1920), p. 346.

12. Edward M. Miggins, "A City of Uplifting Influences: From 'Sweet Charity' to Modern Social Welfare and Philanthropy," pp. 141–171 in Campbell and Miggins, *The Birth of Modern Cleveland*; and John J. Grabowski, "Social Reform and Philanthropic Order in Cleveland, 1896–1920," pp. 29–49 in David D. Van Tassel and John J. Grabowski (eds.), *Cleveland: A Tradition of Reform* (Kent, Ohio: Kent State University Press, 1986).

13. Miller and Wheeler, *Cleveland*, pp. 89–93.

14. Edward M. Miggins, "Becoming American: Americanization and the Reform of the Cleveland Public Schools," pp. 345–373 in Campbell and Miggins, *The Birth of Modern Cleveland*.

15. For an excellent analysis of Johnson and his reform effort, see Swanstrom, *The Crisis of Growth Politics*, pp. 44ff.

16. Livesay, "From Steeples to Smokestacks," especially pp. 62–67.

17. Ibid., p. 67.

18. On the lives of the Van Sweringens, see, for example, Ian S. Haberman, *The Van Sweringens of Cleveland: The Biography of an Empire* (Cleveland: Western Reserve Historical Society, 1979).

19. Van Tassel and Grabowski, *Encyclopedia of Cleveland History,* p. 884.

20. See also the excellent overview on this period by Ronald Weiner, "The New Industrial Metropolis: 1860–1929," in Van Tassel and Grabowski, *Encyclopedia of Cleveland History,* pp. xxix–xliii.

21. Kenneth L. Kusner, *A Ghetto Takes Shape: Black Cleveland, 1870–1930* (Urbana: University of Illinois Press, 1976).

22. U.S. Bureau of the Census, *Seventeenth Census of the United States* and *Twenty-First Census of the United States* (Washington, D.C., 1950 and 1990).

23. *Annual Report of the Cleveland Chamber of Commerce* (April 1920), and *City of Cleveland, Ohio, Annual Financial Report for the Year Ending December 31, 1980.*

24. It is important to note that Cleveland historians, such as David Van Tassel and John Grabowski, use almost an identical scheme of periods to speak of Cleveland's history as it unfolds, though they do not make the same analytical claims for the nature of economic and political institutions as I do in this work. See Van Tassel and Grabowski, *Encyclopedia of Cleveland History.*

25. Miller and Wheeler, *Cleveland,* p. 46.

26. Ibid., p. 51.

27. City Documents, City of Cleveland, 1866, p. 49.

28. The actual ratio is \$1,688,643/\$28,657,253, ibid.; the bottom figure comes from data contained in *A History of Cleveland and Statistical Exhibit of the Trade, Commerce and Manufactures of the City of Cleveland for the Year 1871* (Cleveland: Cleveland Board of Trade, 1871).

29. City of Cleveland Documents, 1856; 1857; and 1866; and Reports of the Various Departments of the City of Cleveland, 1876; 1886; and 1896.

30. *Annual Report of the Departments of Government of the City of Cleveland for the Year Ending December 31, 1895.* The figures are \$34,924,308 and \$132,639,905 for municipal and private property, respectively.

31. *Annual Report of the Departments of Government of the City of Cleveland for the Year Ending December 31, 1914.*

32. " 'The watch-word of the Johnson remnant upon re-entry was "efficiency," the more readily attainable and more generally acceptable portion of the Johnson reform,' " Robert L. Briggs, *The Progressive Era in Cleveland, Ohio: Tom Johnson's Administration 1901–1909,* (Ph.D. diss., University of Chicago, Department of Political Science, 1961), as quoted in Swanstrom, *The Crisis of Growth Politics,* p. 50. One of the points on which many observers of this reform period in American history agree is that the main achievement of reformers, like Tom Johnson in Cleveland and the Social Democrats in Milwaukee, was greater efficiency in the operations of government. Melvin Holli was one of the first to notice this fact and spoke of it in terms of the difference between social reform and structural reform. Holli uncovered it in the case of Mayor Hazen S. Pingree in Detroit, as reported in Holli, *Reform in Detroit: Hazen S. Pingree and Urban Politics* (New York: Oxford University Press, 1969). Also see Martin J. Schiesl, *The Politics of Efficiency: Municipal Administration and Reform in America, 1800–1920* (Berkeley: University of California Press, 1977).

33. See *The Report of the Chief of Police, 1903.* As Fred Kohler, chief of police, noted in his message, "it is … very gratifying to note the commendable disposition on the part of the

rank and file of the force to assist me in *bringing efficiency and discipline ... to a high standard*" (p. 14, my emphasis).

34. *Report of the Cleveland Chamber of Commerce* (1925), p. 318.

35. Weiner, "The New Industrial Metropolis," in Van Tassel and Grabowski, *Encyclopedia of Cleveland History,* p. xliii.

36. *City of Cleveland Annual Comprehensive Financial Report for the Year Ending December 31, 1990.*

37. Annual Reports of the City of Cleveland, 1943 and 1990.

Chapter 10

1. *Austin Growth Watch.* Data are for city only; the SMSA (standard metropolitan statistical area) population stood at 800,000 in 1990. (City of Austin Department of Planning, Annual Edition, 1991.)

2. This narrative account is based largely on my earlier book, *Power, Money & The People: The Making of Modern Austin* (Austin: Texas Monthly Press, 1987). Also see the excellent but highly controversial biography by Robert Caro, *The Years of Lyndon Johnson,* Volumes 1, 22 (New York: Alfred A. Knopf, 1982–1990).

3. As quoted in Orum, *Power, Money & The People,* p. 10.

4. U.S. Bureau of the Census, *Ninth Census of the United States,* Volume 1 (Washington, D.C., 1870); and *Twelfth Census of the United States,* Part 1, Table 26, 1900.

5. Orum, *Power, Money & The People,* pp. 13ff.

6. See, for example, the discussion in Joe R. Feagin, *Free Enterprise City: Houston in Political and Economic Perspective* (New Brunswick, N.J.: Rutgers University Press, 1988), chapter 3.

7. Orum, *Power, Money & The People,* chapters 3 and 4 especially.

8. Ibid., especially pp. 37–44.

9. Ibid., chapter 4.

10. Ibid., pp. 99–109.

11. "Payrolls Without Smokestacks," *Texas Parade,* November 1950, pp. 13–18. The same points were made by Smith in my interview with him in 1986, the tape of which is now located at the Austin History Center.

12. Orum, *Power, Money & The People,* chapter 9.

13. Ibid., chapter 7.

14. In a sense, this difference also confirms the general theoretical bearings on the city proposed by Manuel Castells in his *The Urban Question: A Marxist Approach* (Cambridge, Mass.: MIT Press, 1977); originally published as *La Question Urbaine* (Paris: François Maspero, 1972).

15. *Austin Growth Watch* (City of Austin Department of Planning and Development, 1992).

16. On this matter, see, for example, the Introduction in Richard A. Bernard and Bradley R. Rice (eds.), *Sunbelt Cities: Politics and Growth Since World War II* (Austin: The University of Texas Press, 1983), pp. 1–30. One must also note that well before the city's aggressive annexations of the 1970s and 1980s, there was a recommendation of the University of Texas Institute of Public Affairs that Austin work hard to annex adjacent areas in order to overcome the problems faced by the metropolitan regions of the North; see John Gillespie,

Government in Metropolitan Austin (Austin: University of Texas Institute of Public Affairs, 1956), chapter 5.

17. In 1950, when the population of Austin was 132,459 people, the City of Austin reported that it employed 1,750 people; by 1990, when the population of Austin had more than tripled (to 465,222), the number of City employees had increased to 10,262—about six times the City's workforce in 1950. These figures are available from the City of Austin annual reports (1950 and 1990). Moreover, there seems to have been a gradual increase in the percentage of people employed by the City, as a proportion of the total population, over this period of time. It grew from 1.3 per 1,000 in 1950 to 1.5 per 1,000 in 1970, and then to 2.2 per 1,000 in 1990.

18. These data are calculated for the City of Austin budgets from 1950 through 1990. The complete array of figures are as follows: 1950 = $85.47; 1960 = $77.54; 1970 = $286.75; 1980 = $1,296.83; and 1990 = $2,145.30.

19. The 1986 survey is available at the Austin History Center and goes into great detail on recommended changes. The extent to which those recommendations were followed was revealed to me in several conversations with Sue Barton, an analyst in the Planning Department of the Austin Police Department.

Chapter 11

1. See, for example, *Money,* September 1993, pp. 124–142. According to this report, among 300 cities considered, Minneapolis–St. Paul rank 3rd, while Milwaukee ranks 16th and Cleveland 155th. In the 1992 survey, Milwaukee ranked 52nd. It remains puzzling as to why Milwaukee ranks so high, but the rankings are based on rather unsystematic coupling of criteria.

2. I am especially indebted to John Adams and Barbara VanDrasek for letting me read an advance copy of their important work, *Minneapolis–St. Paul: People, Place and Public Life* (Minneapolis: University of Minnesota Press, 1993). There are also a number of other key works on the two cities, including Calvin F. Schmid, *Social Sage of the Twin Cities* (Minneapolis: Minneapolis Council of Social Agencies, 1937); Ronald Abler, John S. Adams, and John R. Borchert, *St. Paul–Minneapolis: The Twin Cities* (Cambridge, Mass.: Ballinger Publishing, 1976); John R. Borchert, David Gebhard, David Lanegran, and Judith Martin, *Legacy of Minneapolis: Preservation Amid Change* (Bloomington, Minn.: Voyageur Press, 1983); Judith A. Martin and David A. Lanegran, *Where We Live: The Residential Districts of Minneapolis and St. Paul* (Minneapolis: University of Minnesota Press, 1983); Lucile M. Kane, *The Falls of St. Anthony: The Waterfall That Built Minneapolis* (St. Paul: Minnesota Historical Society Press, 1987); and Virginia Brainard Kunz, *Saint Paul: The First 150 Years* (St. Paul: Saint Paul Foundation, 1991).

3. U.S. Bureau of the Census, *United States Census of the Population, 1870* (Washington, D.C., 1871), Volume 1.

4. *United States Census of the Population* (Washington, D.C., 1870 and 1910), Volume 1.

5. The police and the fire departments of the Twin Cities, for example, show the same pattern of growth and development—i.e., change from a volunteer to a professional force—as do those of the other cities. *History of the Police and Fire Departments of the Twin Cities* (Minneapolis: American Land and Title Register Association, 1899).

6. *Summary of Demographic Information for the Twin Cities Metropolitan Area* (St. Paul: Metropolitan Council, August 1992).

7. On the history of the efforts in the Twin Cities, see Judith A. Martin and Antony Goddard, *Past Choices/Present Landscapes: The Impact of Urban Renewal on the Twin Cities* (Minneapolis: University of Minnesota, Center for Urban and Regional Affairs, 1989).

8. The most compelling statement on behalf of retaining historic landmark buildings is to be found in the very moving work by Larry Millett, *Lost Twin Cities* (St. Paul: Minnesota Historical Society Press, 1992). It is notable that neither Cleveland nor Milwaukee seems to inspire the *extent of rich historical and contemporary works* that are so inspired by the Twin Cities.

9. For this history, see Stanley Baldinger, *Planning and Governing the Metropolis: The Twin Cities Experience* (New York: Praeger Publishing, 1971); John J. Harrigan and William C. Johnson, *Governing the Twin Cities Region: The Metropolitan Council in Comparative Perspective* (Minneapolis: University of Minnesota Press, 1978); and John E. Vance, *Inside the Minnesota Experiment* (Minneapolis: University of Minnesota, Center for Urban and Regional Affairs, 1977).

10. Interviews with several people in Minneapolis and St. Paul suggest that there exists some unhappiness with the current composition of the Metropolitan Council and with the way the council has worked—or failed to work—for the past decade or so. There are various recommendations now being discussed for improving the effectiveness of the council, including one that calls for an elected rather than appointed membership.

11. For one rendition of this argument, see *Minneapolis: The Market of the Northwest* (Minneapolis: Minneapolis Civic and Commerce Association, 1917).

12. Adams and VanDrasek, *Minneapolis–St. Paul,* chapters 1 and 3.

13. I am indebted to Professor Joseph Galaskiewicz of the University of Minnesota for sharing his insights with me on this matter.

14. But note that in recent years, the size of the African-American and other minority populations has begun to increase substantially, leading to alarms about growing poverty in the inner cities as well as potential ethnic divisions. See, for example, *Trouble at the Core* (St. Paul: Metropolitan Council, 1992).

15. *Summary of Demographic Information for the Twin Cities Area* (St. Paul: Metropolitan Council, 1992).

16. Of course, the absence of heavy industry is only one such factor that limited black in-migration, as such in-migration also came comparatively late to Milwaukee as well.

17. See, for example, Adams and VanDrasek, *Minneapolis–St. Paul;* Baldinger, *Planning and Governing the Metropolis;* and Abler et al., *St. Paul–Minneapolis.*

18. Baldinger, *Planning and Governing the Metropolis,* chapter 2.

19. See, for example, Adams and VanDrasek, *Minneapolis–St. Paul.*

20. Baldinger, *Planning and Governing the Metropolis;* and Adams and VanDrasek, *Minneapolis–St. Paul,* chapter 5.

21. "How Does the Twin Cities Area Compare?" 1990 Census Socio-Economic Characteristics, Rankings of the 25 Largest Metropolitan Areas. Publication Number 620–93–041 (St. Paul: Metropolitan Council, April 1993).

Chapter 12

1. David Rusk, *Cities Without Suburbs* (Baltimore: Johns Hopkins University Press, 1993).

2. See, for example, Paul E. Peterson, *City Limits* (Chicago: University of Chicago Press, 1981).

3. Rusk, *Cities Without Suburbs.*

4. See the report in the *New York Times,* October 18, 1993, p. A8.

5. Ann Roell Markusen, *Profit Cycles, Oligopoly, and Regional Development* (Cambridge, Mass.: MIT Press, 1985).

About the Book and Author

Why do some cities grow and expand, while others dwindle and decline? Why is Milwaukee a town of the past, while Minneapolis–St. Paul seems reborn and infused with future dynamism? And what do Milwaukee and the Twin Cities have to tell us about other cities' prospects, the trials and destinies of industrial Cleveland and post-industrial Austin?

Anthony Orum's new book tells the story of these cities and, at the same time, of all cities. Here the urban past, present, and future are woven into one compelling tale. Orum traces the shift in the sources of urban growth from entrepreneurs to institutions and highlights the emergence of local government as a prominent force—indeed, as an institution—in shaping the trajectory of the urban industrial heartland. This complex trajectory includes all aspects of urban boom and bust: population trends, economic prosperity, politics and culture, as well as hard-to-pin-down qualities like a city's collective hope and vision.

Interspersing social theory, historical ethnography, and comparative analysis to help explain the fates of different cities, Orum lucidly portrays factory openings, labor strikes, elections, evictions, urban blight, white flight, recession, and rejuvenation to show the core histories—and future shape—of cities beyond the particulars presented in these pages. The reader will discover the key people and politics of cities along with the forces that direct them. With a rich variety of sources including newspapers, diaries, census materials, maps, photo essays, and, perhaps most captivating, original oral histories, *City-Building in America* is ideal for anyone interested in urban transformation and for courses in urban sociology, urban politics, industrial sociology, social change, and social mobility.

Anthony M. Orum is head of the Department of Sociology at the University of Illinois–Chicago. He is author of, among other titles, *Power, Money, and the People,* about Austin, Texas.

Index